Talking to the Audienc

This unique study investigates the ways in which the staging convention of direct address – talking to the audience – constructs selfhood for Shakespeare's characters. By focusing specifically on the relationship between performer and audience, *Talking to the Audience* examines what happens when the audience finds itself in the presence of a dramatic figure who knows it is there. It is a book concerned with theatrical illusion and with the pleasures and disturbances of seeing 'characters' produced in the moment of performance.

Through analysis of international contemporary productions, *Talking to the Audience* demonstrates how the study of recent performance helps us to understand both Shakespeare's cultural moment and our own. Its exploration of how theory and practice can inform each other makes this essential reading for all those studying Shakespeare in either a literary or theatrical context.

Bridget Escolme is a lecturer in Theatre Studies at the University of Leeds. She has published essays on American and European Shakespeare production, theatre for young people and local community theatre practice, and has worked as dramaturg on Shakespeare production at the West Yorkshire Playhouse.

Talking to the Audience

Shakespeare, performance, self

Bridget Escolme

First published 2005
by Routledge
2 Park Square, Milton Park, Abingdon, Oxon OX14 4RN

Simultaneously published in the USA and Canada
by Routledge
270 Madison Ave., New York, NY 10016

Routledge is an imprint of the Taylor & Francis Group

Typeset in Baskerville by Taylor & Francis Books Ltd
Printed and bound in Great Britain by MPG Books Ltd, Bodmin

British Library Cataloguing in Publication Data
A catalogue record for this book is available from the British
Library

Library of Congress Cataloging in Publication Data
Escolme, Bridget, 1964–
Talking to the Audience: Shakespeare, Performance, Self /
Bridget Escolme.
Includes bibliographical references and index.
1. Shakespeare, William, 1564–1616 – Dramatic production.
2. Theater audiences. 3. Acting. I. Title.
PR3091.E83 2004
792.9'5–dc22
2004012724

ISBN 0–415–33222–2 (hbk)
ISBN 0–415–33223–0 (pbk)

TO MY PARENTS
Bob and Hilary Escolme

Contents

List of figures

Acknowledgments

I would not have embarked upon this project without the guidance of
Amanda Price, whose never-failing passion and rigour made me rethink everything I thought I knew about performance. The work was
supported in all its incarnations by the staff of the Workshop Theatre,
University of Leeds, particularly Frances Babbage and Philip Roberts,
and by our colleagues in the School of English, particularly Martin
Butler. The School and the Workshop Theatre facilitated the practical
experimentation that underpins much of the research here, and I
particularly want to acknowledge the contributions of Josephine
Bamford, Dan Bye, Rachel Bowen, Hannah Emanuel, Amy Nugent,
Amy Sackville and Dan Snelgrove and of Leeds-based theatre practitioner Barnaby King. Barnaby King needs two acknowledgments, as he
also provided invaluable help with proofing, as did Eric Langley and
Frances Babbage.

Theatre practitioners and academics alike have been remarkably
generous in giving time, information and work. Terence Hawkes, Kate
McLuskie, Simon Shepard and Sam West all let me have unpublished
texts, now either published or acknowledged in notes here. Barbra
Berlovitz, Gilda Biasini, Neil Irish, Tom Piper and Sam West and
answered questions both complex and trivial on the phone and in
person at busy times in their working lives. The responses of the readers
to whom Routledge sent the work were invaluable, particularly Barbara
Hodgdon's remarkably insightful and detailed commentary. Many
thanks also to the staff of the Shakespeare Birthplace Trust Library,
paricularly Karin Brown, and to the Globe research team, particularly
Jaq Bessel and Alison MacLeod.

Highly influential, though not analysed here, has been the work I did
in the early stages of the project with Paul Hunter of Told by an Idiot,
and the work he has done with our students at Leeds since. My time
observing the rehearsal process for Jane Collins and Peter Farley's

'Webster's Women' at the Tron Theatre, Glasgow and the Museum Of
... was also crucial to the early stages of the project, as was my time as
dramaturgical advisor to Ian Brown's production of *Hamlet* at the West
Yorkshire Playhouse. I am only sorry that it hasn't been possible to
include detailed analysis of all this work here.

I would like to pay tribute to the tireless support and tolerance of my
family – Bob and Hilary Escolme, to whom this book is dedicated, and
my brother John. Many thanks also to Talia Rodgers, Diane Parker and
Barbara Duke for their patience and encouragement. I want to
acknowledge the intellectual and emotional support I have received
from Nicholas Ridout, discussions with whom have been an inspiration
throughout the period of research and to thank Rich Barlow for all his
optimism, and for letting me take over his work space during the
summer of 2003.

1 Actors, academics, selves

As rehearsals start for the RSC's *The Winter's Tale*, Anthony Sher faces a problem:

> A big problem. One that has taxed not only every actor and director who has tackled the play, but countless scholars, audiences and other Bard-watchers over the centuries. What causes Leontes's jealousy? His life seems terrific. He's the king of a prosperous country, happily married to a good woman, Hermione, with one child, another on the way, and enjoying a reunion with his boyhood friend, Polixenes. But then – bang! Out of the blue and with no evidence, he decides Hermione is screwing Polixenes, and, ignoring all denials, destroys everything in sight. I find his violence – a kind of domestic violence – more shocking than that of other Shakespeare characters I've played. At least Richard III is driven by ambition for the crown, Shylock and Titus by revenge. But Leontes's violence seems motiveless. This has affected his reputation, and he is sometimes branded with crude labels: wicked king, mad tyrant, fairy-tale monster.[1]

Sher's search for a solution takes him to the consulting rooms of a neurologist, a psychoanalyst, a psychiatrist and finally to a professor of psychiatry at the Maudsley Hospital, who suggests, without having read the text, that Leontes is suffering from a condition known as 'morbid jealousy'. This condition, victims of which become suddenly and irrationally jealous, misinterpret the innocent actions of their partners, indulge in violent fantasies, then suffer periods of remorse, appears to replicate Leontes' behaviour exactly. Sher can now start rehearsal with the 'new conviction in the role' that knowing about 'morbid jealousy' gives him:

It feeds a need – something which is perhaps invisible to an audience, but crucial – my own trust in the script. Maybe it's the writer in me trying to challenge the greatest of them all. C'mon Will, I'm not sure you've given Leontes proper motivation here. In fact, what seemed like a rather fantastical creation by Shakespeare is revealed to be an utterly realistic one.[2]

Sher wryly offers his imaginary exchange with Shakespeare as a joke against himself: of course, in the end, when the proper research has been completed, 'the greatest of them all', has written nothing so crude as a mere tale, despite the play's title. Shakespeare renders up the fully rounded characters expected of him: characters that late twentieth century theatre audiences should recognise, for indeed they can be imagined taking place in any period. The RSC's *Winter's Tale* is set in 'the early 1900s, a time of intense sexual repression'.[3]

Sher's Leontes is very well received. Everything he does and says seems perfectly consistent and utterly plausible. For *The Times* it is 'one of [his] most intense, most fully achieved performances'.[4] After addressing his early suspicions about Hermione and Camillo's 'paddling palms and pinching fingers' (1.2.115) to the first rows of the Royal Shakespeare Theatre with a touching intimacy – this large proscenium arch theatre will not permit such intimacy any further into the auditorium – he produces a virtuoso performance of psychological realism, 'a characterisation crammed with interpretive points' as the *Observer* has it.[5] He withdraws into his world of morbid jealousy and becomes a nervous, inward-looking figure in a dressing gown, who is deaf to his wife's plea of innocence because only his sickness is now meaningful to him. Hermione is wasting her breath; Leontes is not in need of her spirited self-defence but of anti-depressants. I find the performance oddly cold. In the video/DVD casebook on the performance, Sher expresses a desire that the audience should empathise with Leontes and find it possible to forgive him. But his is a world of mental illness quite impossible to penetrate. It is not a matter of forgiving this Leontes: he is a sick man and thus not guilty from the outset.

The next time I see Sher on stage it is in another production also directed by Greg Doran, *Macbeth*, this time in the RSC's Swan theatre. Having seen Jude Kelly's highly psychologised version at the West Yorkshire Playhouse, in which Lady Macbeth is discovered kneeling centre stage, rocking back and forth and cutting up babygros with scissors, and Macbeth plays every line with a seething tension that indicates immanent breakdown, I anticipate irritation. What kind of power-hungry insecurities or emasculated neuroses might Sher's Macbeth be about to demonstrate? At the Swan, however, there is no sense of a

Figure 1.1 Anthony Sher as Leontes in *The Winter's Tale,* dir. Greg Doran, RSC. Photo: Malcolm Davies © Shakespeare Birthplace Trust

character shut away in a world of private troubles. Sher takes every opportunity to address us directly, shares with us what even Lady Macbeth must not know, pulls us into his deed without a name by confiding, confronting, joking with us. When Macduff and Lennox enter Duncan's castle in 2.3 to complain of the unruly night of storms and portents through which they have just struggled, Sher looks conspiratorially out at us from his upstage balcony on his line 'T'was a rough night' (2.3.61), and we, who know what a night of bloody daggers it has been, laugh at the understatement. When he speaks Act 5's famous lines of nihilistic despair, he walks into the auditorium, leaving a bare stage to figure the meaninglessness of the action in which we have been complicit from the start. The stage has been full of sound and fury and now signifies nothing. If this has been a tale told by an idiot then perhaps we are idiots for watching. This production has offered its audience something quite different to Sher's Leontes, and not simply because these are two quite different leaders of quite different kingdoms. Leontes has been carefully crafted from Sher's research and imagination; Macbeth is something I feel I have had a part in making myself. Once again, it is hard to judge this figure, but not, this time, because he has been given the get-out clause of psychological disturbance. I can't judge Macbeth, because I have enjoyed *Macbeth* so much. I can't judge Macbeth because I feel partially responsible for the figure he becomes in the act of performing to me.

This book is an examination of the kinds of dramatic subjects or selves produced in Shakespeare by different staging conditions and practices. It focuses particularly on the performer/audience relationship and the convention of direct address. It is a book about the pleasures and disturbances of seeing dramatic subjectivity produced in the moment of performance. Though by no means all the productions I include here are by the Royal Shakespeare Company, it's significant that the book has been written at a time in the company's history when the performer/audience relationship appears to have been a growing concern, both in the sense of something to be concerned about, and something profitable. Adrian Noble has left the post of artistic director amidst controversy over the fate of the Royal Shakespeare Theatre in which the Sher/Doran *Winter's Tale* took place. His vision of a flexible theatre space, more suited to the performer/audience dynamic for which Shakespeare's plays were written than the 1930s proscenium, was welcomed by some. Others were appalled at the notion of making so free with public money and destroying a theatre with its own important architectural and performance history. However, Noble's concern for young people sitting in 'second-class-citizen' seats far from the RST stage speaks to his desire for the kind of direct encounter that can't be produced there[6] – and for the RSC, the first years of the twenty-first century seemed like a time for direct encounters. As plans were hatched for the RST's demolition, the Sher/Doran *Macbeth* and a production of *Richard II*, directed by Steven Pimlott with Samuel West in the lead, were using the company's smaller spaces in ways that pushed intimate meta-theatre to new limits for the company. Actors entered the auditorium, opened the theatre's doors to the world outside, demanded that the audience speak, stand, and encounter them directly.

It will be clear by now that the acknowledgment of the theatre audience by actor and *mise en scène* is something I welcome, and prefer to the naturalism of the Sher/Doran *Winter's Tale*. Though I do see talking to the audience as a key convention of Shakespeare's theatre, I don't want simply to take up the cry of the stage-centred critics of the 1970s and

1980s and argue that we can learn from Elizabethan and Jacobean staging conventions and conditions of production. I rather want to ask what it is possible for the human figure to mean when, pretending to be someone else, he or she addresses or acknowledges those who are not pretending – who are always, sometimes somewhat recalcitrantly, themselves. My experiences of talking to British and American actors, reading their own descriptions of their work and watching them in rehearsal, is that they honour and respect their audiences: for these actors, the performance's clarity and accessibility is paramount. However, the relationship between the audience and the fictional figure each actor portrays is rarely seen as productive of that figure's meaning. It is the need to find 'proper motivation' and 'utterly realistic' characters that is the actor's starting point. I want in this study to think about other possible, meta-theatrical starting points for Shakespeare production, and the versions of selfhood, of subjectivity, of humanity they might produce.

The notion of 'proper motivation' and 'utterly realistic' characters in Shakespeare plays has had its academic counterpart. 'The age of Bradley', asserts Michael Taylor in his guide to *Shakespeare Criticism in the Twentieth Century*, 'in its insistence on the special value of character criticism as a means of understanding Shakespeare's plays, constitutes ... one of those eternal moments in criticism that will survive the predations of its competitors'.[7] The 'competitors' in Taylor's account are, no doubt, the self-consciously historicist and materialist academics writing during the last quarter of the twentieth century, who have proposed that characters in plays by Shakespeare might be products of a history and culture with a different sense of what it is to be human to our own. During the 1980s, while actors continued to be trained in the discovery – or production – of Shakespearean characters with inner lives and consistent psychological objectives, many of Sher's 'countless scholars' were *not* concerned with what, in psychological terms, causes Leontes' jealousy. Let us take two examples that have become paradigmatic of British cultural materialist and American new historicist accounts of subjectivity. Francis Barker opens *The Tremulous Private Body* with an extract from Samuel Pepys' diary and offers private diary-writing as the paradigmatic activity of a bourgeois subject that, at the time Shakespeare was supposedly 'creating characters', was not yet fully imaginable.[8] In his epilogue to *Renaissance Self-Fashioning*, new historicist Stephen Greenblatt tells his readers that whereas, in beginning his project, it had seemed to him 'the very hallmark of the Renaissance that middle class and aristocratic males began to feel that they possessed [a] shaping power over their lives', he has come to the conclusion that moments of 'pure, unfettered subjectivity' were in fact politically inter-ested social constructs, 'the ideological product of the relations of power in a particular society'.[9]

These historicist, materialist critical movements have taken little account of what the actor is to *do* in the face of the otherness of early modern subjectivity, however. More recently, there has been a resur-gence of academic interest in character and the inner life in the early modern drama which the actor trained in character study might find more sympathetic. Katharine Eisaman Maus' *Inwardness and Theater in the English Renaissance* challenges what she perceives to be a post-structurally inflected 'attract[ion] to the notion that selves are void'.[10] John Lee has published a furious denunciation of the political interests and anachronistic impositions he sees at the heart of any project that would rename Shakespeare's characters 'subjects'.[11] Bert O. States, appealing to a theatrical common sense, insists that 'the moment an actor cannot find a *self* to play, however deluded his character may be about what selves are, the character is gone and the actor is alone on stage, as it were, by himself'.[12] This study explores the possible mean-ings of moments when actors *are* left onstage, as it were, by themselves. The conventions of rehearsal within which Sher is working, are psycho-logically consistent, self-contained, imaginable apart from the audience for which they were conceived, 'utterly realistic'. Here I want to explore alternatives to character study in Shakespeare production, and the dramatic subjects produced by such alternatives.

Shakespeare and naturalism, illusion and anti-illusion

> [A] convention that seems less than natural today is the tradition of direct address to the audience. Falstaff's catechism on honour is a relic of the clown's role of 'interloqutions with the Audients'. Like explanatory prologues, the explanatory soliloquy or aside to the audience was a relic of the less sophisticated days that developed into a useful and more naturalistic convention of thinking aloud, but never entirely ceased to be a convention.[13]

Andrew Gurr's *The Shakespearean Stage* is still one of the most detailed and useful accounts of early modern theatre production in the field. It offers the reader a way into the material conditions that produced performance four hundred years ago – before hushed audiences seated in the dark, before directors, before lengthy rehearsal processes, before institutionalised actor training. Yet embedded in Andrew Gurr's description above is a post-nineteenth-century assumption about theatrical progress: that at some point around the turn of the sixteenth century, the unsophisticated relics of a performance practice that predates London's first designated theatre spaces begin to 'develop' into 'useful and more naturalistic' conventions of character representation. In Gurr's account, such 'relics' do not entirely disappear from the Elizabethan stage. After all, it would take around three hundred years before theatre technology and acting methodology would attempt to erase all traces of the performer's embarrassing and 'conventional' presence in the theatre. According to Gurr, however, the first steps towards the sophistication of theatrical naturalism are taken, to all intents and purposes, by Shakespeare and the King's Men.[14]

A more radical perspective on this shift, one that frames it in terms of dialectical tension rather than useful progress, is offered by Terence Hawkes. In a development of Robert Weimann's analysis of a move from playing to acting at this time,[15] Hawkes writes of a 'non-verbal, "performative" dimension of public display which our notion of the play as a written "text" has systematically, over the years, obscured from us'.[16] He cites John Stephens' 1615 complaint against a 'common player' who,

> When he doth hold conference vpon the stage; and should look directly in his fellows face; hee turnes about his voice into the assembly for applause-sake, like a Trumpeter in the fields, that shifts places to get an eccho.[17]

The player is evidently more concerned with making an impression on his audience than with the mimetic representation of a conversation between two people. Hawkes uses Stephens' evident distaste for this practice to support the argument that a text-based notion of drama, advocated by Hamlet in his advice to the players, marks the beginning of a suppression of a more open, populist, participatory performance practice.[18] For Hawkes, this shift to the (literary) text shuts down the relationship between performer and audience, enclosing the performer within the authorised fiction.

Our own period, then, reaps the benefit or suffers the consequences of this progress or suppression, depending on one's ideological perspective. The conventions of what Gurr calls naturalism are either regarded as 'useful' in their apparent freedom from convention, or the shift from presentational playing to representational acting is seen as a move towards the eradication of what is radical and popular in Elizabethan theatre practice. Either way, the historical trajectory is clear: the 'newly emerging text-based notion of drama' provides 'the grounding of the one we inherit.'[19] Accordingly, it is with the Elizabethan theatre that recognisably naturalistic conventions of acting begin: conventions adequate to the performance of self-contained characters, people who talk to themselves rather than to the audience. Hawkes' argument draws upon the work of Robert Weimann who, in *Shakespeare and the Popular Tradition in the Theatre*, uses the term *locus* to denote stage space used for action contained within a play's fictional world 'which could assume an illusory character', and *platea* to describe 'an entirely non-representational and unlocalised setting' from which position the performer can acknowledge and talk to the audience.[20] Weimann revisits these concepts in *Author's Pen and Actor's Voice*, where, though he finds 'both continuity and discontinuity between these two types of space' in the Elizabethan theatre,[21] he maintains that 'the *locus* convention foregrounds an apparently self-contained space serving the picture of the performed, not the process of the performer performing'.[22] In this later work, the *locus* appears to be encroaching onto the *platea* in Weimann's theatrical mapping; he suggests that around the time of the first performances of *Hamlet*, theatre becomes more self-contained and authorially controlled.

In this study, I want to readjust the theatre history hindsight that underlies these arguments. I don't assume to challenge the clear evidence offered by Weimann, Hawkes and others[23] that a 'text-based notion of drama' is newly emerging at this time. However, I do want to suggest that in performance, these dramatic texts are dependent for their effects of subjectivity upon the potential for direct encounter between performer and spectator within a continually foregrounded theatre building. I would like to blur *locus* and *platea* more than Weimann does, and argue that if the text is emergent in Elizabethan theatre, the performer is far from merely residual within that text.[24]

References to 'effects of subjectivity' and to what might be 'emergent' and 'residual' in a given culture or discourse mark this study as (at least residually) sympathetic to a critical movement with a particular political project: cultural materialism. The project – to me still a useful and ongoing one and still one that gives rise to a great deal of academic irritation – is best defined by the title of Alan Sinfield's monograph *Faultlines*.[25] It is a critical movement that has endeavoured to find the ways in which cracks and fissures in dominant ideologies show themselves in the cultural artefacts produced by an historical moment. Because it is a 'materialist' critical movement, it speaks of production rather than creation, of historical conditions rather than authors, of subjects in ideology rather than characters and the object of the academic irritation it has produced is primarily its supposed anti-humanism. While the discourse of this critical movement is certainly more than residual here, my own central concern could be regarded as very much a humanist one: it is the potential meaning of direct encounters between actors and the people who have paid to see them act, and the illusions of presence that both permit to occur during those encounters. For though I do not see theatrical illusion as a product of a sophisticated naturalism miraculously anticipated by Shakespeare, nor do I dismiss it as a fledgling form of bourgeois false-consciousness, akin to the kind of illusion of subjectivity that gets the Althusserian subject in ideology up for work in the morning. I want to reappropriate the terms 'illusion' and 'illusionism' here, in recognition of the disapproval they have invoked in studies that have influenced this one. The term illusion became something of a dirty word both in stage-centred and cultural materialist criticism, and I want to redefine what I think are its uses.

In his essay 'Historicising Alan Dessen', Cary M. Mazer critiques the work of stage-centred theatre historicists who have pointed to the interpretive anachronisms that can occur when we read pre-nineteenth century texts without 'shed[ding] the spectacles of realism'.[26] The term 'stage-centred' was coined by J. L. Styan to describe work on the early modern drama that took the early modern stage as its starting point, deriving 'aesthetic theatrical principles from the "external" evidence of theatre architecture and the "internal" evidence of the surviving playscripts'.[27] Mazer situates the work of the stage-centred critics historically. He points to systems of theatrical signification, the use of which by the RSC during the 1970s coincided with Dessen, Styan et al.'s call for a privileging of Elizabethan staging convention in the theory and practice of Shakespeare production. In his excellent essay, Mazer argues that Alan Dessen 'acquired his understanding of Shakespeare's theatre from the same larger cultural practices that shaped the thinking of the theatre directors of his day',[28] and I find it surprising that he only briefly mentions Brecht. Mazer asserts that 'the spectacles through which Dessen sees the Elizabethan theatre were the same spectacles worn by directors and theatregoers in the 1970s, ground and fitted at the Royal Shakespeare Theatre, the Aldwych and the Other Place'.[29] However, the makers of these spectacles can be said to have taken their design blueprints from Brecht, whose theatre aesthetics had inflected both work on Shakespeare and new writing in Britain since the 1960s. In a 1978 essay for *Theatre Quarterly*, Peter Holland describes the development of a

Brechtian aesthetic in British political theatre. He traces this development through the work of William Gaskill, who produced Brecht's plays
and 'Brechtian' versions of the classics for the RSC, the National
Theatre and the Royal Court during the 1960s, and describes Edward
Bond's use of gestic objects – objects that define human relations
through the transactions that take place over and around them.[30] During
the 1960s and 1970s, progressive theatre becomes associated with the
anti-illusionist theatre of Brecht, and theatrical illusion is associated with
a kind of theatrical false-consciousness, a reproduction of the illusions
inherent in society's dominant ideologies which insist that current social
systems are the only possible, natural ones. Brecht:

> Too much heightening of the illusion in the setting, together with a
> 'magnetic' way of acting that gives the spectator the illusion of
> being present at a fleeting, accidental, 'real' event, create such an
> impression of naturalness that one can no longer interpose one's
> judgement, imagination or reactions, and must simply conform by
> being one of 'nature's' objects. The illusion created by the theatre
> must always be a partial one, in order that it may always be recog-
> nised as an illusion.[31]

Mazer remarks of the RSC's work during the 1970s that 'each time
they experimented with a technological or grandly conceptual solution,
they almost immediately pulled back from the experiment' when
remounting productions. 'In each case', he continues, 'the directors and
designers invented a mechanism for foregrounding the actor, the object,
and the gesture; and every time they did so, they ultimately discovered
that they could still convey the foreground without using the new mechanism'.[32] Mazer suggests that this new sparseness is a move *away* from
Brecht – he cites Terry Hands decrying a 'Berliner Ensemble naturalism' left over from the 1960s that insists on real and conspicuous
mud on the boots of a traveller, real moss on a tomb'.[33] Brecht does
indeed repeatedly insist that, while set should approximate location,
properties and costumes should be full of 'carefully worked out
details'.[34] However, the foregrounding of the actor, the object, the
gesture, and a consciousness of the meanings produced by the juxtaposition of these elements, appear to me not so much a rejection as a
development of a British Brechtian aesthetic.

Usefully for the 1980s cultural materialists, Brecht draws upon the
Elizabethan theatre as an example of anti-illusionist drama. Margot
Heinemann centres her essay for Dollimore and Sinfield's *Political
Shakespeare* on connections between Brecht and Shakespeare[35] and a

Brechtian political and aesthetic sensibility is continually echoed in cultural materialist writing. In the early modern theatre, argues Graham Holderness, 'the audience would always sustain an awareness of the constructed artifice of the proceedings, would never be seduced into the oblivion of empathetic illusion'.[36] Francis Barker associates theatrical 'illusion' with a 'bourgeois naturalism'[37] and asserts that '[t]he audience were never captivated by the illusion because the spectacle never produced itself as other than it was'.[38] For Catherine Belsey, the late Elizabethan theatre contained elements of 'emergent illusionism',[39] which she associates with a liberal humanist/bourgeois subjectivity, while presentational elements are associated with emblematic morality play figures with no 'unifying essence'.[40] For Brecht, 'illusion' suggests a naturalistic set of stage conventions, and cultural materialist writing assumes them to be productive of a unitary, self-contained and inward-looking subject.

I want to argue that the plays examined here can produce illusions of subjectivity, albeit fleetingly, which are not necessarily illusionistic in the ways that these critics mean. It is possible to conjure theatrical illusion while at the same time making evident the work behind the illusion, its conditions and means of production. This sense of having one's illusionist cake and eating it theatrically, quite alien to much current Western theatrical sensibility, is one to which I will return. Suffice it to say at this point that 'illusionism' is often used to mean the effacement of theatrical convention and the production of a particular kind of dramatic subject. Early modern dramatic illusion is not necessarily dependent on such an effacement, or productive of such a subject. It is easy to forget that Brecht recognises 'partial illusion' as integral to the theatre experience.[41] But I want to go beyond the implications of the quotations above – that Shakespeare anticipated Brecht, or Brecht rediscovered Shakespeare. I want to argue that the cracks and fissures in dominant thought that cultural materialism has sought in the early modern drama are to be found at moments when the illusion of a being face to face with fictional presences in the theatre is at its strongest, and that this illusion is produced 'outwardly', in the encounter between performer and audience.

Zola, Stanislavski and the anti-theatrical prejudice

It is interesting to note that Sher describes his research as 'feed[ing] a need – something which is perhaps invisible to an audience, but crucial

– [his] own trust in the script',[42] a trust evidently not attained until that research is complete. He reads it, finds Leontes to be unlike people he has observed in his own twentieth-century life, and must therefore search until he finds a plausible doppelganger for him out there. If Shakespeare is 'great', we must find *ourselves* in him, through a process of comparing his characters to the control experiment that is the world outside the theatre. His distrust of 'wicked king, mad tyrant, fairy-tale monster' figures is part of a dominant tradition of psychological realism that I am, riskily, going to call naturalistic: riskily, because the terms naturalism and naturalistic are used in bewilderingly loose ways in a range of places, and I have already implicitly accused Andrew Gurr of taking them out of their historical context. The student of theatre studies looking for a definition of these terms will usually be told to use them only in a strictly historical sense: naturalism was a nineteenth-century movement that emerged from a number of scientific and philosophical meta-narratives that sought to understand man in his social environment. As an artistic movement it began with the novels of Tolstoy, Balzac, Zola, the last of whom, in the much-cited and anthologised essay 'Le Naturalisme au Théâtre' demanded that its principles of scientific accuracy of description be transferred to the stage:

> I am waiting for the time when there is no prestidigitation of any kind, no more waving of the magic wand, changing persons and things from one minute to the next. I am waiting for the time when no-one will tell us any more unbelievable stories, when no-one will any longer spoil the effect of true observations by imposing romantic incidents, the result of which destroys even the good parts of a play.[43]

Amongst theatre companions and guides there is some dispute as to which actual plays are to be counted as historically 'naturalistic'. Bandying the term 'naturalism' about when one is actually referring to a broader and more historically fluid 'realism' is warned against, however.[44] A flexible, three-tier definition has been provided by Raymond Williams, who recognises that the term naturalism is used as a general one for accurate or life-like reproduction, to mean 'a philosophical position allied to science, natural history and materialism' and, for Williams, its most enlightening usage, to refer to a movement which fuses both accurate reproduction and a philosophical position.[45] Sher's search for Leontes owes much to such a movement. His position is scientific, positivist and takes him on a journey to a range of professionals in order to find a phenomenon in the world that he might accurately reproduce in his performance. It also shares with Zola's essay 'Le Naturalism au Théâtre' a desire to erase from the performance what is showy, embarrassingly theatrical, produced only in theatres or in stories. Zola holds up his belief in the transparent reproduction of individuals and society as they really exist, 'without one lie' and their scientific examination in the theatre, 'in the same way that the science of chemistry is the study of compounds and their properties',[46] against the easy moralism of 'symbols of vice and virtue'.[47] Where the new naturalistic theatre, like the good scientist, will honestly show forth its results in truthful and unbiased fashion, the old theatrical forms are condemned as deliberately attempting to deceive the spectator, rather as when we are children, we might be deceived by simple tricks or enthralled by fantastic stories of wicked kings, mad tyrants and fairy-tale monsters. The theatrical heritage that I am going to call naturalistic, then, offers a serious theatre, theatre for grown-ups. It is ultimately an anti-theatrical set of assumptions about what theatre should be, as the dramatic subjectivities it produces are to be imagined by the actor as living outside the theatre in which they are produced, not there merely for our (rather childish) entertainment. I want to add to Raymond Williams' third definition of naturalism – that fusion of life-like reproduction and positivist philosophy – this anti-theatrical strand. As Patrice Pavis' definition suggests 'the natural, though man-made, denies that it is an artificial production'.[48] Naturalistic theatre is that which attempts to erase its own theatricality.

Shakespeare production in Britain is at an odd moment in relation to the history of anti-theatricality in the theatre. The proscenium arch facilitates its own erasure, offering a window through which to spy on a slice of life; the RSC has been disputing whether to rid themselves of their proscenium arch at the RST. Designers have recently worked against the proscenium's performer/audience divide, building a Japanese *hanamidri* out into the auditorium at the RST for *Hamlet*[49] and turning the houselights on for 'to be or not to be', placing ladders up to the balcony to scale the walls of Harfleur in *Henry V*.[50] The inherently meta-theatrical Swan, with its thrust stage and audience half-lit by the spill from the stage lights, has been pushed to the limits of theatrical self-consciousness for *Cymbeline*: the floor of the playing space has been taken up to reveal not lovely wooden boards to match the split-beam authenticity of the auditorium, but a grubby board underlay, scored with the traces of sets past.[51] It is a production that leads Michael Billington to pronounce that 'hyper-theatricality is a symbol of the new Stratford'.[52]

Actors, however, are still trained in character study, and the starting point for character study is certainly the text, not the theatre or the audience. Though the design of theatre buildings, sets and lighting has taken us far from the detailed naturalism of the Moscow Arts Theatre, and there are a whole range of routes to character chosen by the modern actor (including Sher) that don't pass through the psychiatrist's consulting room, I think W. B. Worthen is right in his assertion that '... Stanislavskian principles – continuous characterisation, an organic connection between scenes, the need to develop an inner life for the role, a consistent through-line of action – suffuse thinking about acting today, and particularly suffuse actors' descriptions of their work'.[53] For all he eschewed the term, Stanislavski, father of modern acting, is part of a naturalistic, anti-theatrical tradition that produces dramatic subjects that erase their own theatricality, even when standing on sets that do not. I am going to turn, then, to Stanislavski's writings on how not to leave the actor standing on stage by himself, before continuing with a project that suggests that that is where they might productively be left.

Like Zola before him, 'waiting ... for the time when no-one will tell us any more unbelievable stories',[54] Stanislavski demands truth from his theatre, truth of a particularly consistent and psychological kind. His theory of the 'super-objective', the thematic backbone of every good play, inextricably links consistency of character with coherence of theme. A good actor, sensitive to the authorial voice within the text, will be able to discover a play's super-objective[55] and embody it through his character's own 'unbroken line' of fictional objectives.[56] There is no differentiation made between thematic coherence and psychological consistency, a point we will return to in examining twentieth century critiques of the fragmented and psychologically inconsistent *Troilus and Cressida*. The actor's purpose in Stanislavski's teaching is to create a character that is both true to the author's super-objective and psychologically 'truthful'.[57] Within his system of rehearsal and production, there is no *in*consistency in the two notions that characters are both 'natural', whole, independent ('the conception and birth of a new being – the person in the part ... is a natural act similar to the birth of a new human being')[58] and creations of an author working to a thematic super-objective. The thematic drive of a great work of art will always be best expressed through psychologically consistent characters, and it is assumed that this is what great authors set out to create.

Where, in *An Actor Prepares*, Stanislavski gives an example of a super-objective, its title relates to the objective of a central character:

> Suppose we are producing Gribodyedov's *Woe from too much Wit* and we decide that the main purpose of the play is to be described by the words 'I wish to strive for Sophie' ... But you can describe the

super-objective in terms of 'I wish to struggle not for Sophie, but for my country!' Then Chatski's ardent love of his country and his people will move into the foreground.[59]

The main purpose of the play is encapsulated in the 'wish' of a single 'I' and this is the case even where a play's super-objective includes broader social themes, as Stanislavski evidently recognises that it does here. Brecht's political objection to theatrical naturalism was its tendency to foreground human feeling – 'Chatski's ardent love' – over social processes, in this case, say, those processes and class interests that might produce Chatski's nationalism.[60] The challenge to Stanislavski's legacy contained in this study is rather different. I am concerned with the tendency in his writing to oppose human feeling and theatricality:

> ... [T]his impetus towards the super-objective must be continuous throughout the whole play. When its origin is *theatrical* or *perfunctory* it will give only an approximately correct direction to the play. If it is human and directed towards the accomplishment of the basic purpose of the play it will be like a main artery, providing life and nourishment to both it and the actors.[61] (original emphasis)

Stanislavski's theorisation of the objective figures the theatrical as a set of lifeless conventions, while the psychologically inflected consistency of the super-objective is human, nourishing, real, convention-free. Consistency of purpose for both playwright and character is central to Stanislavski's writings, and such purpose cannot be primarily theatrical in nature.

However, as Kathleen McLuskie argues, the early modern theatre can be viewed as having less lofty priorities:

> ... representation in commercial culture does not depend only on the connection between on-stage and offstage: between the image and some kind of identifiable social reality. That connection is often made by critical and historical analysis but it is a connection which depends upon a prior desire for aesthetic and historical coherence. Early modern representation seems to me a much more hit and miss affair, an eclectic bricolage designed to fulfil more immediate practical ends of getting the play on and getting the book out.[62]

'The practical ends of getting the play on', the labour of theatre production, are what theatrical naturalism endeavours to erase. Its imperative is to produce a transparent representation of 'real' human feeling, emerging spontaneously from an 'individual, delimited, organic, non-commodified, spontaneous psyche',[63] an integral and organic part of the play's thematic drive. It is impossible for the naturalistic theatre to offer character 'say, as an interested, rhetorical representation of subjectivity, a limited model of agency' as W. B. Worthen puts it,[64] as 'rhetorical representation' suggests the practical ends of interested persuasion rather than truthful, transparent mimesis.

According to this binary of human/good, theatrical/bad, plays such as *Troilus and Cressida* and *Hamlet* can only be bad plays. As I will argue, these early modern dramas show a marked tendency to privilege 'the practical ends' of entertainment and plot development over unbroken psychological through-lines and to 'leap from one thing to another', to borrow from Zola again, in their need to carry out the work of engaging their manifestly present audiences. Rather than reverting to a Shakespeare-anticipates-Brecht model, however, I am going to argue that it is dramatic subjectivity rather than alienation effects that are produced by a drive towards theatrical objectives and their self-evident presence on stage. Just as I find the term 'illusion' a useful one in describing Shakespearean theatricality, Stanislavski's notion of the objective is not a baby to be thrown out with his anti-theatrical bath water. Shakespeare's fictional figures undoubtedly have desires and interests that differentiate them one from another. In Chapter Two, I introduce the notion of the 'performance objective' and argue that, whereas in the naturalistic theatre it is impossible for any character to desire or have an interest in anything outside the fiction, Shakespeare's stage figures have another set of desires and interests, inseparable from those of the actor. They want the audience to listen to them, notice them, approve their performance, ignore others on stage for their sake. The objectives of these figures are bound up with the fact that they know you're there.

Interestingly, much performance that has happened in Europe and the US over the last twenty years has returned to the overtly, embarrassingly theatrical as both an aesthetic and a theme. Sheffield-based Forced Entertainment have sat amidst the shoddy remnants of sleazy performances in imagined theatres and clubs; they have read from untidy piles of visible text, or grinned endlessly at us in hideous theatrical make-up, or done silly tricks in gorilla costumes. Dance-theatre choreographer Pina Bausch has dressed her performers in the pretty tea dresses of the first half of the twentieth century, all slightly too big for their wearers like children's dressing-up clothes, and had them line up to entertain us, hilariously and desperately asking for our attention. The Wooster Group have put the realist classics of the American theatre in quotation marks with blackface and hula dancing. In various ways, the post-modern turn in performance practice has drawn attention to the performance of subjectivity in the world by demanding that their audiences watch it being performed on stage. These companies refuse to let us take any performing human figure for a transparent window onto another self, and ask us to rethink the moments in the theatre and in the world when we 'recognise' another human being, when we think we know what someone else *means*. I would like to think of play texts written four hundred years ago doing some of the same work. Like the work of Mazer's stage-centred critics, this study is situated within a performance history which is not only the history of Shakespeare production. As the post-modern turn in performance practice permits us simultaneously to know and not know ourselves, the combination of theatrical familiarity and historical distance in the plays under examination here might also permit productive ways of re-examining the kinds of selves we think we are. In Mazer's essay on Dessen there is an implicit accusation of ahistorical naivety in a criticism that finds ourselves everywhere in the past. To acknowledge that performance conventions produce meaning, and to explore the meanings that a convention used in the past might produce today, is to avoid that naivety, I hope.

Political Shakespeare?

Whilst sympathetic to the political thrust of W. B. Worthen's argument that 'Stanislavski or no, it would be difficult to expect actors any more than the rest of us to stand outside this dominant mode of ideological transmission, producing the world by producing us as its subjects invested in particular notions of what subjectivity entails',[65] I would like to speculate about a theatre that permits some imaginary steps outside this Althusserian entrapment. I suggest here that a good reason for continuing to produce four-hundred-year-old plays is their potential for permitting us, albeit in a fleeting and fragmentary way, to do exactly what Worthen finds difficult: to stand outside our own ways of being, embodying, performing the human, brought up sharp by other efforts at performance, efforts from the past. I could be accused of an historical romanticism here, in much the same way that the Globe reconstruction in London has been. 'A nostalgic citation of absent origins' is what Worthen regards as animating that theatre's direct performer/audience relationship,[66] and in Chapter Three, where I too give an account of the Globe's 2000 *Hamlet*, I want to heed his warning. I don't want to suggest that what we encounter in a Shakespeare production that openly acknowledges the presence of the audience is unmediated access to early modern subjectivity. An actor might usefully study, say, the psycho-biology of the humours as a means of understanding the sudden shifts in emotion demonstrated by early modern dramatic figures, alien to our notions of depth psychology;[67] sh/e might find even more interesting early modern notions of an externally constructed self – notions of role and personage that modern psychology tends to trope as mask or surface rather than as integral to selfhood.[68] But if an individual actor attempts to play Hamlet as if he believes his black bile is out of kilter, or speaks the line 'It is I, Hamlet the Dane' with a confidence in his social position rather than as an assertion of 'individuality', then the audience may be none the wiser. The actor may indeed have simply re-found the historicist naturalism propounded by Method practitioner Stella Adler, who demanded that the actor's imagination in creating character be governed by the sociological circumstances of the dramatic fiction.[69]

There are no examples given here of moments of perfect historical insight, moments when lines of communication to the dead, to echo Greenblatt,[70] are established without interference. What I have found both most pleasurable and most disturbing in the Shakespeare productions that form the case studies here are moments when my position as spectator has moved from recognition of some fragment of humanity that I can claim as my own, to bewilderment at an historical being who stands on stage and demands a recognition I cannot give – when the encounter between performer and audience shift from an inclusive, communal warmth to something more aggressive and combative, for example; or where a figure on stage appears to demand that I enter into an empathy or a conspiracy over something I find morally repugnant. In Brechtian terms, these could be described as historical *Verfremdungs effekts*. However, because these are moments when I have also experienced the most powerful effects of theatrical illusion, I am not going to name them as such. I am going to speculate about the cracks and fissures that the productions studied here open up between the Shakespearean text and the audiences that go to watch them being performed four hundred years after their first performances. I am going to speculate as to how far the meaning produced by the shifting distance between performer and audience might be constitutive of the ways in which the plays produce meaning. Awkward, unpredictable as well as easy, conventionalised encounters between performer and audience appear to me to be demanded by the texts studied here. New historicism and cultural materialism have insisted that the fictional figures on Shakespeare's stage are not always familiar to us; but in those unfamiliar moments, they are still being familiar *with* us. They conspire with us, plead with us, confront us, bully us, vow to please us, and I want to argue that the unpredictability of our reactions – the multiplicity of our readings, the uncertainness of our pleasure and support – are integral to the readings that the plays make possible.

Shakespeare

The focus on Shakespeare's dramatic subjects here, as opposed to a broader range of early modern dramatic figures, is both deliberate and contingent. With regard to contingency, it will be obvious to the most casual theatre-goer that there are many more Shakespeare plays in current British production than works by any other dramatist, early modern or not, and that so clearly guaranteed are audiences for these performances that large subsidised companies care little about whether their programmes overlap. During the period of this research, both the Royal Shakespeare Company and the National Theatre had productions of *Troilus and Cressida* and *Romeo and Juliet* running simultaneously; the RSC redesigned the Other Place to house *Richard II* as the Almeida converted the Gainsborough studios for the same play. *Hamlet*s of all texts and sizes abounded.[71] Shakespeare thus provides the most readily available examples of current theatrical constructions of the early modern subject.

Along with the cultural status that ensures that Shakespeare has been the most performed playwright in Britain during the past century comes the imperative to make the plays accessible to the elderly theatre-goers, students and schoolchildren that make up much of his audience in Britain today. While dramatic works of, say, the eighteenth century, are more likely to be produced in period or period-inflected costume, Shakespeare, and to an extent his contemporaries, are assumed to be adaptable to a range of periods and styles. This is partly due to the frequency of Shakespeare performances and the imperative for each company producing a well-known text to offer the consumer something different to the last. It is also a means of producing accessibility in a way that suggests that it has been discovered rather than imposed. Where much academic writing has eschewed the notion of Shakespeare's universality, much theatre design and direction suggests that a theatre company can set a play of Britain's best-known playwright anywhere in time or space. An exploration of how stage convention constitutes, rather than reflects, the nature of the early modern dramatic subject does well, then, to take as its material the work of our most reconstituted playwright.

In *Shakespeare after Theory*, David Scott Kastan seeks to historicise Shakespeare's seeming adaptability thus:

> … though [Shakespeare] does live on in subsequent cultures in ways none of his contemporaries do, it is not, I think, because he is in any significant sense timeless, speaking some otherwise unknown universal idiom. Rather it seems to me it is because he is so intensely of his own time and place. His engagement with the world is the most compelling record we have of that world's struggle for meaning and value … In his historical specificity, then, we discover ourselves as historical beings.[72]

This study adds to this notion of a Shakespeare intensely historically situated, that of a Shakespeare intensely theatrically situated. The drive behind this research has been a pleasure in the ways in which Shakespeare's plays of the late 1590s and early 1600s push at the limits of what the human figure can mean within the boundaries of particular stage conventions, particularly those that lead to direct encounter between performer and spectator. It is, perhaps, the range of ways in which Shakespeare's plays produce a role for the spectator in the production of meaning that has allowed countless subsequent writers and theatre practitioners to claim that his concerns are identical to those of their own historical period. The possibilities of direct contact between dramatic figure and spectator inherent in these theatre texts may, ironically, have been what has led theatrical naturalism to limit that very engagement. Desiring to experience ourselves as self-originating and coherent psychological subjects, we project this desire onto the work of the playwright who has found the most engaging and direct conventions through which dramatic figures may talk to us. It is not, then, a notional openness to interpretation that this research points to in the Shakespeare plays under examination but rather a theatrical openness to the audience for whom the plays were first written. However, although the paradigm of theatrically conscious staging to which I continually return is the mode of direct address to the audience, the early modern stage itself does not provide the primary research material of this study. The 'nuts and bolts of theatre' that Jonathan Bate defines as the performance critic's field[73] are not, in this particular piece of performance criticism, primarily sixteenth- and seventeenth-century ones. The analyses that follow are of productions that took place between 1998 and 2003.[74] This study explores ways in which addressing and not addressing the audience produce or limit dramatic subjectivity in recent theatrical production of Shakespeare. It speculates as to alternative, more theatrically conscious activities for actors in Shakespeare production than those demanded by the conventions of stage naturalism; it does not suggest that one such activity might be to replace imagined psychiatric syndromes for Leontes with imagined Elizabethan players.

The plays chosen for examination here are ones that have been subject to particular critical and journalistic assumptions around the nature of dramatic subjectivity during the twentieth century. A central aim of this study is to challenge critical and theatrical projects that would make a psychologically coherent subject out of Cressida, plumb the depths of Hamlet's mystery and find character development in Richard II's descent from royal power. Chapter Two, 'Bits and bitterness: politics, performance, *Troilus and Cressida*', challenges the notion that the coherent psychological subject is a prerequisite for performer and audience engagement with an early modern dramatic text. In it, I examine two productions of *Troilus and Cressida* by Britain's largest subsidised theatre companies, the Royal Shakespeare Company and the National Theatre. Both British productions are inflected to varying degrees by naturalistic assumptions about coherence of character, and this affects and inflects the politics of each production. Though I touch upon Wekwerth's production for the company founded by Brecht, the chapter does not abandon Stanislavski, but extends his notion of character objective and super-objective from the naturalistic frame in which they were conceived, to a more theatrically self-conscious notion of 'performance objective'. It examines the kinds of subjects that might be staged in this play when a dramatic figure's relationship with the audience is privileged over psychological consistency.

Chapter Three, 'The point or the question? Text, performance, *Hamlet*', begins by situating textual debates around *Hamlet* theatrically, focusing on two productions, and through them, two texts: the First Quarto, produced by Red Shift theatre company as *Hamlet: First Cut* and the First Folio produced at the Globe reconstruction. It interrogates the issues of theatrical and psychological self-containment that hover around critical accounts of the later published texts of *Hamlet*, the Second Quarto and the Folio editions and it challenges the theatre history that insists that, while a direct relationship with the audience is embedded in the philosophically simpler Q1 text, a self-contained, introspective performance style is demanded by the more complex Q2 and F. I argue instead that the most complex effects of subjectivity in *Hamlet* are produced in moments of direct address to the audience. The chapter then moves to *Hamlet* texts produced not by the Chamberlain's men or early modern memorial reconstruction, but by companies producing *Hamlet* at the turn of the twentieth century. The Theatre de la Jeune Lune's collation and Peter Brook's radical transpositions offer *Hamlet*s that hover at the brink of a theatrically produced subjectivity but at the same time challenge and shift the premises of this study by staging Hamlet as an anti-theatrical figure.

Chapter Four, 'The theatre and the Presence Chamber: history, performance, *Richard II*' is an analysis of the Royal Shakespeare Company's *Richard II*, a production whose carefully systematised use of stage space and direct address produces theatrical effects whereby audience and dramatic figure are experienced as simultaneously present in the theatre and in the play's fiction. The chapter focuses on the presence of the performer in this production, and the ways in which that presence constitutes both dramatic and audience subjectivity. The chapter contrasts these theatrical presences with the naturalistic 'absence' of the dramatic subject in the more naturalistically inflected Almeida production at the Gainsborough film studios. It explores the notion of the theatre as a fictional and theatrical Presence Chamber, where performative speech is enacted upon both audience and dramatic figure and where historical action can be brought into the theatrical present without the aid of a *mise en scène* that insists upon specific modern parallels.

Chapter Five, 'Performing human: the Societas Raffaello Sanzio' concludes the study with suggestions for a theatrically conscious theatre practice in Shakespeare production. Here I have been inspired by the work of the Italian company the Societas Raffaello Sanzio and their presentation of Shakespeare's dramatic figures as perpetually performing humans with vulnerable subjectivities, constituted fleetingly in the moment of performance. From the question that underpins the earlier chapters – does the actor need a 'self' to play in the plays examined here? – the study moves in this chapter to the questions these plays might ask, under theatrically conscious conditions of production, about what kinds of selves can be played in the world.

I have not attempted a survey here – of these plays in production or of their twentieth/twenty-first century critical reception. The examples and samples I have used offer a way of reading theatre theoretically, and of reading Shakespeare texts theatrically. I have taken a quintessentially practical matter – the ways in which an actor in a Shakespearean role might talk to the audience – and a notoriously theoretical one – the construction of the dramatic 'subject' or self – and have attempted to make the practice speak to the theory and vice versa. I hope that the work will provide a theatrical way into theoretical constructions of self-hood which the theatre practitioner might otherwise find irrelevant or wilfully obscure; I hope it will offer ways of using theatre performance to illuminate theoretical constructions of selfhood.

2 'Bits and bitterness'

Politics, performance, *Troilus and Cressida*

... It is not surprising that this piece is seldom played for it does not hang together in any real sense. The Scenes lead nowhere and appear to exist in and for themselves ...

When they have discovered what this play of bits and bitterness is all about, visitors to the Memorial Theatre at Stratford upon Avon should find in Anthony Quayle's production of *Troilus and Cressida* ... certain elements which reach very near nobility ...

Birmingham Mail, 1948

Troilus and Cressida by Shakespeare and *Candide* by Voltaire both present a war-torn world in which destructiveness and corruption appear to overwhelm what is good and pure .... The central characters of Troilus and Candide are both searching for the meaning of truth, loyalty and beauty in a world which seems empty of all value.

National Theatre Publicity, 1999[1]

In Michael Boyd's Royal Shakespeare Company production of *Troilus and Cressida*, Act 5 begins as Achilles circles the stage, ritualistically scattering the blood and feathers of a large white chicken. He and Patroclus light incense and burn a little of the chicken blood in a metal bowl. The significance of the chicken is not immediately clear. It appears to have become something of a joke amongst the performing company, or at least for the stage manager who named 5.1 'Chicken Tonight' in the prompt copy.[2] During the regional tour of the production, the company dropped the dead chicken, or rather reduced it to the essential parts of blood, feathers and a single foot. How is the spectator to read the chicken, or its parts? The white feathers of cowardice are a recurring image in the production. Achilles' generals have scattered them earlier as part of their attempt to provoke him into rejoining the battle against Troy. So perhaps the sacrifice of a white-feathered chicken serves to emphasise Achilles' defiance of Agamemnon and Ulysses. Or perhaps it is simply further proof of

Achilles' decadence: he refuses to fight because of a promise he has made to his female lover; here he is having spent a wild night in at his tent, sacrificing chickens with his male one, Patroclus, played by actress Elaine Pyke in the production's only example of cross-gender casting.

Startling though it is in its first incarnation as whole carcass, this is a naturalistic chicken. It is Achilles' (Darren de Silva) personal prop, on stage to tell us something of his character. It is part of the fictional environment created for the character from costume, sound, set – a suit jacket over a bare chest, crackly snatches of Hawaiian music played at his tent. Later, the chicken – or at least its blood – shifts sign systems, as Cassandra (Catherine Walker) smears the blood from Achilles' sacrificial bowl over her face. We are presumably not expected to imagine that the Trojan princess had been wandering around the Greek camp and stumbled upon the remnants of Achilles' revels. The chicken has a fictional reality, whereas the blood is symbolic. Cassandra is a doomed prophetess; her bloody prophecies are now written on her face. Cassandra herself, in this production, also belongs to two theatrical sign systems. She is not *merely* the prophetess fated not to be believed but appears to have psychological motivations and disturbances quite outside her mythic status – and quite outside the text, in which all her dialogue is prophecy. In 2.2, Paris (Jack Tarlton) angrily snatches a black bundle from his 'mad sister' (2.2.98). She had been nursing and rocking it like a baby since her first entrance. Paris' exasperated gesture reveals that it is not a child, merely cloth. I overhear two elderly ladies leave the Pit auditorium at London's Barbican Theatre, one asking the other 'Who was that girl who lost the baby?'.

The simple point to be made here is that where a four-hundred-year-old text does not appear to offer psychological through-lines or personal back-story, imposing them can lead to the construction of bewildering narrative blind allies for the spectator, where no doubt greater accessibility to a difficult play is intended. The purpose of this chapter is not to parody the excesses of characterisation in an interestingly eclectic production, however, but to mark an intention to explore just what the concept of 'character' does not allow a production and the actors in it to do.

In his publicity for the National Theatre's ensemble company's 1999 production of the play, Trevor Nunn is clear as to what the play ought to do: it ought to challenge us. Its 'abiding questions … are both relevant and challenging to the world in which we live'.[3] Performance critic Carol Rutter, on the other hand, suggests that *Troilus*'s take on the politics of war can no longer challenge an age that is happy to gaze 'unflinchingly at the deglamorised death of heroism'.[4] It is the play's gender politics that still have the power to disturb. Rutter perceptively points to the ways in which directors find Cressida's betrayal of Troilus disconcerting and 'design their way out of ... confusion', motivating an inconsistent figure into psychological coherence, 'iron[ing] out her contradictions'[5] with props and costumes.

Rutter sees Cressida as a Shakespearean exception, arguing that 'Elsewhere in Shakespeare ... the collection of conventions we call "character" proposes something we recognise theatrically as an essential self ... it's (mostly) coherent, (mostly) continuous'.[6] It is certain that elsewhere in Shakespeare dramatic figures act in ways that permit us to read the coherence and continuity of 'character' more easily than we can when considering Cressida. But I want to suggest that it is the 'collection of conventions we call "character"' that proposes a mis-recognition of the early modern dramatic subject and limits the meanings and challenges that *Troilus and Cressida* as a whole might offer an audience today.

It is the political world in which we live – its leaders, its power struggles, its wars – that late twentieth century productions of *Troilus* have sought to challenge – or, according to a remarkable number of reviews and academic accounts, cannot help but address. Since John Barton suggested in the programme for his 1968 RSC production that '*Troilus and Cressida* is perhaps the most modern play in the canon',[7] commentary on the play's relevance to twentieth century concerns has become a commonplace amongst reviewers and critics. This 'play of shifting values ... is the Shakespeare play closest to the present day mood' in 1976.[8] 'The play has lost none of its urgent topicality' in Sam Mendes' 1990–91 production, 'in a week when we celebrate the hollow victory over Iraq'[9] and in 1998, 'this is a drama which had to wait until this cynical blood-stained century before it came into its own'.[10]

Troilus and Cressida started the cynical and blood-stained twentieth century as the subject of much journalistic criticism for generic confusion and misanthropic bitterness. It 'came into its own' as after the Second World War, then Vietnam, then the Gulf War, reviewers began to read it as 'relevant': a relentless attack on the vested political and personal interests behind military conflict. A play of 'bits and bitterness', as a reviewer of Anthony Quayle's production describes it in 1948, becomes permissibly bitter over the course of fifty years of modern warfare. Whether the play is permitted to be 'bitty' on the other hand is another matter. Jan Kott's late 1960s' reading in *Shakespeare Our Contemporary* is steeped in nostalgia for a moral certainty: *Troilus* is coherent in that it mourns the loss of coherence. For Kott, the play centres on the disillusionment of Troilus. The young hero's loss of an idealised love is the audience and reader's loss: 'There is no place for love in this world. Love is poisoned from the outset .... It has been deprived of all its poetry. It has been defiled'.[11] Nunn echoes Kott in his publicity for his 'millennium' production of the play, describing it in terms of Troilus' struggle through a world that 'seems empty of all value'.

A reading of *Troilus* as nostalgic for heroic values has been standard since Tillyard insisted that the fact that figures in the play fail to live up to their own virtues 'does not mean Shakespeare temporarily despised honour and generosity ...'.[12] It is a reading that recurs in accounts of the play through the 1980s, even as audiences were gazing impassively at the dethroning of heroes[13] and critics of a post-structuralist bent were beginning to rejoice in a fragmented, cynical *Troilus*. In '*Troilus and Cressida*, its Dramatic Unity and Genre', Harold Brooks is quite categorical in his assertion that 'cosmic order and the principle of degree in society, and international justice, founded on the law of nature and of nations' remain 'irreducible' by the end of the play, having once been 'movingly and conclusively affirmed by the greatest Trojan [Hector] and the best among the Greeks'. The 'irreducible' nature of all these supposed universals is located in a homogeneous reaction by an imagined audience, which 'enters into them with full and strong approval' as they are compelled to feel 'the final tragic catastrophe of Hector's death'.[14]

Jan Kott calls his *Troilus* chapter in *Shakespeare Our Contemporary*, 'Amazing and Modern', but the play has been more recently appropriated as 'Amazing and Postmodern'. In an essay on *Troilus* in the collection *Shakespeare and the Question of Theory* Elizabeth Freund remarks, 'in the climate of contemporary critical discourse', it is becoming possible 'to show how the Shakespearean self-reflexive forays of wit match, remarkably, the wit of the deconstructionist enterprise'.[15] For writers of a post-modern theoretical turn such as Freund, *Troilus* is a fragmented play and a play of fragments, and therein lies its power. She uses her essay to critique an 'Eliotic' hermeneutic of moral unity that 'works to subdue and tame ... [its] radically subversive energies of wit to some kind of manageable order'.[16] *Troilus*'s politics – its potential to be radically subversive – lies in its wittiness and bittiness. For Linda Charnes, who cites an exhaustive list of post-modern theorists as her influences in the introduction to her *Notorious Identity*, the play attacks the 'myths of origin' revered by traditional criticism with a refusal to offer figures with single sets of values and motivations.[17] For Barbara Everett, rather than overwhelm its audience with a mournful nostalgia, the notoriety of these fallen heroes produces a sense of lassitude, a lack of suspense in the plot which means that 'the play's primary value becomes its relationship with reader or audience'.[18]

The strength of the play for many late twentieth-century critics is its perception that there is something wrong with society's values. The question that arises from these different readings is whether it offers a set of lost values to mourn, or whether it undermines the very concepts of 'value' and 'values'. Do we have here a play that speaks to a modernist despair in the face of a loss of values, or post-modern playfulness around the concept? The last two decades of the twentieth century produce both readings. What I want to explore here is the politics of these readings as it emerges in production – or as it might emerge, for I am going to argue that Freund's 'radically subversive energies of wit' have not quite made the stage yet, and that recent production has tended towards Kott's nostalgic reading of *Troilus*. The productions under examination here foreground two twentieth century concerns – the politics of war and of patriarchy – but both, to differing degrees make of *Troilus* a modern tragedy of individual loss, with the fictional dilemmas and motivations of character at its centre. I am going to end the chapter by speculating as to what happens when the play's 'energies' – its underlying drives, the intentions of its figures – are assumed to be overtly theatrical. Charnes argues that 'The characters of Troilus and Cressida, like the actors who "play" them, also "show" or "play" themselves within the world of the play: self-histrionicism or theatricality is built into their texts'.[19] What kind of *Troilus* might emerge if the citational self-consciousness that Charnes sees in the play is given theatrical attention, if the dramatic figures also 'show' or 'play' themselves within the world of the theatre?

Millenial Troy

Troilus and Cressida *at the National and the RSC, 1999–2000*

The opening moments of Michael Boyd's *Troilus and Cressida* suggest that this is to be a piece of post-Brechtian directness: rough, immediate theatre with the audience sat close to the performers around a thrust stage. This stage is bare but for an electric light with a battered shade hanging over its centre, a chair with an old, cumbersome-looking camera on it centre right, and a burn mark on the floor. The Prologue is spoken by Thersites (Lloyd Hutchinson), dressed in battered bowler and stained overcoat; his is the pre-set camera. This hack journalist or war photographer takes the audience through a sepia slide-show of the Spanish Civil War, to which is added one of the actress playing Helen, tinted to appear as old as the 1930s photographs. Thersites draws back the grey curtain from across an upstage proscenium to reveal the suggestion of a bombed-out Catholic church stage right – a statue of the virgin, broken stained glass – and a door stage left. Brecht's comments on stage design are recalled: the use of projections,[20] a bare stage with locations only suggested,[21] realistically detailed costumes.[22] I am on the look-out for echoes of Manfred Wekwerth's 1986 production for the Berliner Ensemble in which the 'performances bloom in a set ... of great imaginative fertility and flexibility, achieved by the simplest of means'.[23] However, elements of the decor that may only be conceivable post-Brecht tend to work at a level of decor*ation* in this production. It is dominated by the need to support coherence of character in a production that, despite its semantic shifts, ultimately reads *Troilus* as a play about what War does to Individuals, with war and individuals framed as timeless naturalistic tropes. War is the bleak environment against which the individual must struggle. The tragedy of *Troilus* is the tragedy of Troilus, whose loss of this struggle the audience is invited to mourn.

Of course, one might argue that mourning for the loss of Troilus' idealistic innocence is exactly what the play invites. *Troilus and Cressida* sees him change from a young knight and lover who defends the theft of Helen as 'a theme of honour and renown, a spur to valiant and magnanimous deeds' (2.2.199–200), to a disillusioned soldier, who dismisses as 'Fool's play' Hector's tendency to give Greeks a second chance on the battlefield (5.3.43). Hector calls him 'savage' (5.3.49) and the shift is indeed ripe for reading as a pitiful loss of humanity. The RSC positions Troilus' disillusionment as the play's final catastrophe by cutting the text to give the eponymous hero the last word. The epilogue that, in most modern editions, Pandarus speaks at the end of the play, is spoken earlier, at 5.3.112.[24] Troilus' lines of 5.6, 'Fate hear me what I say! I reck not if thou end my life today' (5.6.26–7), are moved to the end of the play. Will Houston's Troilus sits alone in a spotlight at the end of the performance. He repeats 'Fate hear me what I say! I reck not if thou end my life today', then shouts 'End my life!' once more, into the darkness of the auditorium, followed by a whispered 'today'. Blackout. Like J. M. Nosworthy in 1965, who argues that Shakespeare was beginning a tragic version of the play before being invited to submit a comedy to the Inns of Court for their annual revels,[25] Boyd appears to find Pandarus' Epilogue an inadequate ending to *Troilus and Cressida* and his production concludes not with a speech about prostitution and venereal disease but with the near suicidal cry of Troilus.

Reviewers were at odds regarding where and when Tom Piper's set and costumes situate the Troilus' battles and betrayal. The sepia Prologue photographs are scenes from the Spanish Civil War; the women's dresses and haircuts are 1940s-inflected. The *Evening Standard*, using the Trojans' Irish accents as evidence, decides that the year is '... 1919. The besieged Trojans become IRA rebels at war with Britain';[26]

the *Independent* sees the production 'making reference to World War One',[27] while *What's On*, favours a later date, referring to 'Classical Greek heroes recast as World War Two diplomats'.[28] The *Financial Times* reviewer finds himself in 'a part of the twentieth century just before our own, in some more or less middle class milieu somewhere in the Eastern Mediterranean'[29] while the *Telegraph* reviewer admits that he spent the opening scenes 'fretting about exactly where and when the action was supposedly taking place',[30] eventually deciding that he could enjoy the show without coming to any conclusion.

The production clearly suggests a variety of twentieth century wars – and a variety of (romantic? pointless?) causes to fight for, for which Helen might serve as allegory. The historical and political specificity of the wars on offer means that the possible allegories cannot hold, however. The combination of sepia photographs, 1940s costumes and Irish Trojans serve to add to the nostalgic sense of loss that the production focuses through Troilus. The Greeks appear as a buttoned-up military bureaucracy, dressed in grey uniforms, speaking with clipped English and Scottish accents, holding their council scene over a public address system,[31] whilst the Irish Trojans meet over food and earthenware jugs, around a trestle table and wearing unkempt civvies. They are the oppressed minority where the Greeks are the conquering force. To recall the *1066 and All That* joke about cavaliers and roundheads, here the Trojans are 'wrong but romantic', having abducted Helen, and the Greeks 'right but revolting' in their scheming rationality. Paradoxically, given the association in British culture of Irishness with political struggle, Troilus being one of the (romantically Irish) Trojans serves to further individuate him in comparison to the more obviously 'political', faceless Greeks in their grey suits. Boyd's production evokes a range of historical moments but is ultimately concerned with the terrible things any war might do to a keen and idealistic young man in a generalised past from which we can never learn. We are asked to feel for such a young man, to mourn the loss of his idealistic chivalry, but I would argue that we remain unimplicated in the power structures and struggles that have led to his end – an end that is only in this production the end of the play. When Will Houston as Troilus calls for fate to end his life, he cries out into the special space for soliloquy that has been imagined by naturalistic staging and facilitated by modern lighting. It is a dark space, a space without an audience in it, a theatrical metaphor for a self that the actor can talk to without facing the problems of plausibility that arise from delivering complex iambic verse as if actually 'talking to yourself'. As an audience member, one has the impression of being talked through rather than talked to; Houston speaks out into the auditorium but his 'circle of attention' remains, as Stanislavski instructs,[32] unbroken by anyone in it.

I want to turn now to Trevor Nunn's National Theatre production, whose run overlapped the RSC's and which made even more marked use of textual transposition.[33] Here, the Trojans are similarly fated romantics, the empathetic but flawed centre of the play. The epic theatricality of the *mise en scène*, however, shifts the focus of this production somewhat, from personal dilemma to social construction. The National's *Troilus and Cressida* takes place on the open, circular stage of the Olivier Theatre, which is covered with reddish earth and gravel.[34] The boundaries of the playing space are the same concrete grey as the South Bank's arts complex, so that the set merges with the walls of the theatre, creating a seamless whole, a potential blurring of acting and audience space. This is an arena where Christians might be thrown to the lions for our entertainment, one that suggests – though in a less intimate way than the RSC set – that the audience is to be implicated in the action.[35] The stage is a large empty space in which events of epic proportions might take place, an impression confirmed as large numbers of Greek and Trojan soldiers re-enact the capture of Helen and the ensuing battles, in a series of stylised stage pictures during the Prologue. There is no attempt to 'set' this conflict in a war which might be more familiar to a twentieth-century audience than that of the Homeric epic. The war regalia of both Greeks and Trojans signal 'ancient', deliberately other to the twentieth century.

The RSC's use of 1940s costumes and photographs from the Spanish Civil War has the paradoxical effect of dehistoricising the text by suggesting that it could be set in any war.[36] Design and costume construct war as a timeless trope. It might similarly be argued that returning to a visual version of the Homeric epic is also a dehistoricising mechanism, treating the text as a transparent window onto a history of which the early modern period had a specific and limited knowledge. The conscious theatricality of the moving tableaux created during the Prologue, however, reflects the play's consciousness that we are watching the recreation of a myth on stage and that as such, the images presented are versions of a narrative, historically determined. The high-blown and archaic language[37] of the Prologue may be lost on a twentieth-century audience who, to varying degrees, will find much early modern dramatic language high-blown and archaic. To an early modern audience, the contrast between the Prologue's evocation of 'Priam's six gated city' (Prologue, 15) and his confession that a play cannot contain the enormity of the epic might have been clearer. The Trojan wars are great, glorious, mythical, distant: this is a version of them, a version curtailed to 'what might be digested in a play' (Prologue, 29).

On the Olivier stage, this discursive self-consciousness is reflected in the use of consciously theatrical costumes and decor. The sinister war masks of the Trojans and the exaggerated crests on the Greek helmets remind us that we have to re-invent the ancient world every time we stage it. The lit cyclorama, seen through Priam's six gates as they are hauled open, suggests the vast battlefields across which a camera might pan in a filmed construction of the 'ancient world'. This reminder that we have seen other versions of ancient narratives this century, to 'like or find fault' with (Prologue, 30), is re-enforced by the echoing brasses of the musical score: grandiose, impressive and reminiscent of early Technicolor epics. The music cue listed in the prompt book underlines the consciousness of recent film history that underpins this moment:

> To begin the show: a big flamboyant melodic 'entry of the gladia-tors' – brassy and confident – it says the actors have arrived in this circus like sand pit, as indeed they will, swirling and multiple.[38]

Having offered the Trojan wars as a theatrical construction, this production appears equally concerned with the construction of masculinity in

Figure 2.1 Opening to *Troilus and Cressida,* dir. Trevor Nunn, National Theatre. Photo: Catherine Ashmore.

Troilus and Cressida. The Greeks of Nunn's Council scene sit in a semi-circle on a brightly lit stage, the audience in the Olivier forming the circle's other half. Legs apart, gestures sharp and clear, these actors perform a *gestus* of masculinity, underlined by the scene's jokes at the expense of the cuckold Menelaus (Sam Cox), who is repeatedly ignored when he rises to contribute to the debate. Dancing and kissing are twice used to foreground male self-fashioning in scenes set in the Greek camp. Dance is a homosocial ritual in which Cressida (Sophie Okonedo) is lifted and turned in the 'kissing' scene; it is a homoerotic contest for masculine power when Hector (Dhobi Oparei) meets Achilles (Raymond Coulthard) at the Greek warrior's tent: as the two figures dance, goading each other towards a kiss and cheered on by the other men, it is clear that if one or other submits to the kiss he will have been emasculated, as Troilus is by his love for Cressida, no longer 'master of [his] heart' (1.1.4), as Achilles is accused of being by Patroclus, an 'effeminate man/In time of action' (3.3.220–1), as Menelaus the cuckold is.

The Trojans, on the other hand, are a more mysterious, less examinable group of men. When we meet the Trojan generals the lights dim to a semi-darkness enhanced by flames in bowls. The Trojan council takes place in a circle that excludes the audience. Where the Greeks sit on stools, the Trojans sit on the floor. The Greeks know when each may speak. The Trojans raise their hands, then get onto their feet and break the circle when overwhelmed by the desire to speak. The Greeks wear weatherbeaten leather coats, the Trojans flowing white robes. The publicity material asserts that 'The Greek camp is by turns wily, cynical, stupid and profound' while 'within the walls of Troy, the culture is defined by codes of honour and romantic chivalry'.[39] The Greek camp is also discursive, formal, Western and offers itself for brightly lit examination, while within the walls of Troy the rule is passionate chaos and mysterious, dimly lit exoticism; the Trojans' codes of honour and chivalry are readable as the products of the impenetrable passions of a non-Western culture. Troy appears as Greece's decadent, feminine, black Other. In Nunn's production, all the Trojans apart from Pandarus are played by black actors, all the Greeks by white.

Like the 'Irish' Trojans at the RSC, then, the black performers in the National's *Troilus and Cressida* are exoticised and romanticised by the *mise en scène*, which in turn romanticises the Trojans and their cause. However, where at the RSC we are presented with a Trojan council scene whose figures are individually dressed and motivated like characters from an O'Casey drama, at the National we remain at an epic distance from these romantic Trojans, and rather than focus on Troilus as the disillusioned hero, the centre of the production shifts to Cressida in its closing sequence. Like Boyd, Nunn uses transposed text to re-focus the bits and bitterness of the Pandarus ending, but here we are presented with a mix of personal tragedy and social comment, as, in the very last image of the production, Cressida turns on the spot, her lips painted by Pandarus (David Bamber) as a slash of red. She has become Cressida the notorious whore of myth and, it is hinted, a whore on the fictional battlefield in an imagined extension of the narrative.

Both the RSC and the National's treatment of Cressida point to the directorial dilemma of how to satisfactorily motivate – or explain away – Cressida's betrayal of Troilus. During the first half of the twentieth century, when *Troilus* was deemed by theatre critics to be Shakespeare's misanthropic and inconsistent mistake, productions were frequently judged on their success in motivating Cressida. The fact that 'Cressida herself in the text gives barely an indication that she is to turn out a wanton in the end' is seen as a problem which Ben Iden Payne has 'got over ... very successfully' in his 1936 production, 'by making Pamela Brown play the part with a lisp and an effect of petulance which makes Cressida's early protestations of fidelity ring false'.[40] Heather Stannard in Anthony Quayle's production, on the other hand, is criticised for having failed to impose the appropriate psychological consistency: while she 'admirably establishes Cressida as "a daughter of the game"', she 'cannot keep the wrong kind of emotion out of her love scenes with Troilus'.[41] It is a problem that Boyd tackles in the best tradition of Cressida's with Wanton Lisps, except that, rather than making Cressida a consistently deceitful whore, at the RSC she is a consistently innocent but feisty Irish girl who is handed over to the Greeks by her lover and must reluctantly fend for herself by putting herself under Diomedes' protection. Nunn's version, on the other hand, foregrounds the perceived problem by evading it. In contrast with the brightly lit Greek council scene, where the argument in hand is offered directly to the audience for their consideration, Cressida speaks of her hidden love for Troilus and men's tendency to want what they can't possess in Trojan semi-darkness. 'Then, though my heart's contents firm love doth bear/ Nothing of that shall from mine eyes appear' (1.2.285–6) she confesses – and indeed, nothing does from Cressida's eyes appear in this potential moment of conspiracy between performer and audience, as it is too dark to see her face. A leaf gobo speckles the floor where Pandarus brings the lovers together; the scene would have benefited from the cutting of Pandarus' line 'an t'were dark, you'd close sooner' (3.2.47), as it certainly was dark, as was Cressida's tryst with Diomedes. Politics – wily, pragmatic Greek politics at least – can unfold under harsh Brechtian lighting, it seems, whereas personal intimacies, particularly

Figure 2.2 William Houston as Troilus, Jayne Ashbourne as Cressida in *Troilus and Cressida*, dir. Michael Boyd, RSC. Photo: Malcolm Davies © Shakespeare Birthplace Trust.

Trojan ones, must be shrouded in a residual naturalism. Cressida is brought back on stage during the last sequence of the play – but even the punch of this theatrically and citationally conscious display of Cressida as legendary betraying whore is pulled somewhat. Instead of Pandarus' last speech occurring immediately after Troilus, 'Ignominy and shame/Pursue thy life, and live aye with thy name!' (5.11.33–4)[42], and his subsequent exit, an exchange is staged between Pandarus, Cressida and Troilus, constructed from lines from elsewhere in the text. During this dialogue, Pandarus attempts to reunite the couple, bringing Cressida to Troilus on the line 'But hear you, hear you!' (5.11.32). Troilus (Peter de Jersey) rejects the gesture, angrily ignoring Cressida and pushing Pandarus roughly to the floor. The exchange runs as follows (with original text line numbering in square brackets, action in italics):

CRESSIDA: Ah, poor our sex! This fault in us I find:
   The error of our eye directs our mind [5.2.115–16]
TROILUS: (*crossing down DSL of Cressida and standing with his back to her*)
   My love with words and errors still she feeds
   But edifies another with her deeds. [5.3.110–12]
CRESSIDA: (*to Troilus*)
   What error leads must err. O then conclude:
   Minds full of eyes are full of turpitude. [5.2.117–18]
   (*Cressida goes to touch Troilus; he moves away.*)
TROILUS: Go, wind to wind! There turn and change together. [5.3.109]
PANDARUS: (*crossing to Troilus*)
   A goodly medicine for my aching bones. [5.11.35]
TROILUS: Hence, broker-lackey! (*Troilus roughly takes Pandarus' arm*)
   Ignominy and shame
   Pursue thy life (*Troilus throws Pandarus to the floor*) and live aye with thy name! [5.11.33–4]

This is followed by the re-entrance of Thersites, and the sequence ends with Pandarus' last speech as it stands in most editions of the play. The conventional text is thus resumed with Pandarus' 'O world, world world' (5.11.35–6) and he continues uninterrupted with this, the last speech of the play in most texts, and his appeal to the sympathy of any 'good traders in the flesh' (5.11.45) that might be in the crowd. During this speech, he crawls to Cressida, stands her up, adjusts her hair, takes a pot of bright rouge from a bag and roughly colours her lips, and makes to lead her off stage by the hand. He stops to drink from a bottle and Cressida releases herself and moves centre stage as Pandarus continues off. As the lights dim to black, she makes two slow circles on the spot.

Here, then, is the Cressida myth and history leaves us with, Cressida the whore. The production cannot quite resist making psychological excuses for her, however: in the transposed text, she tries to explain herself to Troilus, but he jealously and impetuously rejects her and her only option as spoiled goods is to become a battlefield prostitute. Alan Dessen describes this last image as 'Cressida alone in darkness with a hard-to-read expression on her face'.[43] It is as if the production wants to leave us with Cressida, but not with any sense of her agency. The pledged glove, which Thersites has got from Troilus in 5.2 of this production and throws onto the stage here, and the rouge with which Pandarus adorns Cressida's 'hard-to-read' face do some of the same work as Wekwerth's 'pledges' in his 1986 Berliner Ensemble production. Troilus' pledge here is a red ribbon, with which Corinna Harfouch ties her hair, then ties again on her thigh as a garter, whence it is taken by Diomedes (Jaecki Swarz) who 'abruptly transforms it into a choker, forcing her tethered neck back into a brutal kiss'. At the end of the NT performance it is Pandarus who drops both this and the glove Cressida has given Troilus onto the stage. Gary Taylor describes Wekwerth's *Troilus* as 'a performance wholly characteristic of the late twentieth century' in its feminist sympathies with a brutalised Cressida[44] and Nunn seems to be following in this tradition. Pandarus' rouge in Nunn's production recalls the red choker at Cressida's neck, a garish sign of whoredom imposed by masculine power. But Wekwerth's ribbon has accrued and shifted meanings through the Berliner *Troilus*. Though there can be no doubt as to the coercive nature of the moment with Diomedes and the choker, Cressida has had varying degrees of ownership of the ribbon, varying degrees of agency in the production. At the National, the rouge appears from Pandarus' bag for the first time in this last image, stamping Cressida with the mark of powerlessness so we can be sure of the production's political credentials.

Cressida at the RSC also makes a last, unscripted appearance. Before Troilus' desperate cry into the auditorium for fate to end his life, she enters singing in a shaft of light, a figment, one assumes, of his disillusioned imagination. At the RSC she is Troilus' tragedy, a personification of everything this production mourns: lost love, lost ideals, lost individuality, as Troilus gives himself up to the fight. At the National, she becomes a constructed version of the female to analyse and disapprove – but the production is careful to render her just as powerless, for fear her fate should be regarded as anything but the result of her position in patriarchy.

Cressida's part in the National's new dialogue with Troilus is transposed from her speech of 5.2, when she has given Troilus' pledge to
Diomedes; Diomedes, has left the stage, and the speech would be a
soliloquy but for Troilus, Ulysses and Thersites who have witnessed the
betrayal from their on-stage hiding places:

> Troilus, farewell! One eye yet looks on thee,
> But with my heart the other eye doth see.
> Ah poor our sex! This fault in us I find:
> The error of our eye directs our mind.
> What error leads must err. O then conclude:
> Minds swayed by eyes are full of turpitude.
>   (5.2.113–18)

Spoken to the audience, the last four lines of this speech serve as a
confessional commentary on the action so far. Cressida has been
directed by the 'error of her eye' and must look the audience directly in
the eye and tell them so. The effect of transposing the lines to dialogue
with Troilus is to blur their meaning, as Cressida appears to attempt to
justify her actions in retrospect. The potentially awkward contrast
between this confession and the passion with which the figure refuses
'moderation' at 4.4.2 when she is to be taken from Troilus is muted. As
Cressida's own lines suggest, there is the potential to stage more than
one Cressida here:

> I have an unkind self resides with you,
> But an unkind self that itself will leave
> To be another's fool.
>   (3.2.143–5)

But the gap that might be left for the audience's role in the production
of who or what Cressida 'is' is closed by the National's ending. A play of
'selves' is at the root of Linda Charnes' Cressida, with her double presence on stage as both famous whore of myth and agent struggling 'to
construct some kind of alterity to [her] "authorised" role'[45] as most
typically false of women. The actor, on the other hand, according to
Bert O. States' distillation of the Concept of Character must find a
single self to play, for fear of being left on stage ' as it were, by
himselves' (see page 6). Leaving Cressida on stage, as it were, by
herselves, is something the National production is not quite willing to
do. It seems that, to avoid an embarrassingly anti-feminist reading of

the figure, Cressida must be a sympathetic victim of circumstances, with understandable motivations to guess at through the darkness.

Being and not being Cressida

Troilus and Cressida *and the performance objective*

I began by suggesting that character limits politics in *Troilus and Cressida*. The National attempts a political recuperation of Cressida, by giving her a scene in which she explains herself. Although what she says in it is that the error of her eye has directed her mind, which might appear to an audience as no excuse at all, what we see is a scene in which a black woman apologises for her infidelity, a white man pushes her away and, having become soiled and rejected goods, the woman is left on stage and on show by a pimp. This emotive image offers a version of Cressida rooted in race and gender politics; whether it challenges the world of the National theatregoer is harder to say. We have not been implicit in the exploitation of Cressida; leaving her displayed as a prostitute is what the men and wars of the fiction have done to her. In the following exploration of the potential relationships between performer and audience in the play, I want to speculate about the meanings that might be produced by a Cressida who makes eyes at us, who directly elicits the audience's approval for her actions or defies their disapproval of them, rather than demonstrating her motivations for those actions through the fiction. This is a Cressida whose intentions make no sense in the naturalistic theatre, whose objectives are character- rather than audience-directed. To situate Cressida in a play that deals directly with the audience in this way, I will turn first to a figure whose relationship with the audience seems more obviously direct – Thersites – and then return to another whose subjectivity is produced by watching and being watched – Achilles.

It would be quite uncontroversial to remark that the clown in the early modern drama can be said to have performance as well as fictional objectives. He is licensed not only to call his politically powerful betters – Lear, Olivia – fool, but to sing songs and make comments on the action to the audience. There is no sense in which he has to 'come out of character' to talk to us; he appears not to know which is the world of the fiction, which the world of the play. According to Hamlet, he can get carried away with this duality, forgetting there is a plot to get on with in his desire to make us laugh. Thersites has this meta-theatrical job in *Troilus and Cressida*. Like Feste, he plays the fool for different masters: he leaves Ajax for Achilles' tent, he 'serve[s] here voluntary' (2.1.92). Like Feste and Lear's fool he is a 'privileged man' (2.3.55), permitted to say what his masters may not wish to hear. Like all English Renaissance clowns, he offers comic commentary on the stage action. It is, of course, a particularly cynical and nasty commentary, and causes some discomfort amongst critics determined to find a stable set of moral values at *Troilus*' core. 'The same ethical standards prevail [in *Troilus and Cressida*] as in the rest of Shakespeare' asserts Tillyard, 'and far from imposing his opinions on us, Thersites has his own foul interpretation of others cast back on himself.'[46] In these millennial productions, Thersites' foul interpretations are rendered untrustworthy through characterisation: he is drunk, and of a notoriously untrustworthy profession for the RSC; Jasper Britton's Thersites is crazy and carries a voodoo doll at the National.

But if Thersites' humour is a reductive one, so is the humour of the play as a whole. The first ten lines of the Prologue alert us to the consciously discursive nature of this text. The audience is offered high-sounding Latinate language appropriate to the play's mythical subject matter, which is then deflated at line 10 with the bathetic 'and that's the quarrel'. The play sets up a rhetorical mode then humorously points out that it is just that, and this foregrounding of discourse as discourse continues throughout the play. The discursive status of seeming universals – the natural order, the value of love – is pointed to by the figures who speak them. Ulysses explains that chaos is the result of disregarding a 'natural' hierarchy (1.3.75–137) then proceeds to devise a lottery which he intends to fix in order to prevent Achilles facing Hector in a duel, where Achilles would be the 'natural' man to select. Hector argues that the men he loses on the battlefield are worth more than the abducted Helen, then in a four-line about-face decides to continue the war on the basis that "tis a cause that has no mean dependence/Upon our joint and several dignities' (2.2.192–3). Principles are constructed in language and undercut in action, or are deconstructed using another set of words. As Cressida gives Diomedes Troilus' love token (5.2.67–120), Thersites' cynical laughter at Troilus' desperation may not make him particularly appealing, but he is only doing what the whole play seems intent on doing: reducing discourse to the body, high-sounding language to vested interest.

That Thersites lies towards the 'bitter' end of a 'sweet and bitter fool'[47] polarity cannot be denied, but his fooling techniques apparently work, at least for Achilles as the clown mimics the Greek generals. I am interested in the notion of a Thersites with whom the audience is invited to collude, who does his job of making us laugh and is less inclined to permit a comfortable distance from his foul interpretations than a drunken journalist or a vindictive madman. To borrow from J. L. Styan, the 'complicity ... in the pleasure of putting on a play'[48] that may have existed between performer and audience under the theatrically self-conscious conditions of Elizabethan/Jacobean stage production might be drawn on by Thersites in ways that are both entertaining and disturbing.

Evoking self-styled stage-centred critic Styan suggests claims are about to be made for historical and theatrical authenticity here. *Troilus*'s uncertain stage history warns us against such claims. A *Troilus and Cressida* that engages its audience with a reductive humour, rather than solely through the personal dilemmas of its characters, fits pleasingly with speculation as to the play's possible performance at the Inns of Court Revels. W. R. Elton lists the presence of mock-rhetoric, illogic and fallacies, a spirit of misrule, mock chivalry and legal references as amongst the elements *Troilus and Cressida* has in common with the Elizabethan law revel and his arguments counter the 'Victorian-conceived' interpretation of *Troilus and Cressida* as a '"dark", "unpleasant", "decadent", "pessimistic", and "bitter" problem play'.[49] An audience of trainee lawyers would have been familiar with a range of formal discourses and with the notion of arguments breaking down, the seemingly coherent and watertight splintering and leaking in the face of adversarial onslaught. Such an audience would also have been familiar with the performance skill of speaking to one in the hearing of all and of speaking to one for the benefit and better persuasion of the court in general.[50] A play in which the contingent, discursive status of seeming universals – social 'degree', the value of love – is pointed to both by the figures who adhere to them and those seeking to undermine them seems made for such an audience. Not only is the Inns of Court evidence inconclusive, however, the responses of any early audience must remain speculative. What such an argument can do for a theatrical analysis of the play is to focus it on the potentially *pleasurable* nature of the discursive self-consciousness of this play and the pleasure to be had in watching it at a variety of distances and with a shifting range of attitudes.

That a reading of Thersites should depend upon speculation as to audience response fits logically with his role as clown. I now want to explore some possible performance objectives for Cressida. I use Stanislavski's term 'objective' advisedly here, because I want to be able to discuss fictional figures in theatrical terms. Rather than suggesting that conditions of early modern theatrical production and the corresponding wealth of meta-theatrical reference in the plays facilitate a continual shift from character to performer and back, I am rather arguing that these fictional figures appear to have theatrical intentions.

In the case of the clown, this is clear. Even Stanislavski, whose fictional alter ego tells his students that 'an actor must have a point of attention and that point of attention must not be in the auditorium',[51] could surely not have objected to Thersites having the objective 'I wish to make the audience laugh at these ludicrous, lustful, corrupted figures', although I am sure a dedicated follower might have found a more fictionally contained motivation. What I am going to consider are the implications of such meta-theatrical awareness by figures with less clearly defined theatrical work to do.

Cressida herself can be inscribed with clown-like performance objectives, and accordingly, the Cressida figure/actor's first function is to reassure the audience that the play has not abandoned the bathetic wit of the Prologue, despite Troilus' recent appearance as perfect, and perfectly serious, chivalric lover. Her wit is the reductive wit that under-mines the discourse of principle, of chivalry, of hierarchy throughout the play. Where Pandarus, watching from the battlements with his niece, reads the returning Trojan fighters as the heroes depicted in the Prologue, Cressida reduces them to 'what may be digested in a play' (Prologue, 29): a play on words, a play about flawed human figures. Explanations can be found within the fiction for her banter with Pandarus here, of course: she has an affectionately teasing relationship with her uncle; she praises Hector because she secretly wants to hear Pandarus praise Troilus. I am imagining her in direct engagement with the audience, however, out-joking the figure played by the older actor with bathos, innuendo and a tendency to read unintended meaning into his most seemingly straightforward speeches.

Cressida is warming up even before Pandarus' entrance. Her manservant Alexander speaks of the warrior, Ajax:

ALEXANDER: They say he is a very man *per se*,
    And stands alone.
CRESSIDA: So do all men, unless they are drunk, sick, or have no legs.

(1.2.15–18)

Cressida pulls Alexander from blank verse into prose. S/he extracts from the heroic image of 'man' standing on the battlefield, alone in his unique heroic qualities, the banal, literal, material fact of man who can or cannot stand up according to his state of health or sexual potency. Throughout this scene with Pandarus, Cressida resists his idealisation of Troilus by making jokes to entertain the audience at her uncle's expense. Whereas Pandarus assumes a shared understanding of ideal manhood, Cressida reduces 'man' to any man: banal, knowable and potentially sexually inadequate:

PANDARUS: Who, Troilus? Troilus is the better man of the two.
CRESSIDA: O Jupiter, there's no comparison.
PANDARUS: What, not between Troilus and Hector? Do you know a man if you see him?
CRESSIDA: Ay, if I ever saw him before and knew him.

(1.2.59–62)

There seems to be some controversy as to whether there is a 'bawdy quibble' here.[52] Whether the phrase means simply 'Yes, I'd recognise a man if I'd seen him before' or has the double meaning 'Yes, I'd know whether a man were a man or not if I'd seen him from the front and had sex with him' must depend to an extent on delivery, as the potential for the second meaning is certainly there. A similar exchange later in the scene suggests that this is the tone of the scene:

PANDARUS: 'Well, well'! Why, have you any discretion? Have you any eyes? Do you know what a man is? Is not birth, beauty, good shape, discourse, manhood, learning, gentleness, virtue, youth, liberality and so forth, the spice and salt that season a man?
CRESSIDA: Ay, a minced man; and then to be baked with no date in the pie, for then the man's date is out.

(1.2.242–8)

Here, Cressida takes Pandarus' image of 'spice and salt' and uses it to unman Troilus, reducing him to bodily functions he may fail to perform. Her technique is in the best tradition of fools, taking a figure of speech from its figurative context and deliberately misunderstanding it. In this case Cressida re-contextualises Pandarus' imagery in the material banality of the kitchen, producing from it another lewd and undermining joke.[53] In this the second scene of the play, then, the 'central character of Troilus', he who is 'searching for the meaning of truth, loyalty and beauty in a world which seems empty of all value', to cite the National publicity once more, has become the mere butt of a series of sexual jokes.

I do not draw attention to this moment in order to replace a sincerely-in-love Cressida with a crude and knowing Cressida. That would be just to replace one psychologically consistent character with another. I am rather pointing to the fact that the text here undermines Pandarus' conventional construction of what it is to be a man and to be a hero, by juxtaposing his lines with the jokes of a figure who is at once Cressida and an entertainer – Cressida the entertainer. At this point, these jokes are what engage the audience; they set up expectations of Cressida in addition to the expectation that she will betray Troilus. The Cressida figure has the potential to make us laugh – this is his/her performance objective at this point – and as s/he does so s/he foregrounds the discursive nature of language and its ability to constitute reality, to produce rather than 'reflect' man.

What are the potential effects of Cressida's engaging the audience through humour thus, making direct contact with individual spectators in clown-like fashion as she scores against Pandarus? A group of theatre students was asked to perform Cressida's soliloquy of 1.2.273–86. Pandarus has exited after the exchange cited above, leaving Cressida to confess that she has loved Troilus unbeknownst to her uncle and is 'hold[ing] off' because 'men prize the thing ungained more than it is' (280). Half the students were asked to prepare the speech for direct address to the audience. Half were asked to find motivations for Cressida to speak it without addressing them, to create a 'fourth wall' Cressida. The first versions were performed in a space lit with no differentiation between performer and audience. For the second versions the performance space was lit, the auditorium in darkness.

When the students used the two conventions of stage naturalism – absorption of character entirely within the *locus* of the narrative and a darkened auditorium – they instinctively brought another convention into play, the naturalistic use of stage props, whereby objects both elucidate character and appear in the fictional environment as if spontaneously inspiring speech. One Cressida sits down for a game of patience, turning up cards which seem to suggest her lines to her – a queen for 'women are angels wooing' (277), the joker for 'Pandar's praise' (276). Another spends much of the speech looking into a hand mirror: 'Women are angels wooing' says Cressida, revelling in her own angelic beauty. The props tell us something about Cressida's 'character', like the RSC Achilles' dead chicken: the 'patience' Cressida is a manipulative loner, biding her time until men are drawn to her; the 'mirror' Cressida is newly vain, discovering the power of her own beauty. A similar, lateral connection of text to prop is found as with the dead chicken. Cressida finds the 'women' and 'Pandar' in her speech from the cards she is playing with, or mentions the 'glass of Pandar's praise' and produces a mirror. Achilles declares that he will 'heat [Hector's] blood with Greekish wine tonight' (5.1.1) and in the RSC production proceeds literally to heat some blood.[54] Other students noted that there is no stage direction for the exit of the servant Alexander until the end of the scene, and addressed the speech to him. Motivation then had to be found for confessing to a servant what Cressida will tell nobody else and the relationship became a flirtatious, in one case downright seductive one.

These Cressidas can be defined as individuals within an environment realistically created by objects on stage. They also, it seems, invite judgment from the spectators watching them: the words 'manipulative loner' and 'vain' came from audience responses to the work. Where the Cressidas used direct address to the audience, however, the students' analysis of the performances shifted from judgments of the character, to commentary on their own reactions as audience. The student spectators began to judge themselves rather than Cressida's morality, suddenly aware of their own role in the production of meaning. They commented that they had been let into a secret by Cressida and enjoyed the sense of power that this conferred. The idea that Cressida, or the performer – and the fact that it was unclear 'who' is significant – was flirting with them, was enjoyable rather than reprehensible as it had been when the character had been judged a flirt within a fictional *locus*. The students found these versions were more engaging than the fourth wall Cressidas, and felt more implicated in the action here, despite the fact that they knew from their studies of Stanislavski that the 'reality effect' conventions of naturalism were created in order to produce empathy and engagement. Having associated direct address to the audience with critical distance and the *Verfremdungs Effekt*, they found this Cressida drawing them in, in a way the impressively constructed, fully motivated naturalistic Cressidas did not.

This suggests both a similarity and a difference between the theatrical consciousness of the early modern stage and Brechtian distantiation; a similarity: that foregrounding theatre and performer provokes the audience to examine critically their own relationship to the action of the play; a difference: that the early modern text does not appear to suggest a critical distance between performer and 'character' so much as a foregrounding of the actor's performance objective to engage the audience with his figure, to persuade them that his or her figure above all is central to their pleasure in the performance.

The Cressida that stands before the audience and tells them that 'Women are angels wooing' might dare to glance at them when she tells Troilus that she has another unkind self would be another's fool. She knows that we are watching her, that 'as false as Cressid' (3.2.191) has indeed become the watchword for falseness down the ages. She asks that we watch her stand in for and stand up for Cressida, performance after performance, sometimes drawing to her the gaze of a Troilus, or indeed a kissing Greek, sometimes asking us what we would have done in her circumstances. The last visitation of the ghostly Cressida on the RSC stage, singing blithely, innocent yet siren-like, and the last turning on the spot of the NT's Cressida, smudged with the pimp's red lipstick, both represent Cressida, but do not seem to let her represent herself. She is the fantasy either of a disillusioned young man or of a more generalised patriarchy.

I want to complicate this notion of the self-representing dramatic subject and her direct, knowing relationship with the audience, by returning to Achilles, of whom the Boyd production makes a study in chicken-sacrificing pathology. One might argue, as Rutter does for Cressida, that both Cressida and Thersites are exceptions to the rules of what the modern audience might recognise as characterisation. Both might be called exceptionally meta-theatrical figures: Thersites has his job as clown, Cressida her 'notorious identity', her struggle for a dramatic subjectivity in the presence of the audience that already knows her. Achilles has, in comparison to these two, little obvious opportunity for direct contact with his audience; he has no soliloquies or jokes with which to seduce us into complicity. He is a great enthusiast for subversive comic performance, to wit his reputed encouragement of Patroclus' satirical posturing in imitation of the Greek generals (1.3.146–84) and his applause at Thersites and Patroclus' 'concluded pantomime' (3.3.300). However, he always appears as a spectator, looking on at other performances, expecting, then demanding, that we watch him watching. An appropriate performance objective for Achilles might be 'I wish to maintain that strongest of stage positions, the on-stage observer'. There are few obvious opportunities for direct address in his speeches, few lines that are not dialogue directly aimed at other figures. His first appearance centres on separating the bickering Thersites and Ajax, then in 2.3 there is a section of banter with Thersites, in which Achilles demands to be entertained at the other generals' expense, so that we see a version of them orchestrated by Achilles: 'Come, what's Agamemnon?' (2.3.40–1). If there is contact with the audience in these first scenes it is by means of eye contact. Unlike Cressida in Charnes' reading, Achilles does not struggle against his 'notorious identity' but rather basks in it. When in 2.1 he dismisses the Trojan proclamation of a dual between Hector and a chosen Greek warrior as 'trash', he assures us that had Ulysses not chosen to put the matter to lottery 'he knew his man' (2.1.125–6). A look to the auditorium might be appropriate on this line before his 2.1 exit, challenging the audience not to know him themselves.

Until 3.3, Achilles assumes that his fictional reputation and the gaze of the audience will be maintained without his active engagement in battle.

His is the high theatrical status of the cynical onlooker. Once he has been snubbed by the Greek warriors who 'lay negligent and loose regard upon him' (3.3.41) as part of Ulysses' plan to shame him into fighting, his position of observed observer becomes more tenuous and he has to begin to work to maintain it. By the end of 3.3, when he has become the object of a series of negligent glances, Achilles' 'mind is troubled as a fountain stirred' (3.3.302) and he is tempted from his tent to see the duel he has dismissed. The exchange with Patroclus that follows the Greeks' contemptuous walk past his tent is worth quoting in full:

ACHILLES: What mean these fellows? Know they not Achilles?
PATROCLUS: They pass by strangely. They were used to bend,
   To send their smiles before them to Achilles,
   To come as humbly as they us'd to creep
   To holy altars.
ACHILLES: What, am I poor of late?
   'Tis certain, greatness, once fall'n out with fortune,
   Must fall out with men too. What the declined is,
   He shall soon read in the eyes of others
   As feel in his own fall; for men, like butterflies,
   Show not their mealy wings but to the summer,
   And not a man, for being simply man,
   Hath any honour, but honour for those honours
   That are without him – as place, riches and favour –
   Prizes of accident as oft as merit;
   Which when they fall, as being slippery standers,
   The love that lean'd on them as slippery too
   Doth one pluck down another and together
   Die in the fall. But 'tis not so with me;
   Fortune and I are friends. I do enjoy
   At ample point all that I did possess,
   Save these men's look, who do, methinks, find out
   Some thing not worth in me such rich beholding
   As they have often given.
                                                      (3.3)

Patroclus characterises the former demeanour of Achilles' compatriots as that of worshippers at a shrine, who gaze humbly up at a silent, all-seeing power. Achilles continues with a discourse on man's dependence on external honours, a dependence that he insists does not apply to him. By the end of the same speech he appears to have discovered that his subjectivity is contingent on others' 'beholding' and this is exactly

Ulysses' purpose. Ulysses of the 'degree speech', notoriously appropriated during the 1980s by Nigel Lawson, Conservative Chancellor, to prove that 'Shakespeare was a Tory',[55] reads Achilles to be proud to the point of madness and easily manipulated. Complaining of his refusal to fight, Ulysses represents Achilles as a self-reliant will, who

> ... doth rely on none,
> But carries on the stream of his dispose,
> Without observance or respect of any,
> In will peculiar and in self-admission.
>   (2.3.160–3)

In the same scene, Ulysses describes him as in the control of the 'humorous predominance' (2.3.127) of blood that engenders pride, an imbalance that Ulysses argues is leading to Achilles' self-destruction:

> ... Imagined worth
> Holds in his blood such swoll'n and hot discourse
> That 'twixt his mental and his active parts
> Kingdomed Achilles in commotion rages
> And batters down himself.
>   (169–3)

If Ulysses' concept of universal order based on 'degree' is to hold, those who carry on the stream of their dispose with little regard for the interests of their equals and betters must be read as sick, mad, hardly in possession of a will at all. A psychologically motivated Achilles who sacrifices chickens and tears the bleeding heart from Hector's body as Darren De Silva does in Boyd's production is easily contained by Ulysses' self-interested reading. Naturalistic character study and the psycho-biology of the humours cohere to explain away his actions in terms of mental illness or imbalance, a decadent disturbance we can judge by Ulysses' rules. Achilles is the alien 'other' against which Greek authority and 'degree' fashions itself. Such an Achilles logically stays within a fictional *locus* and directs his reaction to the Greek snubbing to Patroclus; he protests too much to his friend regarding the worthlessness of externally conferred honour, then cracks in a wounded sulk or snaps defensively on the lines 'But 'tis not so with me,/Fortune and I are friends'.

If Achilles' performance objective leads him to turn to the audience for his self-defence, our relationship with him is subtly different. Whether he delivers the lines defiantly or laces his defiance with a trace of insecurity, in telling the audience that he cares nothing for anyone's looks he produces an effect of vulnerability in the acknowledged presence of those on whose looks he is entirely reliant: the paying audience. His suddenly lowered status within the fiction is pointed to theatrically; it is as though he is *reduced* to having to talk to the audience. Ulysses has suggested that the applause of others may not be automatically forthcoming and has pushed Achilles closer to soliloquy where he may be more certain of it. Then Achilles must work to recuperate his performance objective of maintaining the high-status observer position, and our own superior position as witnesses to the action of the play is interestingly foregrounded.

The next time we see him, Achilles is, at first, the object of Hector's gaze:

HECTOR: Is this Achilles?
ACHILLES: I am Achilles.
HECTOR: Stand fair, I pray thee. Let me look on thee.
ACHILLES: Behold thy fill.

(4.5.233–6)

When Hector undermines his position with a joke – 'Nay, I have done already' (236) – Achilles must regain the status lost in the audience's laugh by reasserting himself as the ultimate disengaged consumer, critically perusing a man that he has reduced to an object for sale:

ACHILLES: Thou art too brief. I will the second time,
    As I would buy thee, view thee limb by limb.

(237–8)

In Achilles' last scene, he sets himself up as audience to Hector's death. When he comes upon Hector on the battlefield, he orders his Myrmidons to 'strike', though the Trojan hero is unarmed and he could presumably have accomplished the deed by himself. Though Achilles appears to take part in the killing, demanding that the Myrmidons send up the cry 'Achilles hath the mighty Hector slain!' (5.9.14) and sheathing a sword 'pleased with this dainty bait' (20), his performance objective suggests that he look on a while at the Myrmidons' slaughter of Hector before dealing the final blow. Within the set of conventions that demand he rips Hector's heart from his body, as he does in Boyd's production, the powerful effect of theatrical arrogance that emerges from a figure demanding that the audience 'watch me play Achilles' is reduced to psychological motivation, so that Achilles becomes self-indulgent to the point of mental disturbance. An Achilles with the performance objectives of the disengaged spectator expects to be watched watching, shares similar pleasures to the audience themselves as the heroes of myth are reduced to mere 'parts', but is, like any player, vulnerable in the presence of that audience. When he returns to the fictional fray, he reinforces and foregrounds his performance objective to maintain the position of cynical onlooker, attempting to recover his on-stage status in the killing of Hector. But the position itself – a position similar to the one in which Thersites has framed the audience – has been irredeemably foregrounded as interested and vulnerable. Here, I am suggesting, is the challenge *Troilus and Cressida* might offer a world that watches wars at a distance.

The production that begins with the theatrical notion of performance objective rather than the consistent, psychologically determined character objective, does not avoid the production of subjectivity effects, but these effects are fleeting and constituted in the moment of direct address, rather than consistent and exclusive of the audience. What it could avoid is the ease of judgment that an audience is permitted when the extremities and inconsistencies of the early modern dramatic figure are explained away through consistent characterisation. A spectator at such a performance should not experience less emotional engagement than when sitting in the darkness watching coherent psychological subjects take the stage. S/he may still experience the deaths and betrayals of *Troilus and Cressida* as tragic, or as something akin to the 'personal tragedy' of modern media reportage. But a production that plays this text from the starting point of the performance objective might permit contradictory pleasures and losses. It will certainly frame us as a variety of audiences: the audience which, like Achilles before Patroclus, can 'make paradoxes' out of universals by laughing at their deconstruction; the audience which experiences a nostalgic loss when romantic closure is denied it; the audience which watches itself watching all this. Achilles of the dead chicken and bleeding heart gives us the perspective of the proscenium arch, even from the Pit's auditorium: a single perspective from which truths about humanity are revealed, not questioned.

If we treat the speeches in this play as arguments which are put to the audience to be both enjoyed and critiqued, then it becomes clear that there is an answer to Troilus' desperate cry at Cressida's infidelity, 'If there be rule in unity itself, this is not she …'(5.2.48–9). There isn't *and* she isn't. There is no coherent, univocal Cressida; the Cressida that Troilus loved is only one part of an actor's performance. He has created her; she is recreated by Diomedes; s/he struggles to create him/herself for the spectator.

'C'mon Will,' says Anthony Sher on his first readings of *A Winter's Tale*, 'I'm not sure you've given Leontes proper motivation here.' But after exhaustive research, 'what seemed like a rather fantastical creation by Shakespeare is revealed to be an utterly realistic one'. [56] Or maybe Sher was right the first time. Maybe these figures are fantastically, unpalatably unmotivated in naturalistic terms and the texts seeks to engage the spectator in other ways than by revealing psychological motivation. Though this can never be an identical pleasure to that taken by a speculative audience of early seventeenth-century male law students, using the notion of the performance objective as a way in to *Troilus and Cressida* enables one to consider it as a pleasurable 'play' – rather than a mistaken collage or mournful condemnation – of bits and bitterness. A Cressida who makes laddish jokes in one scene, declares the passions of the romantic lead in another and betrays her lover in yet another may make no coherent sense. We may find ourselves looking at a human being on stage, laughing in comprehension at one moment, the next moment asking 'who – or what – *is* that?' and being asked who we think we are in return.

3 The point or the question?

Text, performance, *Hamlet*

In cultural materialist accounts of *Hamlet*, Hamlet is to be found struggling for agency within a matrix of constitutive factors: social, historical
and theatrical. His line 'I have that within which passeth show' (1.2.85)[1]
is a desperate grasping for a selfhood that had not yet been fully imagined. For Francis Barker,

> ... interiority remains, in Hamlet, gestural. ... At the centre of
> Hamlet, in the interior of his mystery, there is, in short, nothing.
> The promised essence remains beyond the scope of the text's signifi-
> cation: or rather signals the limit of the signification of this world by
> marking out the site of an absence it cannot fill. It gestures towards
> a place for subjectivity, but both are anachronistic and belong to a
> historical order whose outline has so far only been sketched out.[2]

A year later, Catherine Belsey theatricalises this lack of subjectivity, situating Hamlet on a cusp between morality figure and what we might
more easily recognise as character:

> Alternately mad, rational, vengeful, inert, determined, the Hamlet
> of the first four acts of the play is above all *not* an agent. It is as if
> the hero is traversed by the voices of a succession of morality frag-
> ments, wrath and reason, patience and resolution. In none of them
> is it possible to locate the true, the essential Hamlet. In this sense
> Hamlet is not a unified subject.[3]

Eagleton, a year on, echoes Barker's empty, gesturing Hamlet, with a
Prince who has:

> No essence of being whatsoever, no inner sanctum to be safe-
> guarded: he is pure deferral and diffusion, a hollow void which

offers nothing determinate to be known. His 'self' consists simply in the range of gestures with which he resists available definition, not in a radical alternative beyond their reach.[4]

Eagleton's Hamlet is somewhat different from the one he found in 1967, striving for an authenticity untouched by the constitutive pressures of family and state. In Eagleton's earlier account an authentic sense of self can be found 'neither within nor outside society, since both to step outside the official nexus of the court, and to commit himself to it, involves loss of integrity, disintegration'.[5] However, though it may be unrealisable within the court at Elsinore, the concept of authenticity as self-definition dominates Eagleton's 1960s chapter on *Hamlet*. 'Self-possession', 'remaining solid in [one's own] integrity' and the 'full, independent human being'[6] are set against the negatives of being 'used and exploited', [7] being 'defined totally by the way society uses [one]'[8] and 'having no existence at all outside [one's] role of agent'.[9] In 1967, it is still possible to write about an early modern dramatic figure's 'authenticity': the potential, at least, of a personal integrity outside of ideological construction.

Perhaps the Hamlets that emerged during the 1980s were a Foucauldian blip that accompanied a more general post-modern interest in – or despair over – a shifting, externally constructed, politically disempowered self. More recently, to be sure, *Hamlet* has been read as a more certain step along a road to coherent psychological character than in these 1980s accounts. Bert States' analysis is an obvious case in point; for him, theories of the subject are of no use to the actor who must have a character, or die – in the theatrical sense of a disastrously failed performance – 'on stage ... by himselves'.[10] Katharine Eisaman Maus, who takes Hamlet's 'that within which passeth show' as the starting point for her study of *Inwardness and Theater in the English Renaissance*, sees 'we, the post-modern heirs of Wittgenstein, Lacan, Marx, Austin and Foucault' ignoring a Renaissance obsession with interiority because of an historically determined attraction to 'the notion that selves are void'.[11] Theories of Hamlet's subjectivity have come full circle – the cultural materialists call the notion of Hamlet as character 'anachronism', only to be accused of anachronism themselves.

I have not abandoned the cultural materialist *Hamlet* in this chapter. As Eagleton's 1986 prince echoes Barker's, mine is indebted to Belsey's, or rather, the ways in which I have read the Hamlets offered in recent production echo her notion of a Hamlet traversed by other theatrical voices. Barker's frail, 'tremulous', emergent sense of self, moreover, fits the Hamlets I describe here, with their vulnerability to the audience they both confide in and shrink from. The cultural materialist accounts barely mention the moment of performance, however, and in starting from stage production, I want to theatricalise Hamlet's selfhood further. In this account, subjectivity is constructed in the relationship between Hamlet and his audience. His gestures towards the agency of the modern subject become gestures to the audience; his struggle with the constitutive pressures of court and family takes place in the audience's acknowledged presence.

A range of production decisions, of course, determines the modes of address developed by each actor but I want particularly to focus on *Hamlet* texts and to examine how choice of text and cut constitute Hamlet. Red Shift theatre company's *Hamlet: First Cut* uses the Q1 text defiantly, politically – and Peter Collins' Hamlet is correspondingly defiant and political. The reconstructed Globe is devoted to the First Folio, carefully cutting each scene in proportion and finding a theatrical Hamlet appropriate to the visible presence of the audience in the reconstructed open-air playhouse. The Theatre de la Jeune Lune, Minneapolis, and Peter Brook's Théâtre des Bouffes du Nord, Paris, do not make claims for the historical authenticity of their 'cuts': these are *Hamlet*s radically doctored by the companies, stripped of the play's political context and focused more closely on Hamlet himself. To the material conditions that constitute Hamlet's subjectivity in the cultural materialist accounts, then, I want to add those of editing, cutting, transposing.

The 'bad' quarto and the authority of performance[12]

Interviewed about his experience of acting in a production of the First Quarto of *Hamlet*, Christopher McCullough defends the integrity of the the 'bad' quarto text, suggesting that it points 'much more towards contemporary theatrical practice'[13] than the later editions. The later texts, he continues, represent Shakespeare and the King's Men in a more literary and proprietorial mood, 'after the play's economic life had finished'.[14] Q1, argues McCullough, is truly representative of Elizabethan theatre practice, which he compares to Bertolt Brecht's

> open-ended theatre of debate, where actors could be in character one moment and side-stepping it at another; a theatre that was more about the clash of ideas, exposing contradictions, rather than making seamless wholes.[15]

By default, he suggests that the later published texts on which current editions are based are *not* of that theatre, and are by extension less direct, less politically challenging. 'To be or not to be – I there's the point'[16] he argues, 'can't be said introspectively',[17] implying that the better known 'that is the question'[18] can be. Where Q1 is part of an anti-illusionistic theatre of debate, Q2 and F are the more self-contained, illusionistic and ultimately conservative texts.

Two significant recent analyses of *Hamlet* Q1 cite this interview, in which Bryan Loughrey talks to several theatre practitioners involved in producing the first quarto. They are interesting examples of the authority of performance in academic action. Leah Marcus' chapter on the Q1 text in *Unediting the Renaissance* and Robert Weimann's in *Author's Pen, Actor's Voice* both use these practitioners' voices to give performance credence to a theatre history that shifts from direct, populist, presentational performance to contained, literary, representational theatre during the first years of the seventeenth century.[19] Leah Marcus cites them to support her argument that the later published *Hamlet* texts show, 'literate expectations … slowly winning ground away from earlier oral modes of operation'[20] in English theatrical culture. Like McCullough, she associates a more literary text with more introspective dramatic figures, asserting that '[t]he soliloquies in Q1 are brief and demand to be addressed directly to the audience; the soliloquies in Q2 are more readily interpretable as Hamlet's long and elaborate musings to himself'.[21] Loughrey's interview provides Marcus with evidence that Q1 represents a more theatrically accessible dramaturgy, which is gradually being superseded at the beginning of the seventeenth century by the 'new, more self-contained literary theatre that [Hamlet himself] favours'.[22] Weimann represents the Q2 and F1 *Hamlets* as more clearly contained within a representative dramatic *locus* than those of Q1, and uses the difference to mark the contradictory authorities – those of 'author's pen' and 'actor's voice' – that he argues are circulating in the Elizabethan theatre. Weimann offers a detailed analysis of the dramaturgy of Hamlet's encounter with Ophelia in Q1 and F (Q1: 7.136–87; F1: 3.1.87–161), where he notes that a more presentational style in the First Quarto 'commingles with the representation of character'.[23] Weimann regards Q1 as '"a version specially abridged for performance on tour" … adapted and reconstructed by travelling members of Shakespeare's own company'[24] and suggests that its tendency to the presentational mode of direct address is evidence that, away from London, 'the writer's authority appears to be partially absent or short-shrifted'. For Weimann, the Q1 text is evidence of the touring players' use of presentational modes almost in spite of the playwright's more naturalistic dramaturgy, and Loughrey's interviewees are used once more to support him:

> … [Q1's 'To be or not to be' soliloquy] appears to be more strongly in favour of a mode of presentation that is contiguous

with, and yet different from, that representation which, in the strictest sense of 'impersonation' constitutes an inward self through soliloquy …. As modern actors like Guinness and McCullough have suggested, for Hamlet to say, 'I there's the point' is to address spectators rather than his own interior state of mind.[25]

It would be fairly simple to challenge the assumption that the line 'To be or not to be, I there's the point' (Q1: 7.114) is more suggestive of direct address to the audience than 'To be or not to be, that is the question' (3.1.55). One might argue that the Q1 version could be spoken just as easily as though a thought has just occurred to the speaker as the measured rhythms of the more familiar line, even that the abrupt 'I' could more plausibly be said as if Hamlet were talking to himself than the Q2/F alternative. But this is not the point or the question: both lines can be spoken fairly convincingly as either introspection or as direct address. My challenge is going to be to the broader assumptions about the relationship of stage convention to dramatic subjectivity that are contained in the conflation of challenging language and sophisticated philosophy with the 'self-contained' in performance.

That *Hamlet* Q1 is a simpler piece of theatre than Q2 and F is not at issue here. It is shorter, with shorter and fewer soliloquies, a fact that supports McCullough's impression of its being a faster moving, less philosophical play than the later published versions.[26] Weimann notes the less elevated, more physically concrete language of the Q1 'To be or not to be' soliloquy, which replaces 'purely intellectual, stoical forms of resistance by an entirely plain, everyday horizon of harsh living'.[27] Marcus comments on Q1's simpler moral and religious framework. Both she and Kathleen Irace note that Claudius is more unambiguously the villain in Q1.[28] Gilderstone and Rossencraft are less disturbing figures than their later published counterparts: in Q1, their past friendship with Hamlet is not mentioned and their betrayal appears less personal. Gertred's innocence is less ambiguous; she has a scene with Horatio, not in Q2 or F, in which she makes it clear that she understands her husband's guilt and swears to keep her knowledge from him. Laertes is the impetuous young avenger who leaves the duelling plot in the hands of the villain Claudius, not suggesting the poisoned sword trick himself, as he does in the later editions. The 'undiscovered country' of the 'to be or not to be' soliloquy is something to be feared only by the 'damned' in Q1 (Q1: 7.121). We fail to take our own weary lives because of 'joyful hope' (Q1: 7.122) of an afterlife in heaven, of which damnable suicide would deprive us. In the more familiar soliloquy, salvation is far less certain; it is 'dread' of 'the undiscovered country' (F1: 3.1.77–8) that makes cowards of us all.

The simpler moral and religious framework of the text supports a variety of explanations for the existence of Q1. It could be an earlier draft of the play, closer to an older, less dark and doubtful ur-*Hamlet* now lost, or even the ur-*Hamlet* itself.[29] It could be the more widely accepted memorial reconstruction, perhaps by an actor with a less sophisticated philosophical outlook than Shakespeare's,[30] or a reconstruction unconsciously simplified for less avant-garde audiences than those that patronised the London theatre.[31] I want to argue that, while the F and Q2 texts produce a different kind of dramatic subject to Q1, its *directness* is constitutive: the later texts represent a theatrical development of the human figure that talks to the audience, rather than a withdrawal into an increasingly self-contained fictional *locus*. I am going to posit the idea of an increasingly detailed and sophisticated relationship with the audience embedded in the later published *Hamlet* texts, producing an effect of subjectivity that can be usefully described as less 'self-contained' and less recognisable as consistent character than that produced by the language and dramaturgy of Q1.

Hamlet: First Cut: Red Shift

Figure 3.1 Tim Weekes as Corambis, Peter Collins as Hamlet in *Hamlet: First Cut*, dir. Jonathan Holloway, Red Shift. Photo: Gerald Murray.

Jonathan Holloway's *Hamlet: First Cut* evokes a modern state preparing for war. Its set is a construction of untreated steel, which rusts through contact with the slightest moisture,[32] giving the effect under light of tarnished copper. The leader of a false proscenium and a back wall with gaps and slots define and frame the playing space. It is a jagged, disintegrating, industrial space. The irregular pattern of the back wall recalls a map of the state Claudius is endeavouring to control, particularly when he unfolds a large campaign map in front of it, to pore over during the ambassadors' visit of Scene 7. Performers can be seen behind the back wall, waiting to enter and creating a musical score by scratching metal and wood across it; the sounds are picked up by sensors and amplified to make an abstract soundscape for the piece. Four steel 'obelisks' are used to create a range of locations – the parapets of the castle, a dais for the Danish royal family, Gertred's bed, Ofelia's grave. They are hollow and hinged to provide entrances for figures of the dead, dressed in camouflage fatigues, their faces bandaged. These guide Hamlet to the Ghost; their presence haunts the production. Scene changes are marked by rhythms beaten out with drum sticks on the steel obelisks, lending an urgency to what might otherwise mar the sense that this is '*Hamlet* with the brakes off':[33] steel rostra take some time to move. The scene-shifting undertaken by the actors, though somewhat awkward, is central to the production's rough-theatre aesthetic. It is hard to imagine reviewers wondering where the play is 'set' as they did watching Boyd's *Troilus*. Here, we are always in the presence of actors who make and remake a space for the telling of a story about a state at war.

The beating of the obelisks recalls the Danish shipyards' preparations for war marked by the watch in Scene 1 (1.60–69), and this state of military readiness is reflected in the watch's greatcoats and the khaki uniforms of performers representing the dead. Labour in *Hamlet* and the labour of presenting a play are both foregrounded. Costumes are modern and eclectic, designed by fashion house Red or Dead. Claudius wears a military greatcoat like the watchmen, Corambis (Polonius) combat fatigues and an army beret, Gertred a blue trouser suit that recalls 1980s power-dressing. Hamlet's donkey jacket, with paperback copy of Sartre's *The Age of Reason* stuffed into one pocket, is clearly intended to denote 'student'; Rossencraft and Gilderstone are similarly dressed with the additions of spectacles, college sports shirts and rather more ostentatiously worn college scarves, a comic comment on these more conformist students. Ofelia clings to the figures of the dead to a haunting, 'trip-hop' version of her songs, in a bright pink skirt, slit to the thigh, and heavy laced boots.

Just as McCullough finds parallels between the directness of Q1 and Brecht's epic theatre, so Red Shift and Red or Dead appear to have sought a social *gestus* of costume here, a realism that reflects status and occupation rather than psychology. Those that rule and serve the state are dressed for military action. The bandaged figures of the dead in their tin hats recall a war now associated with class-ridden injustices and ill-judged campaigns. The aesthetic reflects the production's preoccupation with the play's political landscape. Q1 itself, with its shorter soliloquies and more precipitous action, has been described as a version in which 'the problems of the play become less psychological, more circumstantial and contingent'.[34] In Red Shift's version, political contingency is central to Claudius' state of Denmark. The programme notes emphasise the company's broader political agenda in similar terms to those involved in the Orange Tree production; indeed these much-cited practitioners are once again used to point up the 'energy and edge' of Q1 in comparison to F 'in all its refinement': 'What the First Quarto is pointing us towards is not literature but theatre practice'.[35] The quotations from Loughrey's interview are followed in Red Shift's programme by a condemnation of the cultural elitism that has condemned Shakespeare to 'the rarefied domain of High Culture' and the inverted snobbery that has dismissed him as too difficult to be 'relevant'. The notes end with the statement: 'Throughout the population, people are entitled to have their artist made available.'[36] It is presumably the Q1 text, the artist's 'first cut', that is going to achieve this, through its qualities of directness and theatrical authenticity, as opposed to the literary refinement of the longer texts.

Hamlet's relationship with the spectator in *Hamlet: First Cut* is undoubtedly direct. Before the action begins, Peter Collins enters, clicking the lid of a child-proof pill bottle. He opens the bottle, looks up, takes a pill, slowly takes in the auditorium with his gaze and permits the spectator to take him in in return. The action of taking the pill could be described as the *gestus* of a suicidal Hamlet from which this figure appears somewhat distanced. He is a defiant, arrogant student figure, threatening possible suicide. The actions of slowly and deliberately clicking the pill bottle then removing the lid and taking the pill are clearly for our benefit; they are accompanied by Collins' combative stare. Where the theatre architecture on this British tour permits light to spill onto the audience, eye contact is direct. The production thus begins by acknowledging our presence. This *gestic* deliberation cannot quite be read as distance between performer and 'character', however. Collins' gaze into the auditorium is combative, but it appears always to be Hamlet's. Contrary to the assumption that direct address produces an inconsistent or fragmented dramatic subjectivity, his 'character' remains consistent throughout his performance.

Collins' is a young Hamlet, a rebellious student who thinks he knows it all. In Q1, it seems that he does. Q1 Hamlet has less competition for the audience's sympathy and attention than the Hamlet of Q2 or F. The first-published text offers the spectator a more simply villainous Claudius than the other versions. Kathleen Irace points to the fact that Claudius' first speech lacks Q2 and F's first 25 lines, in which the new king reminds his courtiers of their approval of his marriage and dismisses young Fortinbras' view of the Danish state as 'disjoint'. The Q1 text 'thus undermin[es] a possible first impression of an efficient gracious ruler'.[37] Claudius' lines revealing his sense of his own guilt are absent; the soliloquy comprising his vain attempt at prayer is more than halved (F1: 3.3.36–72; Q1: 10.1–13). That is to say, passages where Claudius might appeal to the audience, in both the sense of presenting an appealing figure and the sense of direct appeal to the house, are fewer. Q1 Hamlet comments on characters contained within a world of which he has superior knowledge, implicating the audience in his version of events. This seems to be a Hamlet that can make points rather than one compelled to ask questions. Collins' first soliloquy – 'O that this too much grieved and sallied flesh ...'[38] (Q1: 2.55–75) is spoken with a directness, energy and clarity appropriate for what is actually, in Q1, an expository speech. Claudius' re-announcement of the affair with which the court has freely gone along – his marriage to Gertred – is not made in this version, and it is from Hamlet that we first hear that his mother is now his uncle's wife. The first occurrence of the word 'married' in the soliloquy is five lines into the speech, to which compare Q2 and F's first 'married' twenty-three lines in. Hamlet is our narrator in Q1. His version of the marriage – 'O wicked, wicked speed, to make such/Dexterity to incestuous sheets' (Q1: 2.69–70) – is not balanced with Claudius' description, the structure of whose lines suggests a measured and rational decision to marry after the death of his brother (F1: 1.2.1–16).

In Q1, Hamlet has a clear theatrical purpose: to show us the court and its corruption, and to explain the plot. The first soliloquy expresses his anger at the world rather than explicitly introducing the contemplation of suicide. Compare

> O that this too much grieved and sallied flesh
> Would melt to nothing,
> Or that the universal globe of heaven
> Would all turn to a chaos!
>
> (Q1: 2.55–8)

with

> O that this too too solid flesh, would melt,
> Thaw, and resolve itself into a dew:

  Or that the everlasting had not fixed
  His canon 'gainst self-slaughter.
      (F1: 1.2.129–32)

Red Shift's Q1 Hamlet expresses the young man's furious wish that the whole contemptible world should be obliterated. It is not long dwelt upon: he soon moves on to the back-story the audience are going to need, while the Q2 and F versions of the soliloquy provide one of the play's famed hiatuses, in which he wishes he could obliterate himself. In Q2 and F, the revenge plot proper, to be precipitated by the ghost, has not even begun before Hamlet introduces the idea of his own suicide, calling into question his own 'use' amongst the uses of this world, which are 'weary, stale, flat, unprofitable' (1.2.133), rather like a bad play. Whilst Q1 at first seems the more annihilationist text, calling for '*all* [to] turn to a chaos', it swiftly moves on to exposition, giving an impression of purposeful presence in the figure of Hamlet. The later texts appear to conflate a sense of purposelessness, expressed by Hamlet, with a dramatic purposelessness, where the Q1 Hamlet's expository and commentating role in the dramatic structure is clear. Q1 Hamlet has his uses.

  Red Shift's Hamlet, the darkly humorous, rebel intellectual, is an instantly recognisable, post-1960s archetype. It is an appropriately 'self-contained' response to the simple moral framework and fast-moving suspense narrative of Q1. Collins' student prince has an arrogance appropriate to the revenge hero who takes God's law into his own hands, gaining the audience's sympathy but always already doomed. From the moment he looks defiantly out at us with his pill bottle, there is a sense that this Hamlet is going to be able to say 'I told you so' by the end of the play. Even the extra 'Well' that in Q1 comes before the penultimate line of the first soliloquy, 'It is not, nor it cannot come to good' (Q1: 2.74), gives the impression of self-righteousness, proceeding from a self-confident distrust of the established order in the student figure. This Hamlet can be easily mapped onto the figure of the revenge tragedy outsider, caught between a desire to punish a corrupt world and the religious imperative to leave punishment to God. His dilemma is not so much complex and ambiguous as a basic component of revenge tragedy plot. 'Though un-Senecan moral perplexities beset him on all sides', argues Robert Miola in his study of *Shakespeare's Reading*, 'Hamlet follows the conventional pattern and tries to re-create himself as Senecan revenger'.[39] Within Q1's fast-moving plot, he almost succeeds. Moral perplexities are short-lived: the moral framework of Q1 contains answers to them and the plot leaves them behind.

There is not the sense of pointlessness and lack of purpose that the other texts contain, no discourse on the piece of work that is a man, to be deflated by Hamlet's question, 'What is this quintessence of dust?' (F1: 2.2.308–9). Q1's hero, with his clear revenge imperative, is finally consumed by the overriding moral and religious framework which human revenge contravenes. The student with his copy of Sartre is an outsider in Denmark but has no doubts as to his role within the theatre. Contrary to McCullough's implication that the later published texts represent 'a theatre that was more about … seamless wholes' than Q1's 'open-ended theatre of debate', Q1's more straightforward revenge plot and sympathetic but inevitably doomed hero present a more predictably seamless whole than the Hamlets of the later published texts. Q1's containment within clear revenge tropes permits a modern production to map a simple but consistent character onto its central figure, a recognisably modern one who has points to make rather than questions to ask.

Hamlet at the Globe

Giles Block, who took the quaintly named roles of 'Master of Play' and 'Master of Voice' in the Globe production,[40] tells us that 'Questions abound in *Hamlet*. The very first line is a question: "Who's there?" calls Barnardo, and like most of the play's questions, particularly the most quoted, "To be or not to be", it is never answered.'[41] In Q1, on the contrary, both questions *are* answered. Where in Q2 and F1, Barnardo's question is countered with Fransisco's: 'Nay, answer me. Stand and unfold yourself' (F1: 1.1.2), in Q1 Sentinel 1 opens the play with 'Stand: who is that?' and gets the reply ''Tis I' (Q1: 1.2). In Q1 we suffer the 'scorns and flattery of the world' (Q1: 7.123) 'for the hope of something after death', (131) whereas 'dread' of that same something (F1: 3.1.77) leaves the question of whether to be or not to be open in Q2 and F. For Loughrey's interviewees, for Marcus and for Weimann, it seems but a short jump from the idea that the later published texts ask questions that they cannot answer, to the notion that Hamlet asks these questions of himself. Whatever the debates around the authenticity of the Bankside Globe, however, the reconstructed Elizabethan playhouse with its visible audience – partly mobile and potentially restless, partly seated at eye-level with the actor – clearly demonstrates that talking to oneself is an improbable way of engaging and securing the attention of the spectator. What is the nature of the relationship, then, between the audience and the more complex, philosophical Hamlets of the later published texts?

Mark Rylance's performance in the Globe reconstruction's 2000 *Hamlet* might, in another theatrical context, support the notion of a psychologically consistent character, insofar as his performance offers signs of inner life and emotional struggle. In F1 and Q2, of course, Hamlet describes his grief at his father's death as 'that within which passeth show' (1.2.85), a line not present in the Q1 text.[42] Rylance in his 'suits of solemn black' (1.2.78) cuts a frail figure on his first appearance; he is a lost soul amongst a nightmare of court bombast and sycophancy, he is set apart from the 'show' that is the court. Figures on the New Globe stage tend to look oddly large against the extravagantly decorated *frons scaenae* and pillars that surround them.[43] Claudius and Gertrude wear bright-red velvet, the expanse of which produces the illusion of quite enormous stature. Hamlet is a relatively tiny figure in black whose request to return to Wittenberg, signalled by his kneeling with his arm held formally aloft, is ignored, while Laertes is attended to and his request to return to France granted. Hamlet is a sorrowing figure, whose feelings are tactlessly ignored by the court and who thus appears to be feeling more deeply than its garishly showy inhabitants.

In both this and his 1989 performance,[44] Rylance begins Hamlet's first soliloquy 'O that this too, too solid flesh would melt' (F1: 1.2.129) with his back to the audience. Although he later turns to face us, such a deliberate exclusion of the audience for the first lines of the first soliloquy could certainly be read as 'Hamlet's long and elaborate musings to himself',[45] a manifestation of inner life overheard by the audience, rather than consciously produced in their presence. Rylance appears to want the spectator to consider – or feel – the emotional impact of bereavement as father and son embrace in Hamlet's first encounter with the armoured ghost, a moment not without its phenomenological discomforts for an audience used to dim lighting and dry ice. Hamlet's line calling for his 'tables' to set down that one may 'smile, and smile and be a villain' (F1: 1.5.108) is cut, so that his horrified incredulity at the news from the grave need not be interrupted by so seemingly calculated an action. In his encounter with Ophelia, played with misogynist bitterness and violence in many productions, Rylance speaks to Penny Layden with a tearful sincerity that suggests he really believes that a nunnery would be the safest place for her. His Hamlet is inconsolable at his mistaken killing of Polonius, managing convincingly to obliterate the comic callousness of calling his corpse a 'wretched, rash, intruding fool' (F1: 3.4.31) by weeping through the lines. This is a figure that signals all the emotional depth and sincerity that Stanislavskian performance places in opposition to the superficial, the showy, the theatrical.[46]

The above might give the reader the impression of a production *over*wrought with emotion. Few recorded impressions of performances find it so. Favourable reviews find a quality of authenticity in Rylance's performance and locate that quality in the voice.[47] This may partly be because Rylance understands that in order to be audible in this space it is not necessary to shout, a fact noted in Pauline Kiernan's analysis of the Globe reconstruction's first productions.[48] Not everyone on stage in *Hamlet* is as much at ease with their voices in the space, and Rylance's unstrained sibilance produces an effect of an authentic self 'giving voice'; he appears to be speaking 'that within' spontaneously, against those who appear to be forcing their voices.

Another key to the effect of emotional authenticity produced by Rylance's performance is Giles Block's use of punctuation in his cut of F1. F1's punctuation has a literary tidiness not apparent in either of the Quarto texts, with more prolific use of the full-stop, colon and semi-colon at points where Q2 uses commas or no punctuation at all.[49] While the Globe has based its *Hamlet* text on F1, Giles Block has virtually eliminated colons and semi-colons from his cut. Moreover, in his work on verse speaking, Block advises that '[p]unctuation in speech ... should be thought of in general as giving emphasis to the previous word, not simply as an excuse to pause'. Even for prose, where 'punctuation might indicate pauses that will help to clarify the meaning' he cautions 'against indulgent pauses .... If you can use punctuation to emphasise rather than to pause, this emphasises the muscularity of the text'.[50] 'Rylance's great talent is his ability to speak his lines as if the words had just occurred to him'[51] writes the *Morning Star* reviewer, coining something of a critical cliché. This effect is not created by naturalistic pauses and stutters, however. Rylance's words tumble out with an urgency that suggests, paradoxically, that the only proof to be had of 'that within' lies in the need for its external communication.[52] His performance is one that depends finally on his ability to produce the effect of communication between dramatic figure and audience, rather than the impression of an always half-hidden inner life. He begins his first soliloquy with his back to the greater part of the house, as if absorbed in his own inner world. However, he turns around on the seventh line – 'Oh fie, fie, 'tis an unweeded garden/That grows to seed' (F1: 1.2.135–6), awkwardly at first, as if pained at the act of communication, then speaking and moving more urgently, underpinning the dialogue with an emphatic language of gesture. This gestural technique was particularly disliked by the *Times Literary*

Supplement,[53] yet it was one that emphasised the soliloquy's status as an act of communication, as well as an expression of emotion: as an act of emotional rhetoric in fact.

The Globe production points up Hamlet's relative instability of role in the later published texts. Unlike Red Shift's Peter Collins, Rylance expresses no self-assurance in a role of expository outsider. There is, throughout 1.2, the sense that, despite the expectations set up by his theatrical presence, there is no role here for Hamlet either fictionally or theatrically. He joins his uncle and the court up stage centre at a council table, moves away to kneel and appeal for Claudius' attention, then moves further down stage – out of what Weimann would call the *locus* of the court – where he is ignored in favour of Laertes. He marks himself as without a role in court and does not turn to the audience until he is seven lines into the first soliloquy. 'O that this too too solid flesh would melt' begins with a wish that religious law would permit him not to exist, and Rylance communicates the first lines directly with no-one. On turning to us, having had his will disregarded in the fictional court and having no story to tell that has not been assuredly revealed by Claudius, Hamlet begins to address us as though abashed by such a great crowd. It is as the performer appears to gain confidence in his communication with the audience that the performance of Hamlet gains pace and energy and Rylance begins to move about the stage in desperation to convince us of his perspective on the fiction.

My account slips from 'performer' to 'Hamlet' back to 'Rylance' here. A man on stage signalling discomfort with being before an audience cannot but denote 'performer', while the lines he speaks denote Hamlet's fictional discomfort. It is as if the presence of the audience produces the move away from the contemplation of not-existing, towards more purposeful performative speech, the justification of his perspective on his mother's marriage.

Rylance's performance, then, does not merely replace Q1's simple act of communication with an internalised expression of disgust and grief to be spied upon by the audience. His is a subjectivity produced in the moment of communication with that audience and at a point where the performer's relationship with the audience is most clearly foregrounded, the moment of direct address. Claudius would wish to prescribe for Hamlet the identities of 'Courtier Cousin and ... son'. Instead, Hamlet hovers down stage dressed in black, an outsider in the fiction yet without the clear role of meta-theatrical commentator.

One reviewer describes Rylance's Hamlet as 'addressing us as if we were his conscience'.[54] In fact, he addresses us as what we are – an audience watching a play. A conscience suggests a certainty of moral stance

that Hamlet seems unconfident we will provide here.[55] The term would
be better applied to Claudius, in his prayer of 3.3.36–72, where the
word suggests a simpler moral framework from within which Claudius
admits – to us and to God – that he has transgressed, and assumes that
the spectator, too, will condemn him; or to Laertes as he explains his
doubts about Hamlet's romantic intentions to both Ophelia and the
audience (F1: 1.3.11–44); or to Polonius as reads his precepts for living to
both his son and the spectator (F1: 1.3.58–80). Murderer, father and
brother pray or offer advice within a secure moral framework, of which
the figure of Hamlet has been bereft, and assume that the audience
share that moral framework. Again, they make points where F1 Hamlet
asks questions.

Rylance's relationship with the audience, then, is a more complex
and ambivalent one than that of other figures on stage with him. After
his encounter with the ghost and the putting on of his 'antic disposition'
(1.5.172), he draws attention to the moral simplicity around him with a
more confident mode of direct address, provoking the spectator's
complicit laughter at the expense of Polonius and Rosencrantz and
Guildenstern. This is a shift into a clowning role that some reviews find
uncomfortable, and Rylance is accused of over-simplifying Hamlet's
descent into madness. The *Times Literary Supplement* complains that 'the
production simplifies ambiguity wherever it is found in the play', giving
the example of 'the method of Hamlet's madness (he wears a dirty
night-shirt and shakes his bottom at Polonius)'. According to this review,
'We enter the world of situation comedies where love is cosy and
madness zany and people hug each other a lot'.[56] I am at a loss to think
of a situation comedy that could be likened to the plot of *Hamlet* or that
might exhibit the emotional intensity of Rylance's performance, but
what is significant here is that the *TLS* compares what is regarded as
'zany' in Hamlet's behaviour to a current popular art form that simplifies human relationships and dilemmas. In similar vein, Clive Johnson
complains that 'Hamlet is mad, then, of a sudden he is not … Such a
lack of complexity makes it impossible to identify with the characters,
and … It fatally means that Hamlet's dilemma does not appear a
dilemma at all.'[57] We return to a notion of complexity that is conflated
with the Stanislavskian concept of organic character development,
whereby every line and action offered by a dramatic figure must hold to
a psychological logic contained within the play's fiction.

Rylance's shifts from grief-stricken son, to bewildered performer
uncertain of his role in the presence of the audience, to clown-
commentator, complicate the notion of Hamlet as a clearly defined
character who undergoes psychological development within the self-

contained world of theatrical naturalism. Immediately Horatio and the watch reappear after his encounter with the ghost in 1.5, Hamlet is beginning to elicit laughter from the audience.[58] From staggering tearfully under the burden of the knowledge the ghost has imparted, using his sword as a crutch, Rylance is suddenly provoking laughter at the ghost's quick work under the stage, following the line 'Well said, old Mole, can'st work i'th'ground so fast?'(1.5.162) with an absurd physicalisation of a mole, complete with mechanical digger vocal effects. From the point where he enters dressed in a night-shirt, smeared with brown marks suggestive of excrement – 2.2, his first entrance after his encounter with the ghost of 1.5 – his relationship with the audience leaps repeatedly back and forth from knowing humour to the vulnerability of exposed grief; Rylance's Hamlet's *performance* of madness problematises the stable subjectivity that the reviewers cited above would wish to see break down at a supposedly more realistic pace.

The 'antic disposition' as it is manifested to Polonius and to Rosencrantz and Guildenstern, those chiefly concerned with keeping him under surveillance, is a performed madness that draws the audience into further humorous complicity with Hamlet at the theatrical expense of these, Claudius' spies. This is not to say that audience speculation as to whether or not Hamlet is 'really mad' is closed down but rather that the production offers a dense layering of performer-playing-madman and madness-as-performance that refuses simple solutions to the question of who or what Hamlet is. The bottom-shaking to which the *TLS* reviewer objects, then, is part of a build-up of comic irony at the expense of those that would sound the depth of Hamlet's mystery. This particular action is part of a routine that begins during Polonius' description of the players (2.2.396–402), during which Rylance stands on the table behind him and reduces him to the 'tedious old fool' (2.2.219) of his earlier insult, pretending to control him as a puppet-master, wind him up with a handle, and eventually baring his behind in the parody of the madman Polonius thinks he is. Polonius, the confident voice of the moral truism, thinks he commands the audience with his comments on Hamlet's madness, but it is Rylance's clowning that holds our attention.

Hamlet's adoption of the role of the clown, who 'works' the audience with jokes and commentary, gives rise to an interesting contradiction. The Clown or Fool is the figure most obviously concerned with 'show' of all Elizabethan stage figures, as Hamlet himself complains later. Far from fulfilling its intended purpose of hiding Hamlet's knowledge from the rest of the court, the role actually brings on Claudius' surveillance. If this did not make it an inappropriate enough role for the revenge hero trying to carry out his task, the clown or fool has also, according to Hamlet himself, a tendency to perform improvised comic sequences – including the baring of behinds, perhaps – at the expense of 'necessary questions of the play' (The bottom-baring occurs as Polonius speaks his absurd list of dramatic genres (F.1: 2.2.396–400)). Having encountered the ghost, Hamlet vows to wipe out everything that has formed his 'self' to date and replace it with nothing but Revenge Hero; then in order to conceal his taking on of this role, he takes on another which has a quite contradictory function. Clowning, like soliloquy in this play, draws attention to itself at the expense of plot. Yet Rylance demonstrates ways in which some of Hamlet's lines are specifically written for clowning interaction; an accusatory glance at the groundlings 'who for the most part are capable of nothing but inexplicable dumbshows' provokes them to a good-humoured muttering and booing in order that Hamlet can continue '*and noise ...*' (F1: 3.2.11–12), which provokes loud laughter.

It is worth returning to the Q1 text here, and Marcus' argument that the later published *Hamlet*s represent a move towards the literary embodied in Hamlet's own snobbish remarks. In the advice to the players, the Q1 text has Hamlet speak a series of jokes that he warns the First Player against, but that were presumably meant to provoke laughter in early audiences, whether from the 'barren spectators' in the pit or those 'gentlemen' who according to Hamlet actually go to the trouble of writing the jokes down at home:

> And then you have some again that keeps one suit of jests, as a man is known by one suit of apparel, and gentlemen quote his jests down in their tables before they come to the play, as thus: 'Cannot you stay till I eat my porridge?' and 'You owe me a quarter's wages', and 'My coat wants a cullison', and 'Your beer is sour', and blabbering with his lips and thus keeping in his cinquepace of jests, when God knows, the warm clown cannot make a jest by chance, as the blind man catcheth a hare.
>
> (Q1: 9.21–8)

T. J. B. Spencer's justification for including this passage from the 'bad' quarto in the largely Q2-based Penguin text is significant: 'it is just the kind of passage', he says, 'that would soon become out of date and would therefore be cut in later performances'.[59] Robert Weimann partly predicates his argument that traces of theatrical authority remain in the Q1 text but are absent from Q2 and F, on the absence of this list of jokes in the later published texts. One could also use this absence to support Marcus' view that the Elizabethan theatre is becoming increasingly 'literary' at the turn of the sixteenth century: all traces of the improvising clown disappear in the later published *Hamlet*s so that even jokes at his expense have become outmoded.[60] However, the argument against them in Q1 is not against conscious reference to the theatre so much as the jokes' lack of spontaneity. They are so 'oft repeated' that spectators are able to write them down before coming to the performance – presumably so they can be shouted out, thus calling the supposedly improvising clown's bluff. In Rylance's consciously comic performance it would seem that there is no longer any need for the clown to be the audience's source of theatrical jokes, as his role in *Hamlet* has been taken on by the tragic protagonist.[61]

In moments when he induces laughter at the expense of those who would keep him 'in the cheer and comfort of [their] eye' (1.2.116), Rylance turns surveillance back on the surveyor, offering us a comical and superior position from which to watch Polonius, Rosencrantz and Guildenstern and at the same time producing the effect of a figure working for the impression of individual agency, an overview of the dramatic action. Here his role in the drama is clear and can be likened to Q1 Hamlet, offering a perspective from outside the court. When he is alone on stage, however, and without the role of narrator suggested by Q1, this overview collapses and Hamlet engages the spectator in questions regarding the meaning of his role and the action to be taken in the play. In Rylance's performance, this does not mean that dialogic interaction is continually peppered with humour while soliloquies are always spoken with a bewildered seriousness. The acknowledged presence of the audience means that Hamlet can shift into a complicitous humour at moments where the reviewers cited here might find it least appropriate. The reviewers exhibit a discomfort with the perceived travesty of generic boundaries, but it is in fact the breaking of such boundaries that produces the effect of complex subjectivity in F1 *Hamlet*. Here is Bert O. States on 'the actor's presence':

> It would be unthinkable for a character such as Lear or Macbeth – or even Hamlet, who is brother to the clown – to peer familiarly into the pit because there is something in the abridgement of aesthetic distance that gives the lie to tragic character and pathos. A character who addresses the audience immediately takes on some of the audience's objectivity and superiority to the play's world.[62]

States acknowledges clown-like qualities in Hamlet, presumably because his 'madness' permits him the acerbic licence of the fool to comment on the reducibility of emperors to bunghole stoppers. However, whereas it is the clown's role to make comments for the benefit of fictional figures and audience alike, States' comment suggests that the tragic hero can only be 'brother to the clown' *within* the narrative of *Hamlet*: he cannot play the role of clown for the audience as this contravenes the rules of tragedy. The image of an actor peering into the pit comprises actor, auditorium and the conditions that would make 'peering' necessary: audience in darkness, actor with bright lights shining into his/her eyes. States has made the assumption that the tragedies he mentions are being performed in the proscenium arch theatre with its footlights and darkened auditorium. If I am wrong and what States has in mind is a staging arrangement in which the audience can be seen by the actor, then it is difficult to visualise the effect of 'peering' where there is no need for it. It suggests, perhaps, an arch humour, an 'aside' quite separate from the rest of the play's aesthetic, whereas what is evident in Rylance's performance is a relationship with the audience that is at the root of Hamlet's subjectivity. All Elizabethan drama invites direct address; the later published *Hamlet*s represent a shift in the dramatic subjectivity constituted by this mode of performance towards a more complex but entirely theatrical presence for the performer/figure.

Rylance's delivery of the 'Oh what a rogue and peasant slave am I' soliloquy, a version of virtuoso variety which repeatedly ended in applause, illustrates this point. The speech is full of questions, which Rylance uses to build to a provocation of the audience. In the 'solid flesh' soliloquy, Rylance/Hamlet appeals to the audience for agreement that the whole world is 'weary, stale, flat and unprofitable' (1.2.133). Now that the ghost has provided a point to existence in that world, it is of his own performance that Hamlet requires a critique. Wondering at the player's feigned emotional response to the death of a fictional queen, Hamlet asks,

> What's Hecuba to him, or he to Hecuba
> That he should weep for her? What would he do,
> Had he the motive and the cue for passion
> That I have? He would drown the stage with tears
> And cleave the general ear with horrid speech …
>
> (F1: 2.2.559–63)

Then

> … Am I a coward? [to which compare Q1 'Why sure, I am a
>   coward' (7.368)]
> Who calls me villain? Breaks my pate across?

Plucks off my beard, and blows it in my face?
Tweaks me by the nose? Gives me the lie i'the throat
As deep as the lungs? Who does me this?
Ha?

(F1: 2.2.571–6)

The speech builds from self-condemnatory comparison of his own
'performance' to that of the player, to self-mocking provocation of the
audience as Rylance comes to the very edge of the stage to ask 'Am I a
coward? Who calls me villain?' When an audience member quips back,
Rylance uses the questions that follow to suggest a mock fight with
whoever has replied, so that the questions that follow give the impression of a provocation to a pub brawl: 'Come on if you think you're
hard enough ...'. Spoken to an individual in the audience, the image of
Hamlet's beard being plucked off and blown in his face is a consciously
theatrical one, suggestive of a performance that is so poor that this is
exactly what one of them might do to a theatrical beard worn by such
an actor. On occasions when no-one responds, Rylance provokes a
number of audience members with the lines, then dismisses them with
a gesture as weaklings too frightened to take him on, contemptible
indeed given the pathetic figure he asserts that he himself is cutting.
Hamlet/Rylance demands that the audience condemn him for being an
inadequate revenge hero. Whether an answer is forthcoming from the
audience or not, this combative stance appears to give Rylance/Hamlet
the confidence for a truly virtuoso rant of 'a bawdy villain/
Remorseless, Treacherous, Lecherous, Kindless Villain!/O Vengeance!'
(F1: 2.2.580–2), instantly undermined by the deadpan 'Why, what an
ass am I. Aye, sure this is most brave' (F1: 2.2.582),[63] a switch from
seemingly authentic anger to acknowledgment of that anger as part of
the (inadequate) performance that provoked a volume of laughter at the
Globe in direct proportion to the swiftness of the switch.[64] The undermining of 'O Vengeance!' by the bathetic 'Aye sure this is most brave'
produces the effect of Rylance/Hamlet rehearsing, in our presence and
inviting our criticism, for the performance of the self-contained
dramatic figure known as Revenge Hero, the figure that he has vowed
to the ghost will obliterate all other traces of self. To borrow from
Catherine Belsey, the revenge hero he fails to represent, though 'unified'
in that it is entirely consistent within the theatrical tradition that
contains it, is 'precisely not ... a subject'.[65] It does not produce the
effect of a self-originary will; it has in fact been willed by the Ghost.
The effect of subjectivity *is* produced, however, as Rylance's Hamlet
shows us the stock type and acknowledges the inadequacy of his

attempt to play it. The sense that we are permitted an encounter with the 'real' Hamlet behind the attempted performance is strong.

The effect is a fleeting one, more difficult to grasp than a self-contained subjectivity based in character study. Hamlet expresses a sense of inadequacy to life's tasks, so during the soliloquies we might describe him as a character who reveals that sense of inadequacy. Hamlet expresses doubts regarding the exterior nature of show and performance, so we might describe him as a character who values serious philosophy and 'that within'. On the other hand, he is also to be seen organising plays, dispatching Rosencrantz and Guildenstern and 'playing the fool' with seemingly unproblematic gusto. His solution to the inadequacy of his own performance is to commission another one, 'The Mousetrap', in which he is to play the vehemently exterior role of the clown-commentator. Rylance's willingness and ability to perform each of these moments for what one might simply call their entertainment value but might be more accurately described as the engagement value of the performance objective, is indicative of the inextricability of the early modern dramatic subject from its theatrical setting. The strongest effect of subjectivity is produced when Rylance/Hamlet is most like a performer in front of an audience.

To return to the objections made by the *TLS* and by Clive Johnson's review, Rylance's jump from heightened emotion to clowning is entirely appropriate, given the theatrically constituted, dialogic nature of dramatic subjectivity in F1 *Hamlet*. The communication through humour which clowning entails, draws the audience into further complicity with Rylance/Hamlet, into what I would venture to call a shared dramatic and emotional space that has been prepared by the vulnerability of the performer in the first soliloquy. If the 'purpose of playing' (3.2.21) is regarded as primarily to create self-contained characters with which the audience can identify, then a range of requirements with regard to development and consistency come into play which Rylance's leaps from knowing humour to tearful distress might be said to contravene. Rylance's performance produces the effect of subjectivity quite differently, however. The leaps are those of the virtuoso performer, whose vulnerability to and complicity with the audience are played through the dramatic figure of Hamlet so that the audience is constantly in the foregrounded presence of both. Rylance's performance suggests that Elizabethan 'personation' is a development of the virtuoso story-telling present in earlier theatrical forms rather than a departure from it in which residual, less sophisticated modes remain.

From 5.1, Rylance appears to lose his relationship with the audience. His distress over Ophelia's grave is played with a conviction equal to his performance earlier in the play but little contact with the house remains. Though the punctuation in the text of the 'readiness is all' speech (5.2.21–4) demonstrates the same tumbling syntax of the rest of Block's text, Rylance offers these lines at a more measured pace, giving 'The readiness is all' the weight of a sentence to itself, as it has in modern editions.[66] There are two ways of reading this change. One reading finds that Hamlet, having discovered a capacity for action in his dealings with pirates and treacherous friends, attains the Christian stoic's reconciliation with death in his encounter with Yorick's skull and his musings about the fate of kings as bunghole stoppers. Certainly Rylance appears calmer and more philosophical in this slower and less direct mode of performance, and it may have been the intention to signal that Hamlet has now 'learned something' about the nature of life and death. More in keeping with the production's aesthetic of direct address, however, is a second reading of this scene, as bereavement for the spectator. Hamlet encounters a clown – the first appearance of such a figure apart from the lead himself – and regards the rotting skull of another. The clown role shifts from Hamlet to gravedigger, then is visibly figured as dead. Hamlet can now make what might appear the most obvious declaration of self-contained subjectivity in the play 'This is I,/Hamlet the Dane' (F1: 5.1.257–8) but then, in a complete relinquishment of active will, is reconciled to fight in his uncle's show-duel despite expressed misgivings. As a clown's skull is replaced in its grave, as Ophelia is newly laid in hers, it seems we must also say goodbye to the complex theatrical subjectivity of Hamlet, as he slips back into a simpler moral frame where there can be no questioning of man's inevitable fate 'Be as ourself in Denmark' (1.2.122) says Claudius, the only figure to identify himself with the country apart from Hamlet here. At this point, Rylance appears to obey the command, withdrawing from the 'presence' of his direct encounters with the audience into a more clearly defined fictional *locus* and simpler moral framework, prefiguring his final slippage into the fiction of the friendly duel directed by Claudius.

An ending which makes a simple moral point about what Hamlet has 'learned' is inadequate to the questions with which we have been asked to engage during *Hamlet*. His seeming reconciliation with his fate in Rylance's performance here highlights the relative moral simplicity of 'Not a whit, we defy augury' (5.2.219) depriving the audience of the complex, shifting subjectivity which they have been complicit in developing throughout the play. As Rylance pulls back into a more 'self-contained' Hamlet, the production calls into question the conflation of self-containment and complex subjectivity.

Anti-theatrical Hamlets

Theatre de la Jeune Lune

For the Theatre de la Jeune Lune, there is nothing that 'passeth show'. The self-consciously theatrical aesthetic of its *Hamlet* is one that informs all the company's work. They describe themselves as 'striving to link a past heritage of popular performance traditions – from circus and classical farce to *commedia dell'arte* and vaudeville – to their present function within the local community and the larger international community of cultural production'.[67] Their mission statement recalls the Globe, whose website tells us that 'each year the Globe Theatre Company rediscovers the dynamic relationship between the audience and the actor in this unique building'. Of course there is none of the focus on a single iconic author at Jeune Lune, no obligation for the company to narrate itself for tourist and educational consumption. The singularity and authenticity of Jeune Lune's building is predicated on its very lack of uniqueness, on the fact that it was once something else – of which there are still many in Minneapolis – a Victorian warehouse. Like the Globe, though, Jeune Lune is concerned to link itself with a past in which theatre was less of an elitist form, more of a direct encounter between performer and audience, theatre company and community. Its is the deliberately rough beauty that signals a desire to recapture the theatrical authenticity of these popular forms. On stage, painted figures in rich colours offer theatrical magic with all the tricks exposed against their bare brick-walled space. Its *Circus of Tales* is a display of simultaneous acrobatic and story-telling virtuosity; its *Seagull* breaks its naturalistic boundaries as figures float towards us in dance-like formation through suspended birch trunks to remind us that Chekhov wrote this play about the theatre. The bar and foyer of its converted warehouse are filled with pieces of old sets and coloured bulbs. Performers and co-directors Dominique Serrand, Vincent Gracieux, Barbra Berlovitz and Steven Epp are trained in the European tradition of clowning developed by Jaques Le Coq, and the exuberance and vulnerability of the clown infiltrates every production. The productions offer open pretence, and therefore, the company signal at every turn, no pretence.

Guest director Paddy Hayter's *Hamlet* is a production in a long and recently much drawn-upon tradition of Hamlets stripped of their political context. Alex Jennings at the Young Vic, Simon Russell-Beale at the National, Adrian Lester in Brook's Théâtre des Bouffes du Nord production are all unencumbered by news from the war with Norway and give no-one their 'dying voice' for the succession, as no Fortinbras is announced, or enters to survey the carnage at the end of the play. The combination of this choice and the informality of the Jeune Lune text, collated from Q1, Q2, F1 and their own interpolations, produces a highly empathetic figure in Epp's prince, a Hamlet we can get close to; we are given no distractions from him and he speaks a language we understand. Like Rylance, he appears vulnerable in the presence of the audience before whom he must expose his pain. Unlike Rylance and very much unlike Collins in Red Shift's *First Cut*, his struggle to act does not take place in a formal court or a country at war, where action is circumscribed by hierarchy, etiquette or contingency. Instead, Jeune Lune also draws visual attention to a concept that inspired the company as they began work on *Hamlet*, that of the play as elemental myth. The 'elements' of earth, fire, water dominate the *mise en scène* – the playing space is an expanse of sand, lit with flaming torches and edged by pools of water. A ring of masked Greek chorus figures in sandy-coloured robes open and close each performance and stand looking on at the action throughout, occasionally taking silent roles as courtiers and messengers.[68]

Situating *Hamlet* in a mythic no-man's land was a popular choice amongst audience and critics; it appealed, perhaps, to a desire for millennial *Hamlet*s to be timeless, open, universal. It also invites comparison to Brook's *Hamlet*, whose US tour overlapped the Jeune Lune run. The productions are different in tone – Brook's is the intensely serious 'holy theatre' of his own definition,[69] Jeune Lune's a rougher version, exuberant and carnivalesque. However, the visual conception of both *Hamlet*s, and the frame provided by the sites of their creation, speak of a desire for something timeless, a theatrical authenticity that stands outside politics and history. Both companies' theatre buildings speak their architectural origins; they remind us of their pasts by remaining distinctively unfinished. Both advertise the traces of past occupants and past productions: Jeune Lune leaves its warehouse walls bare and fills the bar with old sets. Bouffes du Nord leaves its paint peeling to remind us of the faded rich-and-gaudiness of past theatrical tradition; the theatre is a ruin of a reconstruction, built in imitation of a nineteenth-century ' théâtre a l'italienne' and abandoned after a fire in 1952, until Brook took it over in 1974. This seductively untidy aesthetic suggests both specific architectural histories and a theatricality that outlives history, or rather offers a return to a timeless, nostalgic space in which theatre was a direct affair and no plush interiors were needed.

Both companies appear to want *Hamlet* to take place nowhere – though in both cases it's a distinctly South Eastern nowhere with a story-telling tradition unmarred by Western theatrical elitism or the distinctly European politics that both productions cut. These are beautifully crafted productions, Brook's most self-consciously so, and their emphasis on story-telling foregrounds the presence of the audience. Both are radically cut and therefore easy on the audience's attention span. Both could be called 'direct'. However, having set up the mode of direct address as a convention that confronts the spectator with her own attitudes to the dilemmas and subjectivities being staged, I am interested in the elements of the Jeune Lune and Bouffes Du Nord productions that pull at the neutrality of their design and editing concepts. For these *Hamlets* are seductively nostalgic, potentially unchallenging. The buildings and the companies wrap us up warm in their theatrical authenticity. There are no embarrassing gift shops or irritating helicopter noises here, no reminders of the pressures of global capital to make us interrogate our consumption of that authenticity. I want to see if they offer any of the discomforts that I think the play contains.

Jeune Lune's *Hamlet* loses Rosencrantz and Guildenstern along with Fortinbras. Every actor in the *Hamlet* company made a contribution to the final draft, choosing lines from the parallel texts primarily on the principle of accessibility.[70] The company's 'Credo' promises a 'theatre of directness, a theatre that speaks to its audience, that listens and needs a response ... a theatre that excites and uses a direct language – a theatre of the imagination', and where a Q1 line seems easier on the ears of a modern audience, Jeune Lune use it. Occasionally the company replaces words with their own more accessible choices, and I find myself mistaking Q1 lines for Jeune Lune interpolations: Q2 and F's Horatio says to Hamlet of the Ghost,

> It beckons you to go away with it
> As if it some impartment did desire
> To you alone
>
> (1.4.58–60)

Jeune Lune replaces the lines with Q1's

> It beckons you, as though it had something
> To impart to you alone.
>
> (4.34–5)

The simplicity sounds startlingly modern.

Jeune Lune's conflations and additions, which not infrequently break up the pentametric rhythm of blank verse passages, render this something of an informal *Hamlet* text, appropriate to the carnivalesque exuberance of Claudius' court. Claudius (Vincent Gracieux) and Gertrude (Barbra Berlovitz) are player king and queen, drummed onto the stage like a cross between figures in a medieval carnival and Chinese new-year dragons. Each is at the head of a train of silky fabric in which they are held by attendants and from which they break, to roll with much playful, giggling sensuality on the sandy floor. All this decadence embarrasses Polonius, who enters, then nearly removes himself at the sight of the embracing king and queen: courtly etiquette is not observed here. At a number of points, formal address between characters is cut or changed, so that Horatio's 'My lord, I came to see your father's funeral' (1.2.176) becomes the rather more abrupt explanation of his presence in Elsinore, 'I came to see your father's funeral', and Polonius is demoted from 'My lord' to 'Sir' when Hamlet asks him about how he 'play'd once in the university'.

This last is a tiny change, and the reader might find it difficult to imagine noticing it in performance, especially as the company do not replace 'My Lord' elsewhere. Using it here in the Mousetrap scene, however, Epp continues with the mode of address he has used to Polonius when, in his 'antic disposition' Hamlet has refused to recognise him. The more casual 'Sir' is an appropriate address by Hamlet the madman to Polonius the Fishmonger, but rather undermines the thin veil of politeness that Hamlet seems able to command elsewhere in the play. This is a Hamlet who feels happy to shout 'A pox on you!' to Polonius when he tells the First Player that his passionate speech is too long. The exclamation is derived from the Q1 lines which read 'A pox, he's for a jig or a tale of bawdry/Or else he sleeps' (7 322–3). Where Mark Rylance shares his contempt for Polonius with the audience alone, Epp throws it in his face, and in another Elsinore, one would be surprised no-one has thought to pack him off to England before.

There are rules observed in this *Hamlet*, but they are theatrical ones. Both this and the Brook production share a concern with entrances. Brook's figures move ceremoniously onto the playing area as if performing a ritual brought into being by Toshi Tsuchitori's music. At Jeune Lune, masked figures enter in a cluster on each new entrance and move aside as if to reveal each new performer. Here is some of the exposed theatrical trickery with which Jeune Lune seduces its audiences – the characters appear as if by magic; we gasp at the magic while we can see how they did it.[71] Characters are brought on in this way throughout the production, and the masked figures stay on stage as courtiers, servants and arrases. Hamlet, however, refuses to obey the rules. He storms on stage by himself after Laertes has had his request to return to France granted – and looks as though he would storm off again, shaking off the joyful attentions of the masked figures who attempt to include him in the celebratory reaffirmation of his uncle's marriage and the theatrical sign system that produces each figure as part of a theatrical tale consciously told. He is stopped by Claudius' lines: 'But now, my cousin Hamlet and my son … How is it that the clouds still hang on you?' (1.2.64,66) and obliged to take part in a courtly and theatrical performance he wants to eschew.

Like Rylance's, Epp's Hamlet appears vulnerable and disorientated in Claudius' court and in the presence of the audience. It appears horrible for him to reveal how he feels about his mother's marriage in front of a paying audience, as he is so evidently bewildered by her 'falling off' himself. 'Must I remember?' (1.2.143) he says, wonderingly, rubbing his forehead as if what he sees in his 'mind's eye' appears there suddenly, distressingly, like the voices of a schizophrenic. Epp, like Rylance, jolts from frail disturbance to knowing clown and, though there is no Rosencrantz and Guildenstern for him to play off, his ridicule of Polonius in the clouds exchange distils the comic conspiracy between Hamlet and audience as he describes weasels, camels and whales in the sky with a deep-voiced mock seriousness. Like Rylance, his advice to the players repeatedly interrupts their rehearsal of the

Figure 3.2
Dominique Serrand as Polonius, Stephen Cartmell as Laertes, Barbra Berlovitz as Gertrude, Vincent Gracieux as Claudius, Steven Epp as Hamlet in *Hamlet*, dir. Paddy Hayter, Theatre de la Jeune Lune. Photo: Michal Daniel.

'Murder of Gonzago' and, as at the Globe, Hamlet wears a clownish costume to the play within the play and provides a percussive punctuation in addition to his verbal interjections. The company did not see the Globe's *Hamlet* but it seems that a focus on overt theatricality leads to a productively inconsistent Hamlet in both cases. Interestingly, the similarities between the two performances extend to the delivery of the 'we defy augury' speech – both Hamlets slip away from us in a moment of self-revelation here; both appear to have found a profound truth in the fatalism of 'the readiness is all'.

Ultimately, Jeune Lune's theatrically conscious *Hamlet* produces, paradoxically, a more anti-theatrical Prince than the Globe's production. Where Rylance bereaves us of his presence with his retreat into Calvinist orthodoxy and his quiet 'readiness', Epp's performance of Jeune Lune's naturalistically fragmented text before a darkened auditorium produces a Hamlet that has always seemed happier to be alone. His vocabulary of gestures is less presentational than Rylance's, his clowning a more desperate front for inner torment. Yet I am going to argue that Jeune Lune's *Hamlet* does not finally privilege the naturalistic psyche, the anti-theatrical 'that within'. Throughout the performance – particularly through the figure of Gertrude and in a moment where the framing device of the mask impinges on the main action of the play, Hamlet's privacy is re-constituted in theatrical terms.

For the women in Hamlet, privacy is repeatedly insisted upon and then violated. Whilst 'sewing in her closet', a moment of domestic privacy even the audience is not permitted to see, Ophelia recounts being burst in upon by the most theatrical of lovers, 'his doublet all unbraced, no hat upon his head ...' (2.1.75–6), gesturing her complicity in a narrative of betrayal she never meant to precipitate. She is instructed by her father to be 'something scanter of her maiden presence', then has her love letters read out and her most intimate moments with Hamlet spied upon by both king and father. Gertrude, of course, is also watched behind the arras in another private moment stage-managed by Polonius, during which she is also observed and commented upon by a dead husband she cannot see, and in which her son threatens to expose 'the inmost part' of her (3.4.20). In modern production, Gertrude is usually wearing a nightdress; Berlovitz's voluminous white gown is no exception.

The 'closet' scene is where the masked figures in Jeune Lune's production do their most meaningful work in the production, as they form the arras and hold up the canopy that denotes Gertrude's room. They remind us that Gertrude has an audience even when, in most productions, she acts as though she thinks she does not. Their presence

Figure 3.2 Barbra Berlovitz as Gertrude, Steven Epp as Hamlet
in *Hamlet*, dir. Paddy Hayter, Theatre de la Jeune
Lune. Photo: Michal Daniel.

on stage foregrounds our own voyeuristic presence at the scene and
foregrounds the histrionic gestural flourish with which she describes
Hamlet to Claudius – 'Mad as the sea and wind, when both contend/
Which is the mightier' (4.1.7–8). Berlovitz's cranking up of the theatricality as she describes the scene in such as way as to protect Hamlet's
cover offers us an image of female strength in performance that
produces a different Gertrude from others I have seen. As Hamlet turns
her eyes into her very soul, leaving her on the floor or bed to her
profound sighs and heaves, one production choice for this moment is to
signal that court pretence falls away, leaving the queen exposed, vulnerable and prey to terrible doubts about her husband. The First Quarto
leaves no doubts here, with its scene between the queen and Horatio in
which Gertrude makes clear that she understands all. There have been
exceptions to an emotionally crumbling Gertrude, notably Brigit
Forsyth at the West Yorkshire Playhouse, whose queen grows in stature
as a result of her encounter with Hamlet and who storms off before
Claudius can beckon her out at the end of 4.1. What Berlovitz offers
here is a re-enforced theatricality that doubles back onto Gertrude's
status. She presents Gertrude as an arch-improviser who, having 'that
within that passeth show' exposed, is able to return to the show of the
court and the theatre with her theatrical presence redoubled. The
performance works excitingly against the grain of theatrical Hamlets
and their closeted mothers, hinting at the possibility of female agency

through performance, albeit a performance forced upon her by the direst of circumstances.

Sarah Agnew's Ophelia is not offered the chance to perform in her own dire circumstances – but then Ophelia never is. When sane, she is told to be scant of her maiden presence, when mad, her songs about sex and death are usually directed inwards, or fleetingly to other figures on stage. Even in productions where direct address is a consistent convention, Ophelia is commonly played as if in a world of her own during her songs and exchanges. She sings and speaks either to herself or to the court, but as if she had other beings in her mind's eye. The RSC's 2000 production, in which the house lights in the Royal Shakespeare Theatre were brought up so that Samuel West could genuinely address the audience during 'To be or not to be', has Kerry Condon sing to herself and to the imaginary birds she feeds with torn strips of Hamlet's letters. Penny Layden at the Globe offers a refreshingly strident and unwavering performance of the songs, set to complex early melodies, but never directed to the day-lit crowd. Even Peter Zadek's German production, which gives each figure his and her moment with the audience (Gertrude tells the audience of Ophelia's death, Angela Winkler as Hamlet falls off the stage in her efforts to reach them) traps Ophelia behind a fourth wall of madness. I have only once seen Ophelia's songs offered directly as performance to the auditorium, in a student production directed by Theatre in Education director and lecturer John Hazlett. Hazlett has Gertrude and Claudius squirming in awkward embarrassment as Theresa White's Ophelia does what young women are not supposed to – engage in overt performance. The indecorous use of direct address works both fictionally and theatrically, as the audience whom Claudius first addresses as his loyal subjects become a crowd of 'ill-breeding minds' that the King fears may respond to her with 'dangerous conjectures'.

Jeune Lune's Ophelia is infantilised in madness, playing in the sand that covers the stage and planting her flowers and herbs there. This is a logical decision – the mad Ophelia reverts to a childhood in which father and brother seem determined to keep her – but the interpretation fails to fulfil the promise of female power in performance offered by Berlovitz. Still more frail is Shantala Shivalingappa in Brook's production, who speaks rather than sings Ophelia's songs over Tsuchitori's underscoring. Ophelia's madness cannot, it seems, be expressed as performance, despite the fact that perform with voice and, according to Q1, lute, is exactly what Ophelia does. To be in the world of Jeune Lune's *Hamlet* is to perform or to resist performance, so perhaps is it right for Ophelia to revert to a state that in modern psychological terms is unself-conscious, pre-performance. I would like to see her madness permit a performance that sanity does not. When Ophelia is mad, her performance objective is to stay on stage and to sing to us. Her exit is drawn out, as if the performer did not want to leave her audience: 'Good night ladies, good night sweet ladies, good night, good night' (4.5.73–4). Hamlet, on the other hand, begins the play wanting to get off: off to Wittenberg and out of the court in 1.2, off stage and out of life when, despite his misgivings, he accepts Claudius' challenge to duel with Laertes.

After the exit of Claudius from the scene of the Mousetrap's theatrical crime, Jeune Lune add two words to *Hamlet* that sent me back to the First Quarto to ensure I had not missed their presence there. 'It worked!' Hamlet calls gleefully to Horatio, and it is a modern interpolation that seems, unlike the company's other additions and replacements, a little patronising. Audience members who have not understood that the Mousetrap is staged in order to test Claudius, and that his abrupt exit and call for lights means that the plot has 'worked', are surely a lost cause. The theatre, on the other hand, does 'work' for Hamlet, as the fictional world of the play does not, so that perhaps this jarring addition works too. Singing and dancing with glee – the unrhyming song of 'Damon dear' and 'a very, very pajock' (3.2.281–4) is not cut, despite its obscurity – Hamlet behaves here as though the whole play were at an end. He has stage-managed the performance of his uncle's guilt, the performance 'worked', and for a moment it is as if this is all he has to do. The play within the play itself is a wildly exuberant affair, as it has to be to top the carnivalesque theatricality of the performance proper. In the first run of the production, the Player King and Queen sing their lines whilst figures in enormous masks, caricatures of Gertrude and Claudius, enact a simultaneous dumb show. In the revival, figures on stilts denote the death of the Player King with red streamers. For the short soliloquy ''Tis now the very witching time of night...' (3.2.388–99), Hamlet wears the mask the Lucianus player has worn for the play, and where 'O what a rogue and peasant slave' has seen Hamlet failing in rehearsal for the role of revenger, here it seems a successful performance might be possible. The privacy that Epp's Hamlet seems to prefer to the 'show' around him precludes action; the overt theatricality of Lucianus' devilish mask denotes a choice of action, an agency behind which Hamlet might hide, his privacy intact.

The fact that the Mousetrap is one of the most engaging moments of Jeune Lune's *Hamlet* is not, I think, a fault of the production. The company's celebratory, carnivalesque aesthetic offers moments of theatrical agency for the figures in *Hamlet*, suggesting that a world of show is the only one in which real decisions about how to act can be made. Hamlet's tragedy in the Jeune Lune production is that he wants to get off rather than engage with the show. The uncomfortable question for the audience, who are engaged with it, lies in what we want Hamlet to do if he stays on stage. Though Jeune Lune strip the play of its political context, they place Hamlet in a theatrical context that offers a tempting alternative to soliloquising inaction. The production provokes an unsettling desire for the kind of simple revenge narrative that the Players might offer, the moral certainties of a revenge hero that could 'drink hot blood' (3.2.390).

Peter Brook and the Théâtre des Bouffes du Nord

I want to move directly here to Adrian Lester's intensely naturalistic Hamlet in Peter Brook's production, and to position myself as spectator as I have in my account of Jeune Lune's production, but it is difficult. It is difficult because I have in my possession a filmed version of the Brook production, showed on the BBC's cable arts channel, BBC 4, and made without an audience. Video recordings of the other *Hamlets* here have been available as *aides memoires*. Their quality, and the audible presence of the audience in each recording, has reminded me, frustratingly, of video's inevitable incompleteness as a record of theatre production and, more productively, of the meanings produced in the moment of performance, particularly when laughter can be heard on the video that is only comprehensible to an audience being addressed or observed directly. Brook's *Hamlet*, unsurprisingly given the sense of theatre history in the making that those names in juxtaposition create, has had a professional film made of it. It has been made in the theatre that produced it, the Bouffes du Nord, with its half-stripped proscenium and peeling red walls, so that it is still self-consciously a film of a theatre production. However, it uses close-up, excludes from every frame the musician, Toshi Tsuchitori, whose live playing underscores and introduces the scenes; it cuts significant moments from the already heavily cut text of the live performance and produces a low-key intimacy that was only one stylistic element of the live version. Film, particularly the close-up shot, intensifies the internalised nature of Lester's Hamlet, so that watching the film tends to obliterate, rather than frustratingly and productively remind one, of the ways in which the live version framed and produced his performance on stage. After watching the film, it is difficult to remember anything but Lester – his quiet tears, his shrugged despair, his expressions of 'that within', from which the close-up paradoxically excludes us. My reaction to the live performance was that its quiet intensity and tiny cast undid, somewhat, the effects of the production's story-telling aesthetic. The television film undoes them almost entirely.

Brook's *Hamlet* centres on the trauma of a man losing a father. In the TV film, a tear runs down his face at the end of the 'To be or not to be' soliloquy, and he is in tears or close to it at various points in the live performance. He does not shake or heave to help the tears come, they simply come, and appear to come from the deadly stillness of a most profound grief. Brook cuts the text in ways that make this grief the play's focus and give it a psychological logic. The stage version opens with a fragment from 1.1, moves to the 1.2 soliloquy 'O that this too, too sullied flesh would melt'[72] after which Horatio enters for the first time, greets Hamlet and tells him of his sighting of the Ghost; the Ghost enters just as Hamlet declares to Horatio that he will speak to it if it assumes his father's person (1.2.243–4), and this moment slips into 1.5's encounter between the Ghost and Hamlet. Brook's flexible staging of red-orange carpet, cushions and fabric-covered stools permits[73] action from anywhere in the play to take place anywhere in its fictional world, so that the entrance of the Ghost as Horatio is telling Hamlet of the watch's first encounter with it does not particularly jar. When Brook's text returns to the court of 1.2, Hamlet has already found that 'the time is out of joint' (1.5.188), has already sworn to avenge the Ghost and has to listen to his stepfather's exhortation to 'be as ourself in Denmark' (1.2.122) knowing Claudius to be his father's murderer. The sense that Hamlet's heart will break because he must hold his tongue is thus much heightened. In the TV film, the opening moment from 1.1, the 'Who's there?' that both opens and closes the stage production, is cut, and the first lines are Hamlet's 'O that this too, too sullied flesh …'. The film begins with a close-up on a man devastated by his father's death and mother's marriage.

The problem with this reordering is that it oversimplifies Hamlet's assertion that he has 'that within that passeth show'. By the time Brook's text reaches the first court scene, we all know what is 'within' that he cannot show in this production: the facts about his father's death. Lester appears utterly numb with grief and disbelief at his uncle's hypocrisy from the outset, undermining even more emphatically than Q1 could possibly do, any impression of Claudius as 'an efficient, gracious ruler'.[74] Camerawork conspires with cuts in the TV version to offer an exceptionally sympathetic Hamlet; close-ups invade his fragile privacy, paradoxically suggesting that there are limits to how close we can get to this grief, how far we can know what it feels like to lose one's father then discover he has been murdered.

The most remarked-upon cut in a radically cut text – Brook calls it a 'condensed *Hamlet*' in his programme notes – is the moving of the 'to be or not to be' soliloquy to after 3.4's 'closet scene' and part of 4.3's confrontation between Claudius and Hamlet over the whereabouts of the dead Polonius. Left alone on stage, Hamlet is made to face the consequences of his actions as a devastated Ophelia enters, the sequencing and her aghast looks suggesting that she knows Hamlet has killed her father. Lester's Hamlet seems to realise in this moment the destruction he has wrought, and it is this understanding that precipitates the 'To be or not to be' soliloquy's meditation on suicide. The soliloquy spoken, Rosencrantz enters with the Q2 line 'Wilt please you go, my Lord?' (4.4.31), to which Hamlet replies with his last line from 4.3, 'Come, for England' and, in evident disgust at his former friends' collusion with Claudius, then speaks the last two lines from Q2's 'How all occasions do inform against me' soliloquy. Suppressing his remorse at the killing of Polonius and almost appearing to guess at the treachery of Rosencrantz and Guildenstern, even before reading their 'commission', he closes the sequence with 'O, from this time forth, my thoughts be bloody or be nothing worth' (4.4.67–8).

Brook's 'condensed' *Hamlet* aims, according to the programme notes, 'to prune away the inessential, for beneath the surface lies a myth. This is the mystery that we will attempt to explore'. The mystery that the production actually explores is that of the effects of bereavement and betrayal on a young man's psyche. The through-line offered by the 'To be or not to be' sequence makes absolute psychological sense. This sensitive, grief-stricken young man witnesses the grief of the woman he loves, who has lost a father, and has lost him at Hamlet's own hands; he contemplates suicide but is wrested from his thoughts by the contemptible lackeys of the king who remind him of his promise to his dead father. There is none of the awkwardness and anti-climax of 'To be or not to be' falling soon after Hamlet's decision to stage the 'Murder of Gonzago'. 'To be or not to be' stops asking philosophical questions in this production and becomes an expression of personal despair.

In an interview with Margaret Croyden, Brook insists that political questions, at least, are not relevant to *Hamlet*. To her question as to why he cuts Fortinbras and Croyden's suggestion that this reduces the play politically, Brook replies

> The idea that if you take Fortinbras out of *Hamlet* you lose the political dimension is just a throwback to the '60s. If you look at the play very coolly, there is nothing in the whole story of *Hamlet* that links his tragedy to political questions. There is a court, and in a court, naturally, there are court plots, and there is a king who is suspicious of a potential rival. But that does not make it a political play. *Coriolanus* is a political play, because the protagonist is involved in choices that are political.[75]

I would argue with Brook that this places certain limitations on the meanings of the term 'political'. What I want to suggest by examining these moments from Brook's cut is that, after the pruning, we are left with nothing so archetypal as the myth that Brook suggests *Hamlet* must reveal when stripped of its conventional Elizabethan closure. The production offers something on a rather smaller and more personal scale, particularly in the television film. Moreover, it is not the low-key sincerity of Lester's performance, or simply the way in which Brook's cut suggests a psychological through-line so suited to this performance, that presents Brook's audiences with what I am arguing is a reduced rather than a distilled *Hamlet*. Brook's beautifully crafted intercultural aesthetic itself, and in particular its musical underscoring, empties the play of the meanings that might – under a broader definition than Brook's – be termed 'political'.

Rustom Bharucha's *Theatre and the World* contains an angry critique of Peter Brook and Jean-Claude Carrière's internationally celebrated adaptation of the Hindu narrative poem the *Mahabharata*. The production has a place in theatre history that marks Brook out as a theatrical genius, and has become canonised as the epitome of 'interculturalism' in the theatre. 'Of the internationally intercultural performances I have seen' says Richard Schechner, himself in no small way responsible for introducing the term into performance studies, 'your *Mahabharata* is the finest example of something genuinely syncretic'.[76] Bharucha, on the other hand, accuses Brook of cultural colonialism, of appropriating Indian culture with little sensitivity to the philosophical and religious content of its texts or the narrative structure that content produces, of arbitrary characterisation and of imposing a spurious sense of 'timelessness, mystery and eternal wisdom'[77] on the religious, historical and cultural specifics of the *Mahabharata*. Bharucha dedicates three paragraphs to the music in the piece. He is irritated by the eclectic collection of instruments and what he calls the 'synthetic "Indianness"' of the score. 'Predictably', Bharucha writes somewhat wearily, 'Brook was happy with Toshi Tsuchitori's score which [according to George Banu's much more positive account] wasn't quite Indian, nor non-Indian, a kind of music that has a "taste" of India'.[78]

In considering Brook's *mise en scène* and musical choices for *Hamlet*, I return to Bharucha's objections to the *Mahabharata* and his critique of the interculturalism of practitioner-academics such as Schechner and their universalist notions of sociobiology, 'pre-expressivity' and ritual. Bharucha asks the question, 'Can a story be separated from the ways in which it is told to its people?'[79] His answer is clearly no, not if one wants to avoid compromising its aesthetic and cultural integrity. I am not trying to suggest that exactly the same questions of integrity apply when a modern European director takes on a four-hundred-year-old play whose aesthetics and cultural context are always already separate from his. However, there is a universalist neutrality about this production similar to that which Bharucha argues 'prevents Brook and Carrière taking a position to the problems of the text'[80] of the *Mahabharata* and, like the problems Bharucha suggest Brook is evading in the Hindu epic, these problems in *Hamlet* do centre on its historical and cultural specificity.

Brook's *Hamlet* is a two-and-a-half hour cut for eight performers and one musician, Tsuchitori, who worked on the *Mahabharata* and who plays his own score. Cushions, low seats and rugs are moved on and off the larger carpet that delineates the playing space with a relaxed dexterity by the cast, creating a fluid space for the telling of this story. Tsuchitori is in view throughout the live performance, though not in the TV film, marking entrances with a variety of percussion and moving onto the playing space itself during Ophelia's 'mad' sequence, which he underscores with a traditional Japanese cello-like instrument. As many reviewers remarked, the production is highly theatrically conscious, with scene changes and doubling foregrounded by the bare stage and small cast. Ophelia's funeral is created with cushions for a grave and a piece of cloth to represent her corpse; Laertes' poisoned sword is simply marked with a red-painted tip. On one level, one could argue that here is a production highly aware of its own origins. What could be more appropriate than the staging of an early modern drama on a nearly bare stage with live music and obvious doubling? There is no doubt, moreover, that the production's simplicity adds to its clarity. My critique of the production centres on similar concerns to Bharucha's of the *Mahabharata*: that this *Hamlet*'s insistence of a supposedly universally comprehensible mythic core to the play makes it difficult to engage with it on any other level than a feeling of tremendous sympathy for Adrian Lester's Hamlet, wrapped up in a generalised awareness of something aesthetically pleasing but ultimately unchallenging unfolding on the screen. I mention the screen again here because there are moments in the live production that do different kinds of work, to which I will return.

In the TV film, Tsuchitori's score becomes part of a *mise en scène* that suggests there is no politics or history in *Hamlet*. It is used in two ways: to announce entrances and, less frequently but significantly, to underscore speech and action. It is sparse; except in one significant place, the score does not attempt to short-circuit the representation of strong emotion with swelling strings or ominous drumbeats. The heralding of entrances is a simple device that serves the narrative rather than attempting to prescribe the spectator's attitudes to characters or action. It gently suggests the kind of scene one is about to witness rather than creating atmospherics. The faintly sinister rattle on the Ghost's entrances is an exception, but a productive one. The phenomenological discomfort felt by a modern audience when a 'ghost' walks onto a stage not darkened by modern lighting can be distractingly rather than productively alienating, and Tsuchitori's delicate intimation of other worldliness combined with Jeffery Kissoon's stately pace onto the playing space offers just enough ghostliness without having to resort to blue gels and dry ice. At other points, the stringed instrument heralds intimate scenes, rapid drumming suggests an acceleration in the action. Rather than doing the actors' work for them, these introductory phrases acknowledge audience expectation in a way that sits well with an early modern drama. We know, for example, that at the end of a tragedy the action hastens towards death; the score acknowledges this without prescribing the emotions we might experience in the face of that fact. The system of announcing entrances musically is appropriate to the theatrical consciousness of the live production, where Tsuchitori is always visible; here are a group of eight actors telling the story of Hamlet, with a live musician telling us that a new part of that story is beginning and making his own narrative commentary. On film, the score works rather differently, particularly during Ophelia's mad sequence.

In Brook's production, Ophelia does not sing but speaks her songs, sometimes seeming to be in genuine dialogue with Laertes, asking him directly about her father's death: 'And will he not come again? No, no, he is dead …' (4.5.191–2). She speaks over Tsuchitori's strings and, as a number of reviews suggest, the music seems to be expressing Ophelia's internal state, 'an anguish that Ophelia is no longer capable of expressing'.[81] Here, the performance of madness, potentially alien to modern sensibilities and certainly shocking and embarrassing to early modern court ones, is offered as an internalised, essentially feminine performance of grief. Shivalingappa's Ophelia is bravely understated, but the music makes statements for her that returns us to a safely familiar world of psychological distress, particularly where Tsuchitori cannot be seen. Brook describes his first encounter with Kathatkali, the Indian dance form in which moments from the *Mahabharata* are traditionally performed, and says that he found it to be 'something mythical and remote, from another culture, nothing to do with my life'.[82] Ophelia's madness, a madness comprising a combination of raving and lute-playing according to Q1, is from another historical culture. The use of underscoring combined with the spoken rather than sung words serves to re-familiarise it, however unfamiliar much of its audience might be with the Japanese instrument Tsuchitori plays.

For Brook, interviewed about *Hamlet*, all culture appears to be 'our culture'. He produces the play using Japanese instrumentation, a mixed race cast, a slow and ritualistic style of entrances and exits that together with the narrative score are reminiscent of Kabuki, an internalised signalling of grief based in Western naturalism. Defending his international cast Brook suggests that

> Some people could look over *Hamlet* and say 'what are they doing exploiting our English *Hamlet* with all these mixed races?'. Other people receive an experience that takes them into what I call an essential myth. Who would dare say for a second that this myth belongs only to pure Aryan white people from the region of Stratford-upon-Avon? If you follow this logic even a Jew from Birmingham is an outsider and can't play Shakespeare, let alone a man or a girl from Trinidad.[83]

Put like this, and into the mouths of imagined reactionaries from Stratford, who indeed would dare voice objections to Brook's *mise en scène*? He says in the same interview that he has 'heard people say "Oh you have taken the Mahabharata, you're exploiting India, oh, you are pinching an African legend." But true themes link people'.[84] Again, the statement seems too obvious to counter. However, Ophelia's anguish-through-strings and Hamlet's psychological through-line of grief reduce anguish and grief to comfortable truism rather than, say, confronting the audience with the discomfort of a mad woman performing within a frame that might shift our perceptions of madness or femininity. Far from being essential or universal, the 'myth' evoked by Ophelia here has culturally and historically specific roots in Victorian notions of madness as feminine, fey, internalised, where Ophelia in *Hamlet* shifts back and forth from the bawdy to the plaintive, from internal anguish to potentially comical demonstration.

This last description of a potential Ophelia provides a neat re-entry into Lester's performance in the live production of Brook's *Hamlet*. The rhythms of the TV film rarely shift from those of Hamlet's intense though barely exposed grief. Moments in the live performance that jar with this rhythm are almost entirely cut; these are moments where Lester's performance is physically larger, more overtly comic, in more direct contact with the audience and therefore difficult to film without one. The camera has a difficult relationship to moments in the play that are obviously intended as direct address but that have not been cut from the film: when Polonius comments on Hamlet's 'antic disposition' he appears, implausibly, to be talking to himself, until the camera shifts awkwardly to make Bruce Myers face it. In the live performance, Hamlet's routine as he warns his friends not to give away his secrets 'with arms encumbered thus, or this head shake,/Or by pronouncing of some doubtful phrase,/As well, well, we know ...' (1.5.174–6) draws in and includes the audience seated around three sides of the playing space, provokes much laughter then degenerates into an imitation of a mad dog. The film cuts the whole sequence. Lester takes off his shirt for an awkward Rosencrantz and Guildenstern, and beats his chest to demonstrate 'what a piece of work is a man' (2.2.304). He attempts to get himself into a meditative state appropriate to a performance as affecting as the First Player's ancient Greek rendition of the Hecuba speech, then undermines his failure comically for the audience on 'This is most brave'. For an amused but disconcerted Horatio, he puts Yorick's skull on the stick used to represent the Gravedigger's spade, so that it becomes a macabre puppet, turning its head to listen to Hamlet then undermining him by looking out to the audience. All these moments, including the whole Yorick sequence, are cut from the film; the difficult question of whether to speak direct to camera and the awkwardness of performing theatrical comedy when there is no-one to laugh are generally evaded. This is understandable but unfortunate, as these moments of conscious performance make perfect and tragic sense of Lester's singular deadpan delivery of the 'we defy augury' speech. Lester's live Hamlet achieves moments of contact with the audience that it is difficult to watch him throw away with the end of the play and his acceptance of Claudius' challenge. It is a rendition of the fatalistic lines that the *Telegraph* reviewer finds unsatisfactory because not in the tradition of Hamlets who Learn Something:

> What's largely missing ...is a *sense of the spiritual growth that Simon Russell Beale recently brought so movingly to the role*. The hard-won peace and understanding that lie at the heart of the play are reduced to a throwaway fatalism.[85]

Lester's performance is unique amongst the Hamlets examined here for daring to play these lines for what I would argue with Charles Spenser that they are – a retreat into fatalistic and unquestioning religious convention. However, the moment on film merely blends with the performative rhythm of a Hamlet too unhappy to attack any of his lines with the energy of conscious performance.

Brook's filmed *Hamlet* has an aesthetic coherence that none of the other performances examined here achieve, and this is a problem. The politics of *Hamlet* is a politics of performance and of subjectivity, set against the less philosophically problematic politics of a war with Norway that Fortinbras wins. The Norwegian prince's simple account of Hamlet as potentially 'most royal' (5.2.398) offers a productively unsatisfying closure to a difficult encounter with a clown, a lover, a revenge hero, all awkwardly embodied by one figure, perpetually confronting us with his dilemmas. These dilemmas might jar us into a new relationship with our own, if permitted to strive awkwardly for expression, as opposed to being smoothly delivered as identical *to* our own. 'One cannot but agree with the premise that the *Mahabharata* is Indian but it is universal' says Brook, and Bharucha disagrees: 'the *Mahabharata*, I would counter, is universal because it is Indian. One cannot separate the culture from the text'.[86] Bharucha's comment recalls David Kastan's argument that Shakespeare 'does not live on in subsequent cultures in ways none of his contemporaries do ... because he is in any significant sense timeless ... Rather ... it is because he is so intensely of his own time and place. His engagement with the world is the most compelling record we have of that world's struggle for meaning and value.'[87] I am aware that of the plethora of millennial *Hamlet*s that might have been chosen for case studies here, I have chosen productions from outside the mainstream, ones that could be judged to be less conceptually and aesthetically whole than, say the National's or the RSC's of the same period. If *Hamlet* is a play that centres on a failure to act, however, I don't want to exit the auditorium able to say 'It worked!'. I want to suggest that the play should be a theatrical struggle. Hamlet himself seems to find it a dreadful play, not nearly as good as the one that happens off stage and which he devises with such facility – ''ere I could make a prologue to my brains' (5.2.30) – in which deceitful friends are tricked to their deaths and friendly pirates save the day. Though the first three productions discussed here have their beauty, Red Shift's choice of Q1, the Globe's inevitably compromised historical authenticity in the presence of the day-lit modern spectator and Jeune Lune's fragmented text, do not allow Hamlet to retreat into a beautifully crafted fiction. These feel like unfinished *Hamlet*s, because a direct encounter between human figures never feels finished in the way a play conventionally should. Perhaps that is why I have found the *danse macabre* that the Globe Company perform as part of their 'curtain call' and Red Shift's dead figures placed on 'a scaffold' (Q1:17.115) upstage strangely moving. They are signals that the play is really finished and that its figures are somehow 'really' dead, Hamlet having failed once more in his gesturing towards subjectivity. Brook set out to explore an essential myth in *Hamlet* but perhaps has found an essential truism instead: most human cultures, most human beings, empathise with a sorrowing man. The other three Hamlets are less able to seduce us into identification; they struggling for recognition and only fleetingly obtain it; they make fewer clear points about a universal human condition, ask more questions about it.

4 The theatre and the Presence Chamber

History, performance, *Richard II*

Samuel West and *Richard II* / Ralph Fiennes as *Richard II*

A 'lethal debating chamber'.[1]
A 'white-walled squash court or science lab'.[2]
An 'anti-septic laboratory'.[3]
A 'mental institution or art gallery'.[4]

'This blessèd plot, this earth, this realm, this England.'
(2.1.50)

The Other Place, Stratford

The set for the RSC's 2000 *Richard II* is self-consciously sparse. It consists of a long, low, wooden box centre stage, with a gold chair on it; not a golden chair, an ornate chair, but a distinctly ordinary-looking chair, sprayed gold. The chair has a crimson jacket hung on its back and a gold circlet on its seat. Centre right is a grave-shaped mound of earth. The box, the chair and the mound are placed in a white room, the RSC's Other Place studio theatre, which players and audience share. We are all dimly lit in fluorescent purple. Large, white double-doors centre stage, with white alcoves either side, provide upstage entrances. There are three more doors in the side walls of the playing space, seemingly not part of the *mise en scène*. One of them has a Fire Exit sign on it. More chairs – plain white versions of the gold one – stand around the walls. A peal of hand-bells sounds. Actors enter through the double doors, wearing, for the most part, jackets and trousers in deep purples and reds; they smack of luxury, of *haute couture*.[5] The actors stand in frozen tableau, looking at the chair on the wooden box. Samuel West, who is to play Richard, enters from the raked seating where he has been sitting with the audience. He has been reading a copy of *Richard II*. He walks up stage right and bolts a door, one of the 'real' doors in the wall of the studio, a door that leads to another part of the building. He sits down on the end of the wooden box and speaks a Prologue, constructed from the first lines from Act 5 Scene 5 of the play – Richard's 'prison' soliloquy:

> I have been studying how I may compare
> This prison where I live unto the world,
> And for because the world is populous,
> And here is not a creature but myself,
> I cannot do it. Yet I'll hammer't it out. (5.5.1–5)
>   … Sometimes am I a king,
> Then treasons make me wish myself a beggar (5.5.32–3)
> Then am I kinged again, and by and by
> Think that I am unkinged …
> And straight am nothing … (5.5.36–8)
> Thus play I in one person many people,
> And none contented. (5.5.31–2)
>   … But whate'er I be
> Nor I nor any man that but man is
> With nothing shall be pleased till he be eased
> With being nothing. (5.5.38–41)

This figure appears at ease in the white room with the audience, though the measured, emphatic delivery of this transposition suggests something of an intellectual struggle with the concepts contained in the speech. The words 'king,' 'kinged' and 'unkinged' are given a weight that emphasises the grammatical strangeness of the second two words. West rises and 'kings' himself, putting on the jacket that has been resting on the gold chair and fitting the gold circlet on his head. He and Alfred Burke as Gaunt introduce the dispute between the magnates Bolingbroke[6] and Mowbray and West ends this first exchange of the play with the line 'Then call them to our presence' (1.1.15) transposed from a few lines later in the scene. He places his foot on the centre stage wooden box and the 'frozen' company of actors shift forward fractionally; it is as though, while waiting for 'Richard' to start the play, they have made the tiniest of false starts to the scene. Then, as West steps onto the box, harsh white lights snap up on both audience and playing space and the actors move to their positions for 1.1.

Gainsborough film studios, London

A large raised stage area at the temporarily converted Gainsborough film studios[7] is covered with turf. Real saplings 'grow' stage right. The space is vast, with bare brickwork and temporary seating in a stalls and balcony arrangement. A crack in the back wall of the stage extends from floor to ceiling; at its base it is a gaping fissure, wide enough to provide a stage centre entrance. It narrows to a slit near the roof of the building, where it disappears into darkness and a haze of dry ice. The audience sits in darkness, a darkness that extends onto the grassy stage in a wide band, separating actor and audience.

A fanfare sounds. Actors, dressed in long, high-necked dark coats and carrying swords, enter and stand stage left and right. Ralph Fiennes is carried onto the stage through the central entrance on a tall, spindly-legged throne, which is set down on the grass. He is Richard II, wearing his crown and a long, pale, high-collared silk robe, open to reveal loose fitting, patterned yellow silk trousers, strikingly pale and more luxurious than the workaday clothes of his courtiers.[8] He looks disdainful, as if faintly disgusted to be out of doors. The fragile chair makes him appear vulnerable and precarious in the vastness of the Gainsborough studios, and in this explicitly outdoor setting the costume reads as expensive and incongruous pyjamas. The king has just risen and is not pleased to have been called to pass judgement on his subjects' disputations.

This is one reading. That of the *Sunday Times* review is rather different:

> The opening image is one of confident, undisputed power. King Richard, resplendent in glittering white and gold and wearing his crown, is carried in on a chair, his face controlled by a slight frown, remote and impassive. The great noblemen of his court stand in weighty silence, clearly aware that something of importance is about to occur.[9]

This comparison of opening moments from productions of *Richard II* gives rise to obvious questions about subjective readings of theatre performance. It is possible to describe, with reasonable accuracy and an attempt at objectivity, the physical conditions in which a performance takes place. It is possible to make a reading of the sign systems at work in each performance which tells us that, while the RSC presents us with at least a suggestion of Samuel West, it is 'Richard' that appears on stage at the opening of the Almeida production. Objectivity as to intended meaning is, of course, more elusive. It seems particularly so in the case of the Ralph Fiennes/Jonathan Kent production. I read Fiennes as deliberately signalling something in Richard that is inappropriate to the task of ruling England, the England so clearly signalled by the real grass on which he is set down: the effete King Richard's facial expression gives something away. The *Sunday Times* critic reads 'control' in this 'slight frown': the resplendent King Richard gives nothing away.

What is of interest here is not whose view of the intention behind Fiennes' facial expression is the correct one, but the kinds of readings each of these productions suggests, from the first entrance of the actors. The Almeida signals that Fiennes 'is' Richard and invites that we read his expression as an outward signal of what Richard is feeling. Richard may look 'impassive', an 'image of power' rather than a psychological subject, but his face is '*controlled* by a slight frown', denoting something suppressed beneath the impassive exterior. Or it denotes disgust and disdain. This is not to say that reviewers of the RSC production do not attempt character study in their descriptions of West's more theatrically conscious performance. Some, however, find that such a reading evades them, so that it is West rather than Richard that is described:

> Most Richards here [during the 'deposition' sequence of 4.1] use a grand manner and/or actorly virtuosity: while his fortune declines, his spirit soars. But West just stays very precise: he grows more ironic, more intense, and shows in dynamic terms how surely he is in intellectual command of each scene.[10]

Some are disappointed in their expectations of the psychological and emotional 'depth' that typically constitute character on the naturalistic stage:

> West has a gift of clarity as well as lyricism, but sometimes he describes grief rather than reaching deep within himself.[11]

> West's Richard ... [has] a heightened self-awareness that makes him seem to dance around his own character. He is hard to pin down and West keeps our sympathy at bay.[12]

> The crucial quality he lacks is pathos. There is a coldness in this performance, as in the whole production ....[13]

I am interested in this assumed divorce between emotional impact – 'warmth' – and theatrical self-consciousness. *Time Out* reads West as not 'reach[ing] deep within himself'; I am going to suggest that the RSC's *Richard II* has found other places to reach, so that the spectator is never in danger of being left out in a purely analytical cold. Sitting in the RSC's white box of a studio being addressed by Shakespeare's medieval kings and lords, my experience is of being drawn in, involved, implicated. What does West represent when he locks the theatre door and sits on the box? How does he read when he begins to speak Richard's lines from elsewhere in the play? The door he locks is a 'real' door so that he reads as an actor, locking the audience in with him before he begins his performance, rather than as a fictional figure closing a door in a fictional *locus*. As soon as he begins to speak the transposed lines, he appears to be playing 'Richard', yet the jacket and circlet that are to denote 'Richard' have not yet been put on. The *Evening Standard* describes the sequence as 'converting the play into a prison-reverie recollection of the King's decline and fall'[14] and sure enough, this 'Richard' speaks of peopling with his imagination the empty world of his prison. The *Observer* review appears confident that 'in Pimlott's version, the play becomes a story told by Richard in which the whole of England is a jail'.[15] However, the crimson jacket and gold circlet remain on the chair behind him until the end of the transposed prologue and he sits talking to us in grey shirt and dark trousers. The prologue foregrounds West's identity as actor rather than king: 'Thus play I in one person many people'. Could this Richard be 'the thing itself',[16] then: the celebrated 'player king'[17] before he has begun the performance that his position requires, stripped of the adornments that constitute kingly identity? Without these external shows is man the 'nothing' with which Richard imagines being 'eased' during the prison soliloquy (5.5.40–1)?

West's own account of the opening is given both from his own perspective and that of the Richard he imagines. Here he is in his essay on the role from the *Players of Shakespeare* series, slipping from 'I' Samuel West, to 'I' Richard II:

> I ... stood up, walked to the doors and bolted them. If I was going through with this I had to make sure that everyone else was trapped inside the box with me, and wouldn't get out until we'd solved the problem. In fact, as I hoped we would prove, the thing about life is that no-one gets out of it alive anyway ... This was to be an exploration of the prison that we are all born into, and from which we are only released at the hour of death.[18]

Where the Fiennes entrance asks the question 'what is this man, Richard II, like?' the West opening asks 'who, what and where is this?'

and, as we will see, turns those questions on the spectator herself: 'who, what and where am I?'. The identities presented on stage remain stable throughout the Almeida production: what we see is Richard II represented by an actor, the presence of whom his own performance attempts to erase. The location is a green piece of land, at once a range of grassy locations,[19] and at the same time England, a green and pleasant land rent by a split in the back wall that prefigures the forthcoming civil wars. Whatever physical or psychic location the RSC's white box suggests, it contains the audience, who are fully lit, and is always also the theatre in which we are spectators. The lit auditorium and West's putting on of parts of his costume in view of the audience have the effect, to borrow from Richard's line, of 'calling [us] to [West's] presence': of calling attention to the presence of an actor who locks the theatre door and puts on the costume, as well as to the presence of the king whom he plays.

Critics found a range of metaphors for this space; the company referred to it as 'the white box'.[20] In this chapter, which returns again and again to this production as a paradigm of self-conscious theatrical presence, I will call it a Presence Chamber. The term is suggestive of both a fictional location – the room in which the king gives audience – and of a place in which 'presence' is both experienced and examined. This *Richard II* produces an intense effect of presence, through its constant play on ways in which actors, audience and fictional figures can be present to one another.[21] When West locks us into the room with him, the West/Richard figure makes a demand of the audience: that it remain present while the play's dilemmas are 'hammered out'. The door-locking foregrounds the presence of that audience: its possible meanings and the political and ethical dilemmas of being present at the events depicted. Paradoxically, the action also draws attention to the fact that if the spectator wishes she may ignore West's/Richard's demand, by leaving the room by one of the other doors. The fact of whether one is present or absent – in or out of the room, on or off stage – is rendered significant by this production in ways that I argue are central to *Richard II* and its production of dramatic subjectivity.

'…[W]ho sits here that is not Richard's subject?' (4.1.122) demands the bishop of Carlisle at Richard's deposition. It has been argued – by director Steven Pimlott amongst others[22] – that a large swathe of Richard's subjects are excluded from *Richard II*, that this is a play about the 'power brokers' rather than the ruled. Pimlott's production brings these 'subjects' into the theatre by addressing the audience as commoners, lords, soldiers. Spectators are also, always, implacably and very obviously in this production, a group of people who have paid to come and see a play and the ultimate impossibility of casting them as fictional subjects produces, as we will see, effects of subjectivity that naturalistic convention erases.

Critical nostalgia vs theatrical present

Before examining in detail the ways in which the RSC production constitutes its dramatic and viewing subjects, it will be worth putting the play in the critical context that produces *Richard II* as an elegy for a lost ideal of England. This chapter is concerned with the ways in which this production makes its historical events and dramatic figures present to its audience, where a long critical tradition reads the play as a study in nostalgia for a distant past. Where reviewers have doubts concerning the RSC production, it was often exactly this sense of nostalgia that was felt to be lacking. The *Daily Telegraph* suggests that

> [t]here is a coldness in this performance, as in the whole production, that isn't completely true to the *elegiac* spirit of the play .... [Pimlott] tends to bend Shakespeare's plays to his own will, imposing a style on them, rather than letting them speak for themselves .... *Richard II* comes across on the page as the theatrical equivalent of a medieval illuminated manuscript. It's very wordy, very poetic and very beautiful, a long *elegy* for a lost crown.[23]

'If you do not find [Richard] regal and glamorous' suggests the *Sunday Times*, 'a golden boy as well as a flawed ruler, there is no *sense of loss* and therefore no tragedy.'[24]

It is interesting to note that the John Barton production of *Richard II*, described by reviewers as 'Brechtian' in style, as is the Pimlott production, received similar critiques in 1973 for what was considered directorial imposition. Robert Shaughnessy's comment on responses to the Barton production could be applied to the Pimlott critics: 'the implication seems to be that a more natural, straightforward and less overtly directorial mode of production would have been a more illusionistic one: an assumption which is as much ideological as it is aesthetic'.[25] In the *Daily Telegraph* review, as in Tillyard's reading of the play as a medieval artefact, *Richard II* is hardly a play at all; it is rather a poem or an illuminated manuscript whose 'aura' compels a nostalgic sense of loss.[26]

That Shakespeare constructs a world that is recognisably *past* in *Richard II* is an academic as well as a journalistic commonplace.

Readings as ideologically distant as Tillyard's and Graham Holderness', the second of which attacks what Holderness regards as Tillyard's nostalgic conservatism, produce a play that is fully aware of the temporal distance of its subject matter from the period in which Shakespeare was writing. Holderness asserts:

> What the [history] plays offer is ... a form of historiography analogous to the new science, in that it perceives human problems and experiences to be located within a definable historical form, a society visibly different in fundamental ways from the society of the late sixteenth century.[27]

Compare Tillyard's more tentative:

> Of course it would be absurd to suggest that Shakespeare pictured the age of Richard II after the fashion of a modern historian. But there are signs elsewhere in Shakespeare of at least a feeling of historical veracity.[28]

The Tillyardian reading of *Richard II* as a 'medieval jewel of a play',[29] only present to the audience as a relic in a museum might be, demands a distance on the action that the Almeida's darkened auditorium and grassy dramatic irony permits. Holderness' version of *Richard II* as conscious historiography better fits the RSC's 'lethal debating chamber'.[30] In *Shakespeare's History*, Holderness challenges 'the conventional understanding of ... the play', wherein Richard's mismanagement of 'a harmonious, organic community, dominated by kings, bound together by order, hierarchy, degree'[31] is what brings about his deposition and the following civil conflict. For Holderness, it is rather tensions within the very system of fealty for which Gaunt is so nostalgic that bring about its demise. In his examination of 1.1, Holderness argues that Shakespeare's understanding of medieval history is more sophisticated than that of critics such as Tillyard and Traversi, who do not seem 'conscious of the fact that that the appeal of treason and the consequent trial by battle are stages of a legal process, conducted in the Court of Chivalry, according to definite procedures which Shakespeare seems to have known and understood'.[32] Thus Richard's long period of silence at 1.1.30–84 signifies not a weakness of character and an inability to control the magnates, but the balance of power held by the king under feudalism. Richard presides over the magnates' quarrel; that he does not judge it is perfectly proper. However, while the king has legal power over Mowbray and

Bolingbroke, in feudal practice it is the reciprocal relationship of fealty, rather than absolute obedience, that they owe him. The balance of power so perfectly symbolised by the stage blocking suggested by 1.1 – king in the centre presiding over the appellants either side of him – is as easily skewed as the stage picture in the RSC's production, when West's Richard is obliged to step down from his 'box' to persuade Mowbray to give up Bolingbroke's gage. Richard's court represents, even at its most ceremonious, the tensions inherent in feudal power rather than an idealised version of a divinely legitimised monarchy.

Although his reading of the first scene does suggest a staging, however, Holderness appears not to regard *Richard II* as a piece of theatre so much as a sophisticated piece of early modern historiography,[33] in keeping with the twentieth-century critical tradition whereby the play is hardly read as a theatrical text at all. Even Phyllis Rackin's more theatrically inflected reading, in her *Stages of History*, is ultimately reliant on Tillyard's clear distinction between a desirable, colourful past of 'ceremonial style' and 'medieval refinement' represented by Richard's court, and a muddied, potentially disordered present,[34] a distinction that figures the first scene of the play as a picture, a parade or a poem, rather than a drama. Rackin asserts that Richard's world 'is displayed as a remote historical pageant ...';[35] 'the medieval trappings of the opening scene, like Spenser's archaic 'medieval' language, use a temporal equivalent of local colour to represent the past in terms of distance and difference'.[36] She goes on to examine how the play might manipulate the audience's complicity, as Richard becomes the despoiler of this desirable medieval world and Bolingbroke becomes the more empathetic figure. She reads the first act of the play as essentially poetic, symbolic, non-dramatic, then suggests that in the second act there is a shift to the 'present' in which the theatre audience are encouraged to endorse the rebellion against Richard, he who has betrayed the attractive medieval world of the first scenes.

Rackin's phrase 'a temporal equivalent of local colour' to describe this pictorial quality is significant in its suggestion of nostalgia for a comfortingly ordered other world. 'Local colour' recalls twentieth-century tourist industry constitutions of the past and the 'local'. Considering, as Rackin does, the Elizabethan public interest in the 'medieval' tournaments that took place to celebrate the queen's Accession Day,[37] parallels might certainly be drawn between the sixteenth-century interest in chivalric reconstructions and today's reification of the past in the theme park and stately home. However, if Holderness is correct in his argument that tensions within the feudal world are present in the play from its opening speeches, then the notion that the first scene provides the audience with a distant, idealised *picture* of a medieval world can be seen as characteristic of a tendency noted by Lee Patterson, to treat the middle ages 'as an all purpose alternative to whatever quality the present has wished to ascribe to itself'.[38] For Tillyard and Rackin, Shakespeare offers the reader and audience respectively a medieval painting of political harmony which they will desire to repossess and which is snatched from their grasp at the dawn of a three-dimensional but troubled modernity. Tillyard accepts this desire, Rackin critiques it and names it 'nostalgia', but both readings tend to strip the early scenes of *Richard II* of their theatrical and political dynamic.

The reviewers of the RSC production cited above find themselves robbed of a lovingly conserved artefact, a fragment of 'This England'. This is a sense of loss the Almeida's verdant *mise en scène* appears intended to indulge, from the moment Fiennes enters through a crack in England's edifice to which he is evidently blind. 'Here Shakespeare begins his long farewell to medieval England with all its certainties and divine seal of approval'[39] says the *Sunday Times* critic, placing his own seal of approval on the Almeida production. Fiennes enters with fanfare and glistening silk costume, precariously set above England's turf, and we are asked to mourn a medieval past of beautiful kings on high thrones which Fiennes' character tragically betrays. West, on the other hand, sets up a simple image of political and theatrical power over which he appears to be in control. When, as we will see, this picture shifts, a loss of theatrical status has the effect of producing a tension in the political world of the fiction. In the RSC's Presence Chamber, action occurs in real time as well as within a fictional location, whereas on the Almeida's turfed stage a fictional location is evoked that is, like 'This England' in the nostalgia of national consciousness, already past.[40] It is interesting to note that, when the RSC company started rehearsals, no decisions as to a temporal 'setting' for the play had been made; they had, in West's words, 'carte blanche and pièce blanche',[41] unusual freedom. Although later in his account of the production he relates that the company eventually 'decided that we wanted the play set now, in the year 2000/2001',[42] the 'now' in which this production takes place reads as both more and less specific.

To 'set' a production in a particular period suggests a design concept with a pictorial quality: an invitation to the audience to look, from the stable perspective of outsider, at a picture in which particular period elements will be recognisably distant, though that 'period' may be the very year in which they are looking. Compare, for example, the costumes for this *Richard II* with the following season's *Hamlet*, also

directed by Steven Pimlott with Samuel West in the leading role. In
Hamlet, contemporary office suits and security badges at Claudius' court
'set' the play, particularly when seen at the inevitable distance conferred
by the Royal Shakespeare Theatre.[43] *Richard II* on the other hand,
dresses its male figures in clothes that, while recognisably of today's
high fashion, suggest status and opulence rather than an historically
specific ruling elite such as the modern bureaucracy (Euro-cracy?) of
the RSC *Hamlet*.

Taking place as the performance does in the white box Presence
Chamber, with all the figures able to contact the audience directly, the
'now' of this *Richard II* is situated highly specifically, not with regard to
period but in relation to the audience. Rather than reading as a set of
parallels between one period and another, the production situates the
dilemmas and power relations of the play in the spectator's present, the
moment of them being seated in the theatre.

Transposing and dis-locating: inside and outside the Presence Chamber

The RSC's *Richard II* sets up two theatrical 'locations' that could be
described as meta-theatrical, or rather extra-diagetic, as they stand
entirely outside the play's fiction. The first is created by Simon Kemp's
purple fluorescent lighting state in which performers speak text dislocated from the 'original'. Under these lights Richard, Queen Isabel and
Bolingbroke all speak lines from 5.5. Richard opens the production with
the prologue quoted above, Isabel and Bolingbroke are given a shorter
version:

> I have been studying how I may compare
> This prison where I live unto the world,
> And for because the world is populous
> And here is not a creature but myself
> I cannot do it. Yet I'll hammer't out.
>
> (5.5.1–5)

This 'blatant tampering with the text'[44] caused irritation amongst some
reviewers, who saw the transpositions of the lines from the 'prison' soliloquy as a lack of trust in that text.[45] Compare these transpositions to
other 'tamperings', with *Hamlet* and with *Troilus and Cressida*: John Caird,
Peter Brook, the Theatre de la Jeune Lune cut all references to the
political world of the play; it is as if the war with Poland and the figure

of Fortinbras were never there. The first half of the National's *Troilus and Cressida* is rearranged to clarify the plot and the last scene played as if an attempted reconciliation of the pair by Pandarus is simply another event in the narrative.[46] The three substantial transpositions in *Richard II*, on the other hand, are signalled very deliberately as outside the world of the fiction, taking place under the fluorescent purple lighting used for the opening prologue. Their 'blatant' nature is crucial to the production's reading of the play.

Richard's Prologue points to the heightened theatrical awareness that West's Richard signals throughout the performance. According to West himself, 'all sense of special knowledge or hindsight evaporate[s] under the lights'[47] as they change from the purple state to glaring white and the play proper begins. The theatrical consciousness of the production works against West's reading of his own performance, however. It is not only the RSC's Prologue that produces a figure with 'special knowledge'. An intense awareness of audience and theatre space creates the sense of fictional figures aware of their own fiction. Rather as Linda Charnes describes Cressida demonstrating an aware-ness of her own notoriety, West's moments of direct address, and his use of comic irony signal, as we will see, an awareness on Richard's part of his position in history and the theatre. He slips back and forth from absorption in the fiction to knowledge of just where his days will end. The figure that can shift into self-awareness in this way is not a familiar one to current theatre, film and television audiences, whose relationship to dramatic figures tends to be one of ironic superiority, or suspenseful naiveté, as they wait for the revelations that are to occur in the narrative's denouement. To frame the performance with a Prologue that foregrounds Richard's theatrical foresight might, then, be a modern necessity.

Another of Pimlott's more blatant tamperings with *Richard II* is the increased presence of Richard's Queen Isabel on the Other Place stage. Catherine Walker is costumed as an archetype of female and queenly restriction, in a corset-like bodice and a crown that appears to have been styled from her own hair. She sits throughout 3.3, the scene at Flint Castle, huddled in a wrap against the wall left of the central doors, and the audience is reminded that there is another figure for whom Richard's descent to the 'base court' will have consequences. Before 3.4, in which the queen overhears the gardeners speak of Richard's deposi-tion, she speaks her five-line version of the prison soliloquy. The use of Richard's lines to convey isolation and the sense of a prison-like exis-tence demonstrates a modern interest in the position of women, with which the sixteenth-century text is less concerned and the purple fluorescent once more draws attention to the transposition. There are concerns we inevitably impose on four-hundred-year-old texts that accompany the presence of a woman on stage, and this *Richard II* correspondingly signals the queen's extra appearance as an 'imposition'. The Presence Chamber of the theatre offers the queen a voice that the king's fictional presence chamber cannot permit her.

Where I want to challenge this use of transpositions is at the point at the very end of the production where the lines are given to Bolingbroke, imposing a more conservative ending than might have been expected from this theatrically and politically conscious production.[48] Having Bolingbroke close the play with these lines from 5.5 gives the impression of a wheel turned full circle, an inevitable kingly fate. Where the rest of the production emphasises power as process, this beginning-as-ending gives a sense of universal fatality to the theatrical proceedings, a sense in which the audience is being invited to empathise with the unchanging tragedy of lonely monarchs which the rest of the project problematises, through West's self-ironising approach to the exhortation to his followers to 'sit upon the ground/ And tell sad stories of the death of kings' (3.2.155–6). I would describe this last transposition in just the terms Robert Shaughnessy uses to challenge John Barton's concept of replacing the groom who visits Richard in prison with the actor playing Bolingbroke, in Barton's own famously meta-theatrical RSC production:

> It was a ... profoundly anti-historical [gesture] ... designed to arrest the movement of history itself by denying historical difference and change .... Framed in the metadramatic terms of a secularised *Theatrum Mundi* this *Richard II* saw the interplay between personal integrity and the pressures of history, and the rituals of power as scripted and choreographed in a tragic, endlessly repetitive pattern.[49]

The 2000 production, on the contrary, invites an analysis of the interplay between personal integrity, the pressures of history and the rituals of power as they are spoken and choreographed in a theatrical present and in which the audience take an active part. However, as Bolingbroke is abandoned during the dialogue of 5.6 – each lord to whom he offers reward for his loyalty walks off stage as the new king addresses him – and left to sit on Richard's coffin alone, the production suffers a potential lurch into the reactionary pessimism that Graham Holderness argues is latent in the text but which this production appears elsewhere to challenge:

The historical approach [a reference to Shakespeare's truth to his historical sources in *Richard II* as compared to the *Henry IV* plays] is progressive insofar as it locates its problems in a self-contained society of the past, neither idealised nor regretted but objectively analysed and evaluated. But the play is also potentially reactionary, since its combination of tragic form and literate, deterministic historiography can too easily collapse into a resigned pessimism, where 'mutability' with its parent principle of universal order becomes an appropriate metaphor for the 'human condition'.[50]

This last transposition reinscribes the RSC's production, too, within generalised tragic universals, outside the historically and theatrically specific processes the audience has witnessed in this Presence Chamber of a theatre. Overall, though, the fluorescent purple, extra-diagetic world foregrounds the hammering out of theatrical and political decisions in this theatre, in this play, rather than washing them over with universalist truisms.

The production's second location 'outside' the fiction is the space outside the theatre building, which is glimpsed through a door not immediately recognisable as part of the *mise en scène*. At the Other Place in Stratford, Bolingbroke leaves for exile and Richard leaves for prison through a door that leads to a space in which parked cars can be glimpsed. What is the effect of showing a world – *the* world – that is so radically external to the fiction and to the theatrical space in which performers do the work of signification?[51] Open doors to the outside world reinforce the audience's sense of being enclosed in the same room as actors and dramatic figures simultaneously. They also serve to underline the ways in which dramatic figures are dislocated from the contexts in which their identities are conferred. This is not achieved through metonymic design elements, as in Gainsborough studios where a split in the wall may be said to stand for the condition of the English state, but rather through a foregrounding of what happens to the actor in the moment of performance. Bolingbroke is banished from England, and thus from the theatre, as England is the only fictional location evoked there. As he declares himself 'a true born Englishman' (1.3.308) he raises his arms in triumphal defiance and, to the sound effects of cheers, walks out into a car park. He is leaving the country in which family and national ties give his figure meaning, for 'the stranger paths of banishment' (1.3.143). Mowbray underlines the decontextualisation and subsequent meaninglessness suffered by the banished as he foretells the 'dull unfeeling barren ignorance' (1.3.168) that must accompany his going into lands where no-one speaks English. Bolingbroke intends to take with him his identity of 'trueborn Englishman' (1.3.308) but cannot re-establish himself as such until he returns to claim his rights as Duke of Lancaster. Out of England/off stage he means nothing. Patrick Troughton/Bolingbroke leaves the space in which his dramatic figure has meaning – the theatre – for the car park outside, and the decontextualisation of his presence as actor impacts back onto the fictional dislocation of Bolingbroke.[52]

This same stage right door is opened during Richard's encounter with Queen Isabel on his way to prison. Northumberland comes to remove him from the presence of his subjects and from the theatrical Presence Chamber altogether, to strip him entirely of the context in which he exists meaningfully as 'king' and as dramatic figure – a political necessity despite Richard's already having deposed himself. We hear the recorded sound of rain as the door is opened and, if this is an attempt momentarily to include the car park space more fully in the *mise en scène*, it fails, fascinatingly. The sound effect is beguilingly realistic and for a moment it is quite possible to think that it must be raining outside. As one can see quite clearly into the world outside the theatre, the effect of the open door becomes doubly alienating when it is *not* raining outside, as the spectator witnesses 'outside' and a simultaneous sound effect of 'outside'. Richard is being taken into a space in which he cannot mean anything, no matter how hard the *mise en scène* attempts to include the car park as part of the fiction at this point. A space in which he cannot signify is exactly where Richard is being taken in the fiction: to the Tower, where away from the public eye he is 'unkinged', can no longer 'make his presence felt' before the people. As Richard is removed to a meaningless space, the *mise en scène* impacts on the fiction, offering the spectator an experience in real, theatre time that can be mapped onto the experience of watching and hearing the narrative unfold. 'Outside-the-theatre' refuses to be encompassed by the *mise en scène* as part of the fiction but that very refusal reinscribes it within the meaning of the production.

The violence done to conventions of inside and outside here produces an uncanny effect of real presence in this production, as the spectator's attention is constantly drawn to that which is happening in the here and now of the theatre. This reality effect suffuses the figures on stage, the words spoken by them, the spaces in which they stand. It draws attention to the dynamic relations between figure, audience, text and space and makes them central to the politics of *Richard II*. To elaborate on this sense of historical narrative made present, I want to return to the first scene, Bolingbroke and Mowbray's 'appeal', which precipitates the political events of the play and alludes to its political back-story.

The word in the Presence Chamber

The verb 'to appeal' in *Richard II* is a transitive one. Bolingbroke and Mowbray have come into the king's presence not to appeal *to* Richard for judgment but to 'appeal each other' (1.1.27): that is, according to Stanley Wells' Penguin edition note, to accuse one another of treason.[53] The derivation from the French verb '*appeler*,' to call, is significant. These are lords appellant (1.1.34), lords who call or name; another gloss on the first appearance of 'appeal' might be 'to call one another traitor': In thus naming one another, Bolingbroke and Mowbray are not only stating an intention to prove the insult in later combat. There is a strong sense throughout the scene of the power of words to act: to make one's opponent exactly what one says he is. Though Mowbray insists that

> 'Tis not the trial of a woman's war,
> The bitter clamour of two eager tongues,
> Can arbitrate this cause betwixt us twain.
>   (1.1.48–50)[54]

The performative function of the word is so far foregrounded in this scene as to produce a tension between presence and the word that complicates the simple binary of womanly words and masculine action. Words are used to 'make one's presence felt' in the simultaneously fictional and theatrical Presence Chamber and to dislocate or absent the speaker's adversary in the 'eyes of men' that make up the audience. West's experience of performing the play in the RSC's 'white box' was that 'anything that went into the box was thrown into huge relief by the white walls – someone said that everything had inverted commas around it'.[55] He refers to the few objects that are used in the production, but might equally have been referring to speech and action. In this production, speech has theatrical and performative effect. I mean by this not that the actors offer highly emotive reactions to what is said to them, but that the precision of the scene's blocking draws attention to the ways in which one figure uses words to undermine another, to change his theatrical and political status, to make him something other, something weaker, than the figure he was when he came on stage.

Performative language, and the circumstances that render it effective or otherwise, are at the political centre of *Richard II*. By calling the magnates 'to our presence', Richard calls them to a performative space in which he may, supposedly, call one of them traitor and close the dispute. Here, I use the term 'performative' in the sense meant by speech act theorists J. L. Austin and John Searle.[56] A performative, according to Austin's account, critiqued by Searle, is speech that performs action, as in a ceremony or ritual; when I refer to a performative space, then, I mean one in which performatives take place or whose function renders speech performative in nature, rather than simply one in which a performance can happen, or a space that appears to perform itself.[57] The king's very presence should produce such a space in *Richard II*, a performative space which the king controls entirely, in which Richard is called only king but may name his subjects as he pleases, calling one 'knight' in the appropriate ceremony, another 'traitor' in a trial. West's Richard does not speak directly to members of the audience in 1.1. His identity of 'King' has been conferred by God and he does not need to justify his position with 'the people', the role in which the audience has been partially cast, as Bolingbroke and Mowbray appear to do. They address the audience directly, each taking a side of the auditorium to win over, shifting between senses of 'appeal': calling each other, appealing to the spectator.

Beginning his appeal, Bolingbroke seeks to legitimise his words first by calling upon heaven as a witness, then by drawing attention to the presence of the king. His first challenge is spoken in religious and chivalric terms and neatly framed by the divine:

BOLINGBROKE: First, heaven be the record to my speech.
    In the devotion of a subject's love,
    Tendering the precious safety of my prince,
    And free from other misbegotten hate,
    Come I appellant to this princely presence.
    Now Thomas Mowbray do I turn to thee,
    And mark my greeting well; for what I speak
    My body shall make good upon this earth,
    Or my divine soul answer it in heaven

(1.1.30–8)

As the exchange between the magnates becomes more heated, the hoped-for trial by combat shifts out of focus as it is the magnates' own words, rather than God's supposed presence at a future trial, that begin to do the work of proving, making, producing each other as traitor. As the magnates turn to an exchange of performative insults, the context that legitimates their speech acts – the presence of the king and the presence of God as witness – is forgotten. They begin to behave as though it is their words alone and the effect these have on their status in the eyes of the audience that can affect victory – as though theirs is, in fact, 'the breath of kings' (1.3.214). West's Richard finds himself in the undignified position of leaving his elevated position on the wooden box and snatching for the 'gage' that Mowbray will not give him. For, as the RSC production emphasises, this is a play in which felicitous performatives[58] are not in fact the sole possession of the king. Once the king has been obliged to intervene by stepping off the box on which the 'throne' is set, the nature of the space is changed from the king's performative Presence Chamber to one in which all are equally embroiled in the politics of the past and of the moment. Mowbray can and does shout at Richard at just the impassioned pitch he has used against Bolingbroke, and although Mowbray does not, of course, insult the king in the way he does his fellow appellant, Richard's descent offers that unthinkably democratic possibility. The king has entered a space in which he can be 'called'. The exchanges between Bolingbroke and Mowbray are made up largely of performative insults, so that for Richard to step down from the central position is to lay himself open to the power of performatives outside his control and to lose the status conferred by centre stage.

The magnates' insults function as performatives in two ways. First, Bolingbroke and Mowbray figure the words they use to name one another 'traitor' as war-horses and weapons capable of physical harm. Bolingbroke will 'stuff … [Mowbray's] throat' with 'a foul traitor's name' (1.1.44). Mowbray, having denied the efficacy of words in combat, suggests that were it not that Richard's presence 'curbs [him]/ From giving reins and spurs to [his] free speech' (54–5) he would return 'these terms of treason doubled down his throat' (57). When Richard demands he take back his gage, Mowbray describes himself as 'pierced to the soul with slander's venomed spear' (171). When the same request is made of Bolingbroke, this 'throwing' of insults reaches a climax that obliterates quite startlingly the figurative status of the magnates' exchange, as Bolingbroke threatens to tear his tongue out with his own teeth and use it as a missile against Mowbray:

> … Ere my tongue
> Shall wound my honour with such feeble wrong,
> Or sound so base a parle, my teeth shall tear
> The slavish motive of recanting fear
> And spit it bleeding in his high disgrace,
> Where shame doth harbour, even in Mowbray's face.
> (1.1.190–5)

Once this point is reached, Richard in the RSC production has left his 'throne' to follow Mowbray for the gage and all pretence at evoking the presence of the king to preside over the quarrel is dropped, replaced by concern for family ties and 'fair name' (167). 'Shall I seem crest-fallen in my father's sight?' (188) asks Troughton of the audience. There is a double sense of competition at work through the magnates' exchanges here: a competition for reputation within the fiction and for the place of 'well graced actor' (5.2.24), for presence in this Presence Chamber of a theatre.

The second function of speech acts in the scene is the dislocation or absenting of one magnate by the other. In *Excitable Speech*, Judith Butler's study of the performative nature of racist hate-speech, Butler argues that 'hate speech exposes a prior vulnerability to language, one that we have by virtue of being interpellated kinds of beings, depending on the address of the Other to be'.[59] In this Althusserian reading of subjectivity,[60] an insult has a direct and immediate effect on the recipient. We are beings who are what they are called, so that an insult acts on the human subject with the direct effect of momentarily reproducing him in the image conjured by the insulter, dislocating him from the matrix of interpellations from which he normally acquires his identity. '[T]o be injured by hate speech' then, 'is to suffer a loss of context, that is, not to know where you are.'[61] In a stage play about a feudal monarchy, interpellation into subjecthood – or at least into identity as the king's subject – is an unavoidable fact of life: the king calls the gentleman his knight, and that is what he becomes; reputation signifies more than life itself – you are the name conferred upon you. Language thus has the power to slip a dramatic figure's identificatory moorings. A sense of insult as dislocation runs clearly through Bolingbroke and Mowbray's (1.1) exchange. To 'maintain' his insults of 'slanderous coward' and 'villain,' Mowbray would

> ... allow [Bolingbroke] odds
> And meet him were I tied to run afoot
> Even to the frozen ridges of the Alps,
> Or any other ground inhabitable
> Where ever Englishman durst set his foot.
>
> (1.1.62–6)

He defies Bolingbroke to challenge him to fight in the most inhospitable terrain of his choice, where Bolingbroke is already figured as the fleeing coward. Mowbray will not, however, go further than an Englishman would dare, suggesting that a only villain such as Bolingbroke might be willing to step outside the boundaries of Englishness. 'To be injured by speech is to suffer a loss of context ... not to know where you are.' Mowbray's speech figures Bolingbroke as one who might well choose such a battleground so alien that 'Englishman' would not dare to tread there. Bolingbroke echoes the insult at lines 93–4 where he swears to prove Mowbray's treason '... here or elsewhere to the furthest verge/ That ever was surveyed by English eye'.

In the RSC production, the presence of the (mainly) English eyes that survey the performance is constantly foregrounded. The lit auditorium draws repeated attention to the spectator's capacity for giving and withdrawing attention. As each magnate talks to the audience in this scene, he attempts to 'take the stage', to leave his opponent standing awkwardly in this performance and performative space while the audience's attention is fixed elsewhere. The performatives in the text are enacted not only by one magnate upon another, with the hoped-for effect of 'making' him traitor, but by the magnates upon the spectators, with the hoped-for effect of producing supporters. The performatives uttered by the magnates are not merely fictional, then: they have effect in theatrical time and space. They are also therefore highly contingent. A lit audience can never be entirely and successfully 'called' commoners or courtiers: they are always in evidence a group of people who have paid to come and see *Richard II*. The felicity or otherwise of the performatives spoken can never be completely known, as the audience's support for one side or another cannot be wholly assured. Part of the significance of the audience's lit presence is that the fictional figures share a space with those who can refuse to answer the call.

The audience in the Presence Chamber

An examination of the prompt copy of the RSC's *Richard II* will confirm that the mode of direct address is central to this production's formal strategy and meaning. Though Pimlott asserts that 'we don't see the ordinary people in this play',[62] the people ruled by the play's 'power brokers'[63] are a continual presence in his production, as the audience are both addressed as Richard's subjects and acknowledged as a group of paying spectators in the theatre. In the stage manager's blocking notes for 1.1, moments when Mowbray and Bolingbroke address the audience are carefully recorded. The experience of watching the scene is very much one of being included in the action by the two appellants, rather than the sense of looking on at a distant medieval pageant or depiction, as the lords appeal not only to the king but to the auditorium, moving as far down stage as is possible, to speak to individual spectators. In 2.1, Northumberland walks up the steps of the raked seating block to justify to the spectators his support of Bolingbroke over Richard, warning them that

The king is not himself, but basely led
By flatterers, and what they will inform
Merely in hate 'gainst any of us all,
That will the King severely prosecute
'Gainst us, our lives, our children and our heirs.

(2.1.241–5)

The audience is included in this 'us', cast as Northumberland's supporters. It is assumed that 'we' will object as strongly to the likes of Bushy and Green as Northumberland, Ross and Willoughby do, although there is again the sense that we need to be persuaded. Bolingbroke, on the other hand, later *demands* that we rise to pray for the soul of the dead Mowbray, with a gesture and an added command (at 4.1.103–4); rather than casting the audience as 'us', this time we are now 'them', subjects to be ruled. Bolingbroke is, after all, about to ascend the throne.

This casting of the audience can never be entirely complete in a lit auditorium, however, where a spectator who is spoken to directly by an actor remains highly conscious of other audience members watching, even laughing at her, in turn highly conscious that it is not a soldier or commoner being spoken to but one of their own number. Asked to rise by Bolingbroke, some audience members are excited by the unexpected command to participate actively in the fiction, others smile wryly, still others are visibly disgruntled and some don't rise at all. Spectators cast as commoners, soldiers or lords are always a potentially disruptive force; they remain resolutely and inevitably their independent selves whose coercion can never be assured. In attempting to produce the audience as courtiers or commoners, this production also stages the potential of its rebellion.

Richard's relationship to the audience appears to be crafted as carefully as Bolingbroke's, Mowbray's and Northumberland's, though not noted in such detail in the prompt copy, suggesting either that it has developed through the run of the production or that West made his own decisions in this respect. While his position as king remains relatively unchallenged during the first act, Richard's relationship with the audience at the RSC is a comparatively distant one. Changes of focus are not noted in the prompt copy as they are for the appellants in 1.1 and his gaze seems to include all in the Presence Chamber, appellants and audience alike. Far from suggesting, as Phyllis Rackin does, that this relationship figures an historical distance, an invitation to look on from the present at a distant medieval world intricately illustrated with poetry as manuscripts are with decoration, West's sweeping gaze across the Presence Chamber and his generalised mode of address is commensurate with his status in a fiction in which the audience is included. He 'casts' us as his subjects and has no need to appeal for our support and recognition as the barons do. When Bolingbroke and Mowbray are called into the king's presence, Richard is not part of the action but presides over it. His eye takes in the whole room, his performative space, where he calls, in both the literal and the interpellative sense, but is not called. His centre stage position is at once one from which the king can survey his fictional Presence Chamber and the position from which the actor may best take in the whole audience. Unlike Claudius, who also speaks in a formal court scene from the authority position, Richard says little. He appears to be above speech, to maintain his presence as king without having to move down stage and address individuals.[64]

Addressing the auditorium but not contacting individuals directly, West avoids the possibility of having his, and Richard's, presence undermined by the recalcitrant spectator reaction that Bolingbroke experiences. It is appropriate that Richard at this point in the fiction should not make direct contact with his 'subjects'. He speaks scornfully of Bolingbroke's 'courtship to the common people' (1.4.24); he was 'not born to sue, but to command' (1.1.196), but his command is not of so absolute a nature that it can brook the subordination of an inappropriate reaction in the auditorium. West's mode of address during the first act is that of a king rather than a 'subject' in both senses of the latter word. The effect of subjectivity is much stronger in the king's subjects, Mowbray and Bolingbroke, who undertake the effortful process of making their presence felt on stage, persuading the audience that they are who and what they say they are.

The effect of subjectivity shifts to West in his own first moment of direct address, in 3.2, wherein he receives news of rebellion and desertion. Here he speaks to individuals in the front row, reminding them that 'Not all the water in the rough rude sea/Can wash the balm off from an anointed king' (3.2.54–5). Richard, it seems, has entered the competition for stage presence that Bolingbroke and Mowbray have begun in 1.1. By telling us directly of his 'anointed' status, he reminds us that we might be inclined to ignore it and support another figure's claims instead, as countless soldiers in the fiction appear to be doing. It is as though, in addressing the audience, the figure makes a shift from the image of kingliness created by the first scene and by his 'sun' analogy of 3.2.36–53 – distant, silent, all-powerful, an eye rather than a voice – to one who must work for attention like any other actor. From this moment and through 3.3, Richard shifts into a narrative mode, referring to 'sad stories of the death of kings' (3.2.156) and occasionally to himself in the third person;[65] where he cannot retain power in the

fiction, he can at least fictionalise his loss of power and place himself at
the centre of a story told in the theatre.

Harry Berger's account of this scene[66] insists that the audience are
not addressed here, that Richard's self-references are not theatrical but
fictional, a performance for the benefit of his on-stage audience only.
West, too, suggests that he feels an actor's obligation to make psychological rather than theatrical sense when he asks of Richard 'Why does he
give in so easily?':

> It can't remain a problem – you have to make sense of it. After
> another exercise when I was held down on the throne by Aumerle
> and Carlisle as I struggled to pull it out from under me,[67] I
> suddenly decided I wanted to stop. It was as if Richard had said
> 'God I hate this – I wish I could give it up', and then it suddenly
> occurred to him that he could.[68]

Once again, West's shifts of personal pronoun are as significant as
Richard's. Who is the 'I' that wants to stop? West certainly refers to
himself as Richard here. But in a production that foregrounds power
relations in the theatrical present, played out in the presence of the
audience, his objective – to stop and give up – reads as a performance
as well as a fictional objective. Richard's position as all seeing sun-god
king is one of obvious theatrical high status as the performer playing
him stands centre stage or up on the balcony, surveying the audience.
High status, however, is a precarious position, as every modern clown or
student of Keith Johnstone's improvisation games will know.[69] Giving it
up may often be the best way to engage an audience. The RSC's
production leaves centre stage to Bolingbroke during the second half of
the play, then West's Richard, once he has 'stopped' and given up being
king, re-usurps it as the best position from which to talk to the audience.

The centre of the Presence Chamber

Samuel West enters for the 'prison soliloquy' dragging his long wooden
box up-ended behind him. He stands in it centre stage. The prison in
which he speaks of man 'with nothing [being] pleased till he be eased /
With being nothing' (5.5.40–1) is clearly to be the coffin in which this
state of nothingness is to be reached, his 'last presence chamber', as
Bosola calls the Duchess of Malfi's coffin twelve years later.[70] Richard
appears as a man standing centre stage in a box, talking to the audience
of being nothing, and of time 'wasting' him: he is least like a king, most

Figure 4.1 Samuel West as Richard II in *Richard II*, dir. Steven Pimlott, RSC © Shakespeare Birthplace Trust. Photo: Malcolm Davies.

like a 'subject', as the play moves towards his physical death and as he speaks of the death of his royal identity. His possession of the centre-stage position marks the end of striving towards a performance objective strongly foregrounded in this production: the objective to take control of stage centre. In a royal presence chamber, this position is always the king's and history demands that this be wrested from Richard. The dramatic structure of *Richard II* is based around Richard's changing the meaning of this authority position, from one where the king gives audience to his subjects to one where the actor talks to the audience.

Act 4 of *Richard II* begins as Bolingbroke attempts to discover 'who performed / The bloody office' (4.1.4–5) of murdering Richard's uncle, the Duke of Gloucester. A series of accusations ensue in which Aumerle is accused so often that he is obliged to borrow a gage from 'Some honest Christian' (4.1.83), as all his have been thrown down in answer to his accusers. If there is a sense in which Richard does not exercise absolutist control over the appellants in 1.1, 4.1 is a chaotic parody of that lack of control. In the Almeida production, all the nostalgic longing for a medieval paradise in the verdant world of 'this England' cannot dampen this scene's comic potential. It is the light relief that this play's working-class figures – the symbolic gardeners – do not provide. The RSC production appears to be equally comfortable with comedy.[71] However, as chivalric gages are flung all over the stage at the opening of 4.1, the company appears unconcerned with the scene's comic potential until the entrance of Richard. The sequence in this production is a resolutely serious one[72] and central to this tone is the use of the stage centre space.

During the challenges that fly thick and fast in the scene's first exchanges, Troughton's Bolingbroke sits against the up-stage-left wall, only moving centre stage to announce that 'These differences shall all rest under gage/Till Norfolk be repealed' (4.1.86–7). If Bolingbroke stands centre stage during the gage-throwing, as he does at the Almeida's Gainsborough studios, the authority that position commands in 1.1 and 1.3 is undermined to comic effect. Bolingbroke sets up a formal appeal in the first lines of the scene then is obliged to stand amidst a storm of accusing magnates and their hurled gloves, about to intervene and set a date for trial by combat when another lord enters the fray. Troughton's Bolingbroke, on the other hand, absents himself from the authority position. The number of challenges made presage future violence, rather than rendering Bolingbroke's inability to control them ridiculous. Not to stand centre stage, then, is a significant political and theatrical decision. It is impossible to stand there without making a powerful statement, and a statement about power, which, as long as there are other figures on stage, can always be undermined. It is an ambiguous position for Bolingbroke throughout this performance, reflecting the ambiguity of his claim to the throne. He repeatedly appears to take control of the space by standing there, 'in the view of men' (3.1.6) that make up the audience, only to have that control undermined. For the arraignment of Bushy and Green (3.1), he stands down stage of the throne's former position, close to the audience, as if still in need of justification by those in the Presence Chamber rather than in complete control of it. Bushy and Green stand sulkily up stage centre of him, contacting members of what should be Bolingbroke's audience and undermining him with sarcastic looks and comic exasperation. Bolingbroke turns and shoots Bushy with a silenced gun, and there is a sense in which the execution is punishment for making Bolingbroke 'seem crest-fallen' (1.1.188) in front of his audience as much as for his misleading the king. Bolingbroke then invites Green to take centre stage, gesturing towards the audience as if to suggest that they are 'all his'; but Richard's favourite is shot almost before he can complete his last couplet. The power of speaking centre stage has been mockingly offered him then snatched away.

The *Spectator* describes Troughton's Bolingbroke as 'no reluctant regicide but a tyrant on the make, a man who insists the audience should get to its feet to endorse his usurpation'.[73] This moment certainly reads as a desire on Bolingbroke's part to take control of the Presence Chamber after the chaos of the gage-throwing scene. However, when York enters in 4.1 with the announcement that 'Richard ... with willing soul/Adopts thee heir' (4.1.108–9), Troughton looks about him stage right, stage left and to the audience as if caught in the central position, unpleasantly shocked to find himself in danger of becoming king. His declaration, 'In God's name I'll ascend the regal throne' (4.1.113), speaks of a determination to replace Richard's place in the conventional blocking of 1.1, his subjects around him and God, whom he invokes as witness, above. However, the remaining action in this the 'deposition' scene centres around his vulnerability in this position, a reduction of his theatrical status which forces him to send Richard to the Tower/off stage altogether, and a play on his not having chosen to sit or stand there at all.

Having taken control of the Presence Chamber by demanding that the audience stand up (to mourn the death of Mowbray), Troughton's Bolingbroke is undermined by the Bishop of Carlisle who steps forward to denounce him. As Carlisle paces the stage predicting civil war, Bolingbroke remains still and silent, and the stage centre position becomes a dock rather than a coronation dais, Carlisle's speech an arraignment. Bolingbroke, having stepped forward with confidence, now appears vulnerable centre stage, open to the bishop's accusations. Rather in the way that Bushy and Green are instantly shot, Carlisle is now swiftly arrested and removed from the stage where he has been able to undermine Bolingbroke's fictional and theatrical position.

Having thus appeared 'crest-fallen' in the 'common view' of an audience he has attempted to command as though they were his supernumerary subjects, Bolingbroke demands the presence of Richard, so that the king's public abdication may justify his own accession. Where Bolingbroke now appears awkward and exposed at the centre of the space, Richard appears entirely in possession of it, slowly and ironically clearing it of fallen gloves as if to suggest that he, unlike these incompetents, knows just how a Presence Chamber should look. West's performance for the remaining deposition sequence shifts from needling comic irony, to tearful grief, to a self-mockery at his own grief; he becomes the consummate performer of critical commentary, drawing the audience's attention up stage right and away from what should be the scene of Bolingbroke's triumph. In comparison to Richard's fluidity, Bolingbroke's performance vocabulary appears limited and awkward. The formal marching from one part of the playing space to another and the soldierly salutes he uses during 1.1 and 1.3 are appropriate for a particular range of performative ritual – a trial, for example, or even a coronation. This is not Bolingbroke's coronation, however, but Richard's deposition, which West underlines as a mock coronation whose rituals he controls. 'God save the king!' he calls, out into the auditorium, then pauses. 'Will no man say Amen?' (4.1.172) he asks a woman in the third row, with a lightly ironic tone that suggests that he has ceased to 'cast' the audience as his subjects, either dutiful or unruly.

This comic moment of direct contact re-engenders the audience as audience and Richard does what Bushy was momentarily able to do before his death: undermines Bolingbroke in the eyes of the spectator in the theatre, making a theatrical spectacle of what should be a formal and fictional one. During the rest of the deposition sequence, Bolingbroke is directed by Richard into playing a role in which he appears more and more foolish: invited to 'seize the crown' (4.1.181) like a kitten being called to play, pushed violently down on the throne where Richard jams the crown on his head. When West moves upstage to the mound of earth to perform a grief that becomes the central performance piece of the scene, Bolingbroke waits, awkward and vulnerable in a centre-stage position that appears to have lost its theatrical status.

Performing in the Presence Chamber

In the deposition scene, West's Richard makes a performance out of a performative. The coronation scene that Bolingbroke wants the audience to witness appears only to exist in his desperate imagination as he stares fixedly into the auditorium, giving a forced performance, deliberately lacking in the 'stage presence' the spectator might conventionally expect of a king. It is Richard who has the audience's attention as he performs simultaneously for them and his bewildered on-stage spectators. He speaks the discourse of ceremony in comic mode, points to the infelicitous circumstances, the unceremonious confusion of roles that the scene entails, the lack of formal centre to the proceedings:

> God save the king! Will no man say Amen?
> Am I both priest and clerk? Well then, Amen.
> God save the king, although I be not he,
> And yet Amen if heaven do think him me.
> To do what service am I sent for hither?
>   (4.1.172–6)

Each time Bolingbroke believes himself safe centre stage and straightens himself ceremoniously as if waiting to be crowned, West undermines his position by drawing attention away from Troughton and centring the ceremony on himself, foregrounding himself as both speaker of performatives and figure performed upon:

> Now, mark me how I will undo myself.
> I give this heavy weight from off my head
> And this unwieldy sceptre from my hand,
> The pride of kingly sway from out my heart.
> With mine own tears I wash away my balm;
> With mine own hands I give away my crown;
> With mine own tongue deny my sacred state;
> With mine own breath release all duteous oaths.
>   (4.1.202–9)

These lines are spoken up stage right of Bolingbroke; Richard performs his own ceremony of disempowerment, that of which 'Not all the water in the rough rude sea' (3.2.54) is capable – and achieves precisely the opposite focus of theatrical attention to that described by York when he follows the 'well-grac'd actor' Bolingbroke on his progress through the streets of London. From assuming that the audience will play the king's subjects, Richard now acknowledges himself as a performer who can shift from direct contact on a comic line to tears upstage by a mound that represents England and a grave, and whose audience may or may not choose to answer 'Amen' when he requests it. He ceases to treat the audience as *his* subjects and talks to them as willing 'subjects'. By the end of the deposition scene, West has reduced the carefully structured performative meaning of centre stage to a mere part of his performance space, the part where he contemplates his fragmented reflection in the glass, here represented by the wooden box up-ended, then from which he demands to be allowed to exit to the tower, where he reclaims centre stage as the best position for direct contact with the theatre audience.

The 'prison soliloquy' is a study in self-constitution that leads, like Hamlet's soliloquies, to thoughts of self-obliteration; in describing the impossibility of constitution outside of socially conferred identity – primarily here, of course, the role of king – the soliloquy produces a strong effect of willed subjectivity. Each of the three sets of thoughts with which Richard plans to people his cell marks a paradigm of self-definition: 'thoughts of things divine' (5.5.12) inscribe the self within God's providential plan; 'Thoughts tending to ambition' (18) define it according to the achievement of power; 'Thoughts tending to content' (23) figure a stoicism like that which 'grunts and sweats under a weary life' in *Hamlet*. Each set of thoughts engenders its opposite. Divine thoughts engender religious doubt: contradictions are found within the supposedly indubitable divine word, so that a questioning Richard is produced outside of religious law:

> ... The better sort,
> As thoughts of things divine, are intermixed
> With scruples, and do set the word itself
> Against the word –
> As thus: 'Come little ones', and then again,
> 'It is as hard to come as for a camel
> To thread the postern of a small needle's eye.'
> (5.5.11–17)

Ambitious thoughts overreach themselves, imagining impossible selves outside of the 'flinty ribs/Of this hard world' (20–1), an image that figures the world, the prison and the body. Imagining a self that has escaped 'this hard world', however, is to imagine death.

> Thoughts tending to ambition, they do plot
> Unlikely wonders: how these vain weak nails

> May tear a passage through the flinty ribs
> Of this hard world my ragged prison walls,
> And, for they cannot, die in their own pride.
>   (5.5.18–22)

Contented thoughts regard the ills the self must endure as mere repetitions of others' endurance, and in thus interrogating this stoical position, Richard again appears to stand aside from the versions of identity that the world permits. The subject that contemplates these thoughts posits itself outside external constructions but, given that these constructions are all the world has to offer, acknowledges that it cannot exist for long. Being 'one person' (31) is to answer the interpellative calls that make a human being God's creature, or part of a power structure, or an endless repeater of burdensome tasks. To refuse to answer the call is to become nothing, to become meaningless within the structures that confer identity. It is unsurprising that the achievement of subjectivity – of a selfhood that stands outside identity and talks about it – occurs in the moment of direct address when Richard appears closest to the actor that performs him, and is swiftly followed by death.

West's position, imprisoned in the box from which it is impossible to speak – the coffin – foregrounds him once more as the performer he 'plays' during the opening Prologue, made up from lines in this soliloquy. Inside this coffin he is, in fact, able to speak: directly to the audience, stripped of ornaments of his royal, fictional identity. Centre stage now becomes the site of an amplified presence, that of Richard as performer. In drawing attention to the performed nature of his identity as king and to the actor that performs him, Richard's text as spoken by West produces an effect of subjectivity beyond what can be produced by the performance of self-contained character. Bolingbroke, who sends Exton to murder Richard, cannot endure this ultimate position of powerful presence in the Presence Chamber. The punishment for taking centre stage is death. We glimpse a 'sovereign subject' only to have it wrested from us.

The RSC's *Richard II* uses a detailed and focused mode of direct address by the performers, foregrounding them as performers talking to the audience and attempting with various degrees of success to cast the audience in the fiction, as courtiers or commoners according to the demands of the text. The audience watch not only the performers but themselves, being constituted as a range of subjects: Richard's subjects, Bolingbroke's subjects, and subject-persons, agents in the production of the drama's meaning. Sat in darkness, the audience at the Gainsborough studios are 'subjects' in none of these senses. They look on at the action with complete 'objectivity and superiority to the play's world',[74] as Bert States would have it; their relationship to the narrative is essentially ironic. Whether he is read as impassive and controlled, or effete and disdainful, Ralph Fiennes is part of a theatrical matrix that characterises him as 'man whose character brings about his downfall' from his first entrance, a characterisation of which Richard is unaware. Central to this production is the tragedy of a king whose 'character' is inappropriate to his social role and who learns a dignified kingliness too late to save England from civil strife. It is a combination of naturalistic convention and the theatrical metonymy of the grass and split wall that invokes this critically conservative reading of the play, a reading which assumes 'kingliness' as a quality recalled with nostalgic regret in the face of a Richard whose character cannot live up to it until, tragically, he learns what the audience have understood all along, is imprisoned and dies. West, on the other hand, shares Richard's demise with the audience quite openly in the transcribed Prologue. The processes that bring about that demise – including Richard's active part in it, from which he is not absolved by historical circumstance – are then examined in ways that implicate the audience, rather than permitting them, as one reviewer so badly wishes to do, to 'savour the tragedy', to sit apart from the action and know what Richard does not. However, the 'heightened self-awareness' marked by the *Independent on Sunday* that permits West to turn knowingly to a member of the audience for the line 'Not all the water in the rough rude sea/Can wash the balm from an anointed king' can instantly give way to a more obviously emotive performance in this production, less suggestive of the critical distance that the more lukewarm reviews found disconcerting. West appears entirely self-absorbed as he contemplates the fate of kings in the same scene, or breaks down in abject misery on the balcony of Flint Castle in 3.3, happy to indulge Richard's much examined self-indulgence as he sinks to the ground and clutches at Aumerle on 'We do debase ourselves, cousin, do we not,/To look so poorly and to speak so fair?' (3.3.127–8). The Samuel West of Flint Castle offers only Richard's perspective on the action, calling upon the spectator to pity only Richard. Spectators may, of course, refuse to obey the call, and their constantly visible presence emphasises this freedom on their part. What they witness, I would argue, is not so much the actor standing aside from his or her character, or dancing around it as the *Independent* review would have it, so much as the presence of an actor standing up for his or her fictional figure, demanding from the spectator that she look at and listen to Richard, this kingly figure, this weeping wretch, this actor. For Richard II is both fictional figure and performer; his super-objective is a performance objective – to reach the point where his own presence in the theatre is more engaging than those who have set about to reduce his fictional power. As in *Hamlet*, an effect of presence is thus produced, whereby the audience appear to be in the presence of Richard himself, as he shifts from an assumption of authority to a struggle to engage their attention.

Richard II's final achievement of a subjectivity outside social constitution is an ambivalent one. His struggle with what he might be if not a king ceases only because he is killed, and this points to the ultimate impossibility of winning that struggle. Having found it impossible to invent selves, Richard in the Tower can only be 'not a king' or, in his last encounter with the groom, 'not Bolingbroke'. What the theatrical consciousness of the RSC production achieves, is a direct encounter between performer and audience that permits Richard a place in the world of the subjects watching the play, the possibility of an imagined subjectivity outside of social construction. Samuel West suggests that the music he hears from his prison cell should be his signature tune, played out of tune.[75] The notion of a fictional figure hearing his own signature tune played in the theatre is just the kind of theatrically conscious gesture that the plays examined here might logically contain: Richard II listening to a tune that announces him as a dramatic figure in the theatre would foreground the simultaneous standing inside and outside the fiction that constitutes dramatic subjectivity.

In his account of the production, West wryly remarks that 'very few people fell asleep in this production'.[76] Its determination to reach outwards instead of 'deep within', its construction of dramatic subjectivities in moments of encounter between performer, dramatic figure and audience produced a sense that all had been called upon to play the role of performing humans in a political drama and a live performance event, a role which, whether one accepted or rejected it, was hard to ignore. West ends his account of his part in the project with a disclaimer regarding historical authenticity: this *Richard II* was 'our response, not (I imagine) Shakespeare's'. This is always and inevitably the case, though those reviewers who express the desire for the text to 'speak for itself' might deny it. In situating the performance in the presence of the audience in the Presence Chamber, the *Richard II* company does have a claim to historical authenticity should it care to make one; it has made a particularly full and detailed acknowledgment that the play speaks to the audience.

As most current introductions to the play point out, early performances of *Richard II* had the deposition scene censored and it was played, according to an apparently disconcerted Elizabeth I, 'forty times in open streets and houses' as incitement to rebellion.[77] The play evidently spoke dangerously clearly to late sixteenth-century London. Making similarly radical claims for a Shakespeare performance in the current English cultural context would be naïve. However, the RSC's move from nostalgic pageantry and character-led tragedy to a play of political and theatrical presence lets *Richard II* articulate questions regarding socially conferred identity and subjectivity as agency that are politically potent. The RSC's *Richard II* did not produce the common effect of simile in Shakespeare production, whereby the spectator is informed by a 'modern' *mise en scène* how like the experiences of those living in England in 1398 or 1595 its own audience's political experiences are. Nor did it present the play as an elegy for a lost world to be savoured (or slept through). Instead, in making the play talk to the audience, the production achieves something more sophisticated. It asks the spectator to consider her position as witness and agent in relation to specific processes of power occurring in the theatre and permits her to do the work of linking them to what are essentially political questions, because they demand to be answered in relation to the power structures unfolding in both real and fictional time and space: 'what, who and where am I'?

5 Performing human
The Socìetas Raffaello Sanzio

In a performance piece that ended its life with a 'cease and desist' order from Arthur Miller's lawyers, New York performance company the Wooster Group performed moments, lines and fragments from *The Crucible*. They performed them sitting behind a table and in a trough beneath it, in period costume and modern dress, with and without microphones, in blackface, in imitation of themselves rehearsing *The Crucible* on LSD. *LSD … Just the High Points* was not a production of *The Crucible*. It interwove its chosen moments from Miller's play with random readings from the writings of Timothy Leary and friends, an interview with Timothy Leary's babysitter, some dance sequences, some quotations from a touring debate between Leary and G. Gordon Liddy. Miller feared that the piece would compromise a Broadway production of *The Crucible*, might be seen as a parody of *The Crucible* and decided that ultimately he did not want to see *The Crucible* used in ways other than stipulated in and suggested by the play he had written. To the company, and to David Savran who wrote extensively and supportively of the company's work during the 1970s and 1980s, *LSD* was no parody of the Miller play.[1] However, *LSD* staged readings of *The Crucible* that were in excess of Miller's intention, pointing to the cultural and political contexts in which he wrote it and putting in heavy quotation marks the naturalistic acting style the play text requires in performance. In *LSD*, Willem Dafoe breaks down weeping as John Proctor, and before he does so, famously puts glycerine in his eyes to represent tears.

The Italian company the Socìetas Raffaello Sanzio (SRS) works with *Julius Caesar* and *Hamlet* in ways that can be said to be and not be Shakespeare. I begin this chapter with the Wooster Group not simply because SRS also makes free with 'classic' texts and provokes controversy by doing so, but in order to return to a question of authenticity that has haunted this study of the Shakespearean dramatic subject so far. *Giulio Cesare* is a severely cut version of the Shakespeare text with a

Figure 5.1 Dalmarzo Masari as Mark Antony, in *Giulio Cesare*, Societas Raffaello Sanzio, dir. Romeo Castellucci. Photo: Gabriele Pellegrini.

speech by Cicero on rhetoric included in it; *Amleto* ... contains only fragmentary references to *Hamlet*. What I am going to argue they are able to do is point to the theatrical work of the Shakespearean dramatic figure, and how theatrical work infects and inflects the meaning of the two fictions. *LSD* appears to me to highlight the work *The Crucible* does in the theatre and in the world. When Willem Dafoe speaks of his glycerine moment, he says that 'you get your cake and eat it too':[2] the pleasure to be taken in a virtuoso piece of acting; the emotional connection to be made with the man on stage 'crying'; the distance from the crying man produced by the overtness of the technique – the Wooster Group offers them all. This is an expressly post-modern theatre practice, one which offers no political stance from which to critique emotional involvement and absorption but which nevertheless allows the spectator to watch herself getting involved and absorbed. Societas Raffaello Sanzio's frightening theatrical landscapes and soundscapes, their raw and dangerous-looking electrics and, most importantly, exposed and un-beautiful human figures, produce an emotional vulnerability in the spectator and simultaneously shows her how she has got into an emotionally vulnerable state. I think of the Societas Raffaello Sanzio's work as having one's emotional cake and eating it analytically, and this chapter examines what that means for Shakespeare in production.

A pair of rough white curtains closes around a stout, bald man in a toga, leaving a gap in which he stands, speaking an Italian translation of Mark Antony's celebrated address to the plebeians from *Julius Caesar*.[3] As he speaks of the rents in Caesar's mantle (3.2.167–95), of Brutus' unkindest cut, he holds a curtain up to the audience, an audience rendered particularly sensitive to the notion of unkind cuts by an open hole in the performer's throat. Dalmazo Masani has had a laryngectomy and speaks with the aid of a man-made voice box positioned just below this hole. His gaze is direct as he talks to the audience, his speech quiet, intimate and evidently effortful. He is not 'acting' effort, or emotion at Caesar's death: it is the hole in his throat that makes breathing and speaking difficult. His struggle to speak, undertaken calmly and unsensationally, produces an effect of subjectivity that maps itself temptingly onto the figure of Mark Antony. The spectator can see the voice coming from the throat, but convinces herself that it comes from the heart, the 'heart [that] is in the coffin there with Caesar' (3.2.107). The effect is more emotionally compelling than many strong naturalistic performances. As with Willem Dafoe's crying man, we are shown the effect of emotion and the elements that make up the effect, but there is no lessening of the effect itself.

Figure 5.2
Paulo Tonti in
Amleto...,
Societas
Raffaello Sanzio,
dir. Romeo
Castellucci.
Photo: Silva.

A performer in shorts and shoes stands behind a roughly hung polythene screen, on a stage covered with wires, car batteries, and whirring, clanking machinery. Bare bulbs hang from the ceiling, attached to the car batteries by more trailing wire. The man in shorts looks out into the lit gymnasium where this performance of *Amleto...* is taking place and makes an open-armed gesture of self-presentation. As he does so, he kicks at his polythene screen and says the words 'For you'. He does not appear to be looking directly at anyone, but the space into which he looks does not read as the space of actorly soliloquy, the unilluminated space of thought or conscience. The way in which this performer talks to the audience is unreadable within the theatrical discourse I have been developing in this study, because it is unreadable within the everyday framework of intentionality that is assumed when human beings make eye contact with one another. There are notes in the programme that juxtapose quotations from *Hamlet* with writings on autism and when I first see the performance, I am unsure as to whether or not Paulo Tonti is actually autistic; I want to read his alienating indirectness as part of a mental condition. If Tonti were autistic, then when he looks at a partic- ular spectator, he may not, according to the 'theory of mind' reading of the syndrome,[4] be reading her as possessing an independent, self-origi- nary set of beliefs and feelings. He does not appear to be testing audience reaction, or assuming that they will react. He does not signal that he recognises us as subjects and is therefore difficult to read as a subject. As with Mark Antony, the elements that go to make up the effect of dramatic subjectivity are there – the performer's body, a text, an addressee – but subjectivity is harder to read.

Giulio Cesare

In the Societas Raffaello Sanzio's *Giulio Cesare*, constructions of subjec- tivity are repeatedly presented as just that. A performer sits centre stage and speaks lines from the first scene of *Julius Caesar*, a cut version of the tribunes' exchange with the cobbler, in Italian. A pile of shoes grows to his left, evidence of the work produced by the plebeians in the scene, thrown desultorily onto the pile from off stage. Above him, subtitles offer the original text as a translation of the Italian voice.[5] The performer inserts an endoscope into his throat. The resultant pictures of his vocal cords at their twitching, convulsive work are projected onto a screen, between him and the text.

On this stage, man and text do not produce the version of the human produced by the naturalistic theatre, whereby the actor appears as a coherent psychological subject, spontaneously uttering a four-hundred-year-old text, while signalling through a complex series of physical twitches and vocal ticks that deep within this unruptured human body is 'that within which passeth show', a psychological subtext. Here, visible text – subtitles – and visible body, are separated from one another by the visible image of the workings of the vocal chords.

This is one step further along the road to the laying bare of what constitutes the subject than some of the audience are prepared to go. There is much shading of eyes in the auditorium. This man is not, as certain voice coaches would have it,[6] filled with Shakespeare, but with viscera. Being forced to look at what is literally 'within' the speaking subject, to see that what produces Shakespeare is not so much a man as a bit of a man, is disturbing. We are not looking at a coherent subject. We are not even looking at a coherent body, or at least this is not the main focus of the spectator's attention; the eyes are inevitably drawn to the large screen with its pulsating vocal chords. Attention is drawn to a variety of elements that go to make up the production of subjectivity effect – words, vocal chords, body – and a pile of objects that point to the indeterminate mass of people who have no such subjectivity conferred upon them when they are referred to later by Brutus and Cassius: they are a discarded and disregarded group of individuals signified by their shoes. Throughout this performance, the spectator is sensitised to questions regarding who and what signifies the human. What does it mean to be human in this play, and who gets to be – or perform – human? These are questions with which *Julius Caesar* is struggling.

Brutus speaks to the masses with a vibrating metal collar around his neck. It is a low-tech affair, disconcertingly like a crude instrument of torture. In fact the performance space is hung with electrical wires and crude lighting that do not look particularly safe or complete. The first time I am in the audience, the news media have been recently saturated with hastily left torture chambers in the former Yugoslavia, so that this *mise en scène* cannot but suggest that some grotesque violation of vulnerable parts of the human body is about to take place. I contemplate leaving. The metal collar causes the voice of the Brutus performer to quaver wildly, recalling actorly techniques used to produce the effect of a troubled interiority – the shuddering and stumbling that signals that there exists 'that within' that is really too painful to show but that we in the theatre are privileged to witness. When Brutus has finished with it, the collar is left on the stage alone, vibrating absurdly. Next time he speaks to the plebeians, a gas canister is laboriously wheeled on and Brutus sucks from it – another insertion into the throat reveals how a voice is produced. This voice is a daft, helium-induced Disney Donald Duck impression and Brutus' speech finally degenerates into a manic quacking. Now we are on safer ideological territory. Here is the patrician spouting inauthentic gibberish to the working class; at least the inauthentic posits an alternative. Perhaps it is to be found in Mark Antony, whose famously manipulative speech seems to have been stripped of rhetorical gloss. His soft voice struggles to offer the words to us. Here is no actorly production of inner conflict but evidence of real pain. Rather than use 'emotion memory'[7] to produce the effect of a dramatic figure with a coherent psychological life, with a past, this actor produces his effects of authenticity in the bodily present, from the presence of his damaged body. How could anyone doubt this voice? We have, after all, seen the work that has gone into authoring it. I observe myself mapping what has felt like a 'real' human encounter between performer and spectator onto that between Mark Antony and the crowd. I am persuaded: Brutus was a murderer. As the audience leave the auditorium – Mark Antony's speech ends the first half of the production – Marlon Brando's rendition of the same lines[8] is played over the sound system. The audience is reminded of other Mark Antonys and of other theatrical constructions of what it is to be human. The work that must be done in order to identify or empathise is doubly foregrounded by this offering of somebody else's work.

Throughout *Giulio Cesare*, actorly versions of the human are evoked, stripped back for examination, reconstructed for our pleasure. It is not only human bodies that are produced as human, moreover. Things that might be anthropomorphised in other film and theatre worlds have their human qualities taken from them, then returned in ways that are both comical and moving. A large, living horse is led on stage and it is difficult for it to signify anything other than a large, living horse; its very presence in a confined space makes us think of the chaos that would ensue if it neighed, kicked or shat. Before Caesar's death, the horse is written on: the words *mene tekel peres* are painted on its side in large white letters and it becomes one of the play's many portents, to be read and misread by the play's dramatic figures. The animal that signifies only itself amidst the carefully arranged sign system in which it is placed, is made to signify that 'the writing's on the wall', or the horse, for Caesar.[9] Later, a large skeleton of a horse whinnies pitifully at the death of Brutus. The sound clearly cannot come from within the skeleton – it is a recording played as the head of the horse skeleton is raised and lowered

– nevertheless, it catapults us into an anthropomorphic, man-centred world in which the voice comes from the heart and humans and animals alike mourn the hero.

Another animated animal figure sits amidst the chaos that makes up the set of this second half of *Giulio Cesare*, a dusty half-obliterated theatre auditorium complete with half rows of seating and canvas flats. It is a stuffed cat. As Brutus mourns the death of Cassius, attention is drawn to its presence as its head begins to spin around; the spinning head comes to a sudden stop, before turning once more, seemingly to face the audience, as if it had some significant comment to make upon the events of the play. Nicholas Ridout analyses the relationship of this animatronic piece of taxidermy to the constructions of the human with which Socìetas Raffaello Sanzio present the audience:

> ... slowly, meaningfully and with absolutely legible intention [the cat] turns its head to look directly at us. Just as the actor with no larynx needs technology to simulate the voice that is vital to his trade, this cat simulates an emotional response to the tragic events being simulated for us on stage. If an animatronically enhanced stuffed cat can communicate on stage with this degree of human complexity we are in some sort of interesting trouble with our identifications of the human.[10]

Ridout sees director Romeo Castellucci's continuing work with non-actors and performers with unconventional body shapes as part of an examination of what passes as 'human' on stage and in society. Indeed, the company seems overtly concerned with ways in which humans themselves are, paradoxically, anthropomorphised, made to read as particular versions of the human, through theatre and specifically through Shakespeare. Ways in which a theatre audience might expect a human figure to behave and look are foregrounded by the company's staging of both animals and humans. Animals appear to behave in particularly human ways, humans produce effects of humanity through the use of technology, or use technology to reveal how the human is performed.

Animals are repeatedly read as portents in *Julius Caesar*. Though, as messages from the gods, they may be supposed to have a transcendental significance, their meaning is in fact always produced in the moment of reading them. As Cicero points out, '... men may construe things after their fashion/Clean from the purpose of the things themselves' (1.3.34–5). Women, like animals, can be involuntary carriers of supernatural signs, where men tend to construe things after their own fashion. Decius interprets Calpurnia's dream of the bleeding fountain to his own advantage and Caesar is happy to accept his exposition (2.2.83–91).[11] Power is achieved by he who can make a sign mean what he wants it to mean, and in *Julius Caesar*, there is no more contested site of significance than the human body, specifically the body of the dead ruler. The Socìetas Raffaello Sanzio's Caesar signifies Caesar rather than playing him. All the dramatic figure's lines are cut; he simply walks onto the stage, a tiny little old man in a red toga, and speaks the Latin tag *veni, vidi, vici* to the audience, a recognisable sign of 'Caesar'. Brutus wants to ensure that this sign in its final state signifies to his advantage. 'Let's be sacrificers but not butchers' (2.1.165) he says to Cassius, reluctant to kill Mark Antony along with Caesar; and on Caesar's death: 'Let's carve him as a dish fit for the gods,/Not hew him as a carcass fit for hounds' (172–3). Caesar's body must suggest a sacrifice, a link back to the supernatural world whence come the portents that fill the play, an irrefutably transcendental sign of the gods' approval, rather than a sign of the material interest that reduces the human to the level of un-portentous butchered animal. What Caesar's body signifies will determine the significance of the conspirators and their actions – will determine, in fact, what their actions are:

BRUTUS: This shall make
  Our purpose necessary and not envious,
  Which so appearing to the common eyes,
  We shall be called purgers, not murderers.
                    (2.1.176–9)

In *Giulio Cesare*, the old man representing Caesar is undressed, washed carefully by Brutus with a sponge, dried – Magdalen-like – with a lock of hair, then laid on the stage and tied down by crossing rope over his prone body between two columns of nails. Then, in a desperate attempt to over-determine this ritual as celebratory and life-giving rather than sinister and predatory, a handful of paper confetti is tossed over the body.

This careful, lovingly undertaken ritual does not serve the purpose it might have served had this naked old man, this sign of Caesar, looked like an actor. The naked body is not a common sight in the classical theatre, let alone the body of a frail old man, who lacks the confident stance and well-fed flesh of the trained actor. The ropes that tie 'Caesar' down emphasise his pigeon chest and concave stomach alarmingly, and the phenomenal pressure this body exerts on the carefully staged significance of the ritual washing, tying, confetti-throwing, will not permit Caesar to mean what Brutus wants him to mean. This is a body closer to death than your average Julius Caesar, closer to becoming the piece of meat that might render Brutus and Cassius 'butchers'. Just as the involuntary convulsions of the vocal chords disorient the association of Shakespeare with humanist constructs of the human subject – whole, self-contained, the fount of self-originary reason – this little old man demonstrates the gap between what 'man' might want himself to signify and his material presence in the world as the body that can be rendered significant by others, written upon.

The presence of the female body, upon which so much has been written, is both evoked and erased in *Julius Caesar* in the figure of Portia. Calpurnia functions as a portent: she has a dream, which she reads correctly, but which Decius and Caesar re-interpret. Portia, on the other hand, writes her own significance on herself with her 'voluntary wound ... in the thigh' (2.1.299–300), drawing attention to a body that is supposed to signify weakness but whose scar links her to the legendary strength of Cato and Brutus. The two female figures from *Julius Caesar* are absent from the Societas Raffaello Sanzio stage. In the second half of the performance,[12] two female performers enter, representing not Calpurnia and Portia but Cassius and Brutus. During the first half of the performance the conspirators are played by men, during the second half by women, women who have made their own 'mark' on their bodies and whose presence on stage is disturbing. The Brutus and Cassius performers are anorexic. Once again, Nicholas Ridout relates the presence of these women to the Societas Raffaello Sanzio's concern with constructions of the human:

> It is Brutus, of course, whose death at the end of the play elicits Mark Antony's 'This was a man!' Well no, this was, apparently a woman, and a woman whose self-identifications appear to be written in the body, the less than womanly body of the anorexic, a body produced by the saturation of images that tell us what it is to be human, what we must do to meet the criteria. ... Self-reduction in pursuit of identity, or in pursuit of some kind of resistance to the dictates of the symbolic universe.[13]

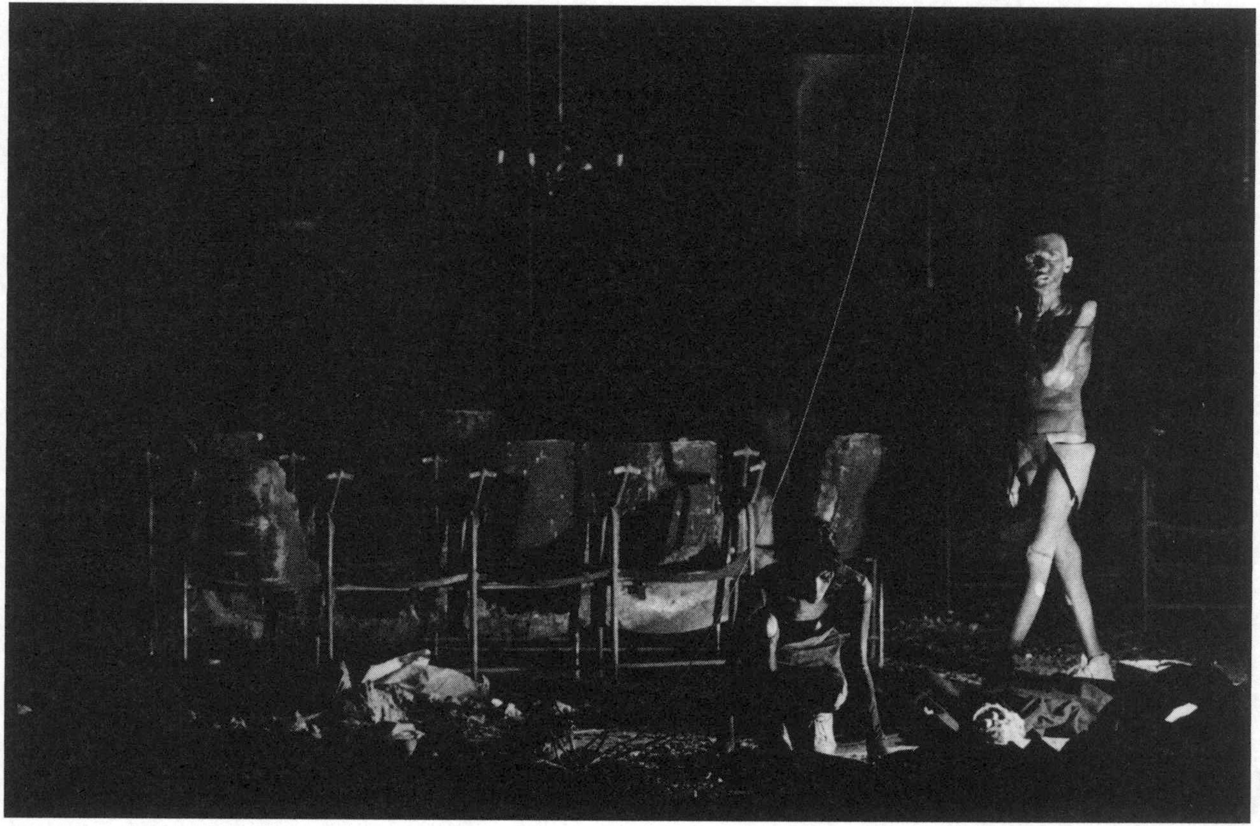

Figure 5.3 Elena Bagaloni as Brutus and Cristiana Bertini as Cassius, in *Giulio Cesare*, Societas Raffaello Sanzio, dir. Romeo Castellucci. Photo: Silva.

Like Caesar's suspiciously thin men, the bodies of this 'Brutus' and 'Cassius' are hard to read. They show distortions wrought on the body by its owner, and foreground the questionable subjectivity of that owner. Who or what determines that these women should be so thin? Are they in pursuit of a socially constructed image of the female, or resisting socially conferred identity? The performance ends as one woman leaves the stage, calling the other by her name. She calls her name as she leaves the stage, as if inviting her fellow performer to follow her to some extra-fictional heaven, disconcertingly suggesting she can only become 'herself' in death:

> Federica, Federica!
> Come here!
> It's beautiful! It's beautiful here!
> Come, come you too. It's beautiful!

Perhaps this staging of a tension in the constitution of female subjectivity through the dysfunctional self-constitution of anorexia is the imposition of a late twentieth century interest in the performance of gender that the original text does not reveal. However, these anorexic women do not only recall the ambivalent agency of Portia's inscription of her own identity/subjectivity into her body, but can be seen as embodying a broader preoccupation with what it is to be human that I am suggesting here is embedded in *Julius Caesar*. The fact that the visibility of these women's illness is uncomfortable to look at sensitises the spectator to the constitution of subjectivity that occurs in both the words of the play and the actor choosing to speak them.

Calling this chapter 'Performing Human' is partly an acknowledgment of the discomfort that this sensitisation produces, a discomfort that reveals itself in a liberal sense of shock that such bodies should be on display. Mark Antony and his laryngectomy in this performance, a woman who has had a mastectomy in the piece *Genesi: From the Museum of Sleep*, the anorexic women and the animals and children that feature in Societas Raffaello Sanzio performances, all give rise to questions of exploitation, and a nervousness hovers around reviewers' accounts of the work. Peter Conrad, whose broadly enthusiastic *Guardian* feature on the company in anticipation of their visit to the London International Festival of Theatre in 1999, finds 'the director's innovations far from gratuitous' but nevertheless refers to the *Giulio Cesare* performers as 'scavenged exhibits', the women in particular as 'specimens of privation'.[14] The word 'exhibit' recalls the exploitative objectification of the

Victorian freak show; a 'specimen' is a thing whose component parts can be analysed or put on display in a science museum without regard to agency or consciousness. Are these people 'used', like the animals full only of stuffing, rather than given free expression as humans full of 'that within which passeth show'?

Linking the work of Romeo Castellucci with Artaud's Theatre of Cruelty, and mistaking the nature of the cruelty Artaud sought to stage,[15] Conrad suggests that the director of the Socìetas Raffaello Sanzio 'sets out to stretch and torment the bodies of his actors, pushing them to the limits of endurance'. According to Conrad, 'the Italian actor [playing Mark Antony] pitifully wheezes and burps his way through 'Friends, Romans, countrymen'. Writing of the anorexic performers, he argues that 'there are risks to this self-consuming strategy: an anorexic member of the original cast died on the job'. Conrad does not deliberately suggest that it was anything but her condition that killed the performer, but the contexualisation of this anecdote implies that her death might have been the result of her work with Castellucci. The calm, measured deliberation with which the Socìetas Raffaello Sanzio performs *Giulio Cesare* is not suggested in Conrad's account. The foregrounded bodies of the company's performers simply and unsensationally foreground the work they must put in to accomplish a performance. What Conrad may find disturbing is that the work of these performers involves their bodies being on show. Bodies that a liberal sensibility would warn us not to stare at, demand that we watch them – watch them in place of the actor, whose standardised physique would normally permit us to imagine that we see only Shakespeare. Where actors erase the labour of constituting the coherent psychological subject, making everything 'look natural', the Socìetas Raffaello Sanzio actors make performance look odd, so that the audience are always aware of the work they are doing – or being made to do. These odd bodies, with their technologically produced voices, their slow, deliberate speech and movement and their presence on stage alongside live and stuffed animals, are not actors so much as performing humans. But although this term cannot fail to connote Conrad's discomfort with the possibility that performers are being treated as 'specimens' or 'exhibits' in a freak show, I am suggesting that they replace naturalistic acting with a performance that liberates the early modern dramatic text from the limitations of psychological coherence. SRS performs, rather than assumes, the human.

In *Giulio Cesare*, this group of odd bodies offers a yet more radical theatrical means of 'get[ing] your cake and eating it' to the Wooster Group's 'simultaneous creation and demystification of effects associated with conventional acting'.[16] The means of production of the humanist conception of 'man' with which *Julius Caesar* is so centrally concerned – rhetoric, the 'whole' male body, a god-like reason that places it above the animals, the ability to respond with empathy to tragedy – are lain bare or pointed to by their replacement with unexpected vehicles of representation – anorexic women, stuffed cats. However, the 'whole picture ... of the crying man' that Dafoe offers his audiences along with its component elements is also maintained in the Socìetas Raffaello Sanzio's work on Shakespeare. The audience laughs at the head of the horse skeleton as it is raised and lowered to coincide with the neighing sound effect at Cassius' death, but *Julius Caesar*'s anthropomorphised cosmos, its neo-classical, man-centred world in which heaven and earth reflect human power struggles, is not merely dismembered as a post-modern joke. We watch the production of the voice that pauses while Mark Antony is overcome with emotion and are shown that it comes not from 'the heart ... in the coffin there with Caesar' but from a combination of an actor's vocal apparatus and a man-made voice box. An effect of direct human encounter is nevertheless produced which takes emotional effect, rather than inviting distanced analysis alone. Along with the Socìetas Raffaello Sanzio's foregrounding of anthropo-morphism and its laying bare of the construction of the human subject comes recognition. To read another as 'human' means taking an ethical relationship to her that would not permit, say, torturing her with the bits of wire that hang in the Socìetas Raffaello Sanzio's setting for the first half of *Julius Caesar*. In laying bare constructions of the human, the Socìetas Raffaello Sanzio asks the spectator to consider whom she regards as 'human'.

The foregrounded physical presence of the working body is not an ideological alternative to rhetoric and constitution in discourse in this company's work. It is rather clear that the body is what human society makes it. The rhetorical act of making one body human and another not, is ever present in this performance, as it is in the text of *Julius Caesar*, where a body can be a sacrifice or a piece of meat, where wounds can be wounds or innocent mouths, according to what we call them. Yet more intensely than in any of the performances examined thus far in this study, an encounter between spectator and performer that can be called 'human' occurs in the Socìetas Raffaello Sanzio's work: an encounter that in laying bare the mechanics of representation insists upon an ethical relation to the four-hundred-year-old text spoken that 'acting' cannot.

Throughout the first half of *Giulio Cesare*, the enormous figure of a man sits with his back to the audience, like a fat male parody of Man

Ray's image of female as cello.[17] He speaks words from Cicero's discourses on oratory.

> It is really a heavy task and difficult duty to assume the responsibility for being the only one to speak – while all the others remain silent – about the most important topics in the midst of a crowded meeting: this is the power of the orator which is mainly the capability of stirring up anger, hate and indignation into human nature and then leading the same nature from those emotions to a state of calm. The same words can be weapons; we might use them to threaten and to hit, or we can handle them only with the aim of producing artistic effects into human nature.[18]

This textual intervention, not by Shakespeare, takes 'blatant tampering' a stage further than Steven Pimlott's transpositions analysed in Chapter Four. It is the production's acknowledgment that its reading of *Julius Caesar* is inevitably a production rather than a reproduction. It is a 'blatant' foregrounding of the performance's concerns with language as a site of power and with its capacity to 'produce effects'. Though I am suggesting here that this is also a primary concern of the text itself, in *Giulio Cesare* there are no pretensions to revealing such a text. The performance is presented as a reading, into which other texts may be inserted for further reading. The enormous male figure's other task is to rock back and forth repeating the word *umano* (human). It is as though if he calls out the word often enough, we will believe him, call him, render him human. *Giulio Cesare* foregrounds not only the variety of constructions of subjectivity present in the play *Julius Caesar* but recalls the audience's powers of interpellation, the process of encounter and recognition on which subjectivity centres.

Amleto. La Veemente Esteriorità della Morte di un Mollusco[19]

As I have suggested in this chapter's opening description of Paolo Tonti as *Amleto*, the encounter and recognition staged by the Soc̀ietas Raffaello Sanzio's treatment of *Hamlet* is rather different. This is because the single performer does not appear to encounter and recognise others in ways that suggest it is entirely possible to encounter or recognise him as a subject. *Amleto* could be described as an evocation rather than a production of *Hamlet*. Indeed, Tonti is listed in the programme as playing Orazio (Horatio), as though the version of *Hamlet* we are seeing is mediated by the friend left to tell Hamlet's story, an 'orator' of Hamlet, rather than Hamlet 'himself'. Although the text of *Giulio Cesare* is drastically pared down, has a passage from Cicero added to it and a performer who calls another performer off stage by her own name, it is recognisably *Julius Caesar*, with performers speaking the lines of the tribunes, the cobbler, Brutus, Cassius and Antony, in the order in which they appear in the text. *Amleto* has only one performer who performs fragments of text, only one of which is recognisably from *Hamlet*.[20] It is divided into five sections, the first four of which correspond to a dramatic figure from *Hamlet* and to a different stuffed animal toy:

i)   Amleto e il padre con l'orso di pezza (Hamlet and the father with the stuffed bear)

ii) Amleto e Orazio con il pappagallo di pezza (Hamlet and Horatio with the stuffed parrot)

iii) Amleto e Ofelia con la bambola parlante (Hamlet and Ophelia with the talking doll.)

iv) Amleto e la madre con il canguro di pezza (Hamlet and the mother with the stuffed kangaroo)

Part v) is 'Amleto e la sua morte' (Hamlet and his death).

Prompted by their juxtaposition in the programme, a spectator with a knowledge of *Hamlet* can make, if they wish, connections between the toys Paolo Tonti uses on stage and the relevant dramatic figures of *Hamlet*. The bear is shown to the audience in a broad gesture of revelation, as if it were an impressive figure of authority to be trusted and obeyed by a child like a father. The parrot has a device inside it that permits it to echo what is said to it, so that when Tonti repeats the hesitant words 'my name is …', the parrot's beak moves and 'repeats' them back to him, and Horatio's task of repeating Hamlet's story after his death is recalled. The doll is fed by Tonti with saliva from a spoon, and speaks, as Ridout puts it, the 'apparently satisfied vocalisations'[21] of the talking doll; she is, perhaps, an infantilised Ophelia, the projected fantasy of a father and brother keen to keep her entirely within their control. Tonti's kangaroo-mother, complete with baby in its pouch which Tonti pulls from its thread and throws away, undergoes a violent torchlight interrogation with 'her' head stuck through the springs of a bare bed frame, a bed frame which Tonti later connects to an electrical circuit, causing it to glow red-hot. *Amleto* makes its strongest commentary on *Hamlet*, however, not so much by virtue of these links so much as by Tonti's performance of autism.

Amleto's stage is divided into sections by wires and car batteries – the inner workings of technology usually concealed in everyday life; even in a rough, Brechtian theatre of exposed theatrical technology, the spectator usually remains safely unreminded of positive and negative leads, earthing wires, the whole lethal business of electrical infrastructure. Once again, the veneer with which actor and naturalistic *mise en scène* cover work and workings is stripped back. In *Amleto* the encounter with the performer in this *mise en scène* is more disturbing still than in *Giulio Cesare*. This is partly because it is not an overtly physical difference or a technological intervention that draws attention to the presence of the performer, but the physical signs of autism displayed by the figure on stage. The repeated gestures that make up the performance – the shooting of blanks from the gun he carries with him, an open gesture of display to the audience from behind a roughly hung polythene screen stage right and his continual stumbling about the performance space, suggest compulsion rather than intention, repetitions that are part of a 'condition' rather than controlled, actorly repetitions made to seem spontaneous. Even the fact that he is able to repeat his actions with meticulous precision – watching more than one performance confirms this – does not entirely dispel the doubts about exploitation that recur more strongly in this performance than while watching *Giulio Cesare*. If part of the autistic condition is a compulsion to sameness,[22] then Tonti's ability to do so does not necessarily suggest intentionality, that he 'knows what he's doing' and is not being treated as a mere 'performing human'.

In fact, Tonti is not autistic. The performance is a virtuoso piece of naturalistic acting, in that it is perfectly possible to believe that he is what he is pretending to be. However, this Hamlet, who stumbles about a playing space in a disused gymnasium that is covered in the Socìetas Raffaello Sanzio's dangerous-looking electrics, speaking only tiny fragments of Shakespeare text, shooting blanks and speaking to a series of filthy children's toys offers us *Hamlet* in ways that naturalistic stage convention does not.

First, the company re-sensitise the spectator to this over-produced text, by reminding her of her own physical being and of the vulnerability of that being, the possibility of its not being. This is not a modern habit of spectatorship. The Hamlet figure totters back and forth amongst the wires and batteries, connecting and disconnecting electrical circuits to light and darken the stage with the bulbs that hang above it. Two lit household bulbs lie on the stage, which he steps upon and breaks. Stage right, a circuit of machinery activates the sound of a siren and a series of loud explosions inside a metal cabinet. The audience are lit: some can be seen sitting with their fingers in their ears throughout the performance. All this noise and raw power puts the body in a horrible state of receptiveness to whatever emotional state the spectator imagines the figure on stage to be in. When Tonti, sitting on the bed frame in which he has previously inserted his toy kangaroo mother-figure, rocks back and forth and mutters, then screams, 'Love me, love me, love me', it is uncertain who or what is demanding an emotional response: Hamlet, a fictional child, a performer, an autistic human. As in the most theatrically conscious moments of *Hamlet* discussed in Chapter Two, the dilemmas of the performer in the theatre and the hero in Denmark are simultaneously presented so as to inflect and infect one another. Here, the spectator's emotional response to each is magnified by the physical assault of the noise that fills the room.

Second, Tonti makes both his performance and the cycle of birth into socially conferred identity, relationships and death, look like hard work. The toys which he shows the audience as if presenting important figures in a play, to which he speaks, shouts, offers food and whom, in the case of a stuffed parrot, he causes to repeat the sentence that is never completed – 'My name is … my name is …' – are filthy with use, from being hurled about the performance space as Hamlet has hurled his lover and his mother in so many other performances. Tonti never ceases to stumble, speak, excrete, attempt to communicate with those that cannot reach him – the toys, the audience. He will not even offer the spectator the relief of taking a bow. At the end of the performance he appears to be hiding behind the cupboard which has emitted the explosions. He will not come out to let the audience know that his performance was not a torture to him, to admit that it was all acting, that he is not condemned to repeat *Amleto* but will now go home and do something quite different.

This is the 'Theatre of Cruelty' with which Castellucci's name has been associated. Life is weary, stale, flat, unprofitable and very painful; it is engendered not in the actor's imagination, nurtured through rehearsal then offered fully formed, coherent and self-contained to the audience, but in the moment of the audience witnessing performance. Artaud, in describing the Balinese theatre he witnessed at the Colonial Exhibition of 1931 remarks:

> [w]e might say the subjects presented begin on stage. They have reached such a point of objective materialisation we could not imagine them, however one might try, outside this compact panorama, the enclosed, confined world of the stage.[23]

Here lies the Societas Raffaello Sanzio's link with the early modern drama the company evokes in *Amleto*. It is the theatrically situated nature of the dramatic figure that permits a level of engagement that goes beyond the empathy demanded by naturalistic stage convention. This Hamlet can only exist in this space, where he is condemned to repeat the story in which the audience is trapped with him.

In other performances analysed in this study, the performer is most clearly foregrounded in the moment of direct address to the audience. To offer the Societas Raffaello Sanzio's *Amleto* as a last analysis of performance in a study that privileges this mode of performance may seem perverse, given the nature of Tonti's acted condition. One of the most troubling manifestations of autism, particularly for the carers of the autistic child, is his or her – more often his[24] – perceived inability to achieve 'direct address', to look into the face of another long enough to signal mutual recognition and the desire to communicate. Tonti appears self-absorbed amidst the wires and batteries of *Amleto*. He does address the audience, in the longest section of text from the play that he uses, Gertrude's description of Ophelia's death. This is spoken centre stage and provides a rare moment of stillness in this perpetually stumbling performance. During the speech, he holds a thick brown lock of hair to his head, as if to represent a woman. At this moment, Tonti does appear to be approaching something like acting. He is doing what actors do – speaking extant speeches and at least gesturing towards the pretence of being somebody else. There is no sense in which Tonti attempts to convince us that this 'is' Gertrude, or Ophelia: the spectator watches him in the most overt possible act of pretence. However, where performers such as Mark Rylance or Samuel West appear to be closest to offering 'themselves' to the audience in the foregrounded moment of performance that is direct address, Tonti defies this delineation of self and not-self as he fails to accomplish what passes as correct human behaviour on stage during the performance, making the other performances examined here appear highly wrought theatrical personae by comparison. At this, his most actorly moment, though it is as far from illusionistic acting as anything hitherto described, he is at his most 'accomplished' in the conventional sense of what passes as accomplishment in performance.

Is it the stumbling, shooting, scrawling Tonti that is Tonti 'himself,' or the Tonti who goes through some pared down motions of acting, in his recital of Gertrude's speech? It is certainly this second Tonti that appears to be 'in control of himself'. Then, at the end of the speech, he begins to urinate, or at least, urine appears to start running down his trouser leg.[25] Tonti drops the lock of hair he has been holding and it becomes wet with the liquid. He has either wet himself – the ultimate lack of self-control – or he has a device in his trousers that permits this illusion and drowns the hair that represents Ophelia, or he is able to exert the self-control needed to urinate at will. The audience are in a perpetual state of not knowing who they are looking at. Tonti's acted condition seems to condemn him to 'be himself' on stage; but the performance repeatedly asks questions about what constitutes a coherent human subject: the ability to exert self-control? The ability to obey rules laid down by others as to how to pass as a fully integrated subject? Or the ability to recognise others as like oneself?

When Mark Rylance asks of the 'groundlings' at the Globe, 'Who calls me coward?' and gets no answer, or Samuel West shares a joke about kingship with a woman in the third row at the Other Place, they appear to be allowing an element of risk into the theatre, the risk of the 'real', face to face encounter which may not go according to plan or provoke the desired response. *Amleto* takes that risk a stage further; Rylance's and West's performances appear supremely safe and under control in comparison. Paolo Tonti's performance risks undoing not only the performance conventions of acting, but the performance conventions of everyday life. In appearing not to be acting, Tonti offers a self that we cannot necessarily recognise as a human subject. In moments of direct contact with the audience, whence comes the theatrical illusion of a dramatic figure standing outside his or her socially constituted identity, Tonti presents an order of being radically different from the other described here. Whether in his reckless stumbling about the set, his disturbingly real excreting to order, his conversations with other figures – the toys – or his direct presentation of some kind of performed 'self' to the audience, Tonti's *Amleto* figure gives rise to questions as to how and with what degree of agency we accept a socially constituted persona.

These questions of subjectivity are peculiarly Hamlet-like. The condition of autism can be mapped onto Hamlet's quite simply. The death of his father precipitates Hamlet into a mourning from which his mother and stepfather exhort him, unsuccessfully, to emerge. Parents have described the most distressing part of the experience of bringing up an autistic child as his appearance of refusing their communicative offerings and his seeming lack of interest or ability to copy their version of what it is to be human. Charlotte Moore, a mother of two autistic sons, writes that her children's condition 'forces you to rethink everything you thought you knew about being human', particularly in terms of how the young human being takes on social identity.

> Normal children are wired to understand social rules. They observe human behaviour intently, and they copy. They are tameable; they carry inside them a voice that tells them how to act. They may ignore or disobey that voice, but that's a choice. Autistic children have no such instinct, no such voice. They cannot be tamed. Through a system of positive and negative reinforcement, desirable behaviours can be boosted and undesirable ones reduced, but this is training, not taming.[26]

The 'voice that tells us how to act' might be described as the superego in psychoanalysis, the internalised interpellations of ideology by Althusser: both are internalised, so that the subject does not appear simply to be repeating what is required of him or her, but to be acting upon authentic choices, with intention. The autistic child does not appear to his mother to have such an internalised voice. Compare Hamlet, refusing Claudius' exhortation to 'be as ourselves in Denmark', constantly repeating his father's funeral in his persistent wearing of mourning. His subjectivity is always in question: is he condemned to repeat the murder of his father in the act of revenge by the supernatural appearance of his father, or does he choose this action? Is he mad or is he 'only acting' his 'antic disposition'? The despair he shares with the audience appears to stem from a concern that all he is being asked to do is repeat, as in the echolalia of the autistic child.[27] In Paolo Tonti's case, the audience not in the know is unsure as to how much of his condition is voluntarily performed, how much an inescapable part of his condition, just as the on- and off-stage audiences for Hamlet's 'antic' role are unsure as to how much method there is in this madness. However, it is not merely that the Societas Raffaello Sanzio has found an apt metaphor for the fictional Hamlet in the condition of autism. Tonti, of all the performers I have described here, comes closest to States' impossible theatrical moment, the moment I have argued in Chapter Two is central to *Hamlet*. He is left on stage by himself.

Whether he is standing behind his polythene curtain, arms opened in gesture of display and saying the words 'For you,' standing centre stage and speaking Gertrude's description of Ophelia's death and urinating or stumbling about in that autistic 'world of his own', it will be clear to the reader that the spectator's experience is not one of watching a 'character' called Hamlet, in the sense of psychological consistency, self-contained acting style or absence from the room in which the audience is seated. Nor is it one of watching the subject that is the performer, standing outside a fiction and commenting upon it. We do not know who Tonti is, and how much of the figure we see is consciously offered. We are rather in the room with a figure who has been named Paolo Tonti and who is also called *Amleto*, a fictional figure whose very way of looking at us interrogates the subjectivity assumed by others.

Although the Socìetas Raffaello Sanzio uses the mode of direct address in their work on Shakespeare, then, there is a sense in which the subjectivity effect produced by the foregrounded performer is yet more elusive than in the highly theatrically conscious Globe *Hamlet* or RSC *Richard II*. Not only is the spectator presented with the raw material that goes to make up the dramatic figure – text, body, *mise en scène*, the work of performance – but the raw material that goes to make up the human self – body, technological equipment needed to render that body an acceptably competent human, a range of relations with other humans, a tone of voice, a range of movements. These elements do not come ready assembled; the performing human is offered to us in pieces. Tonti's gesture of performance behind his polythene screen – he opens his arms, lifts one leg to kick at the polythene and says the words 'For you' – reads as a joke on the competence and communicativeness of performance, and on the competence and communicativeness of 'performing human'. We are offered the possibility that there really might not be a subject to stand outside identity, to refuse to answer the call – only this unknowable collection of performed efforts. The work that must be done to make Tonti's Hamlet a dramatic subject, rather than a mere range of exhausting and repetitious gestures, is virtually all our own. However, in doing that work, the spectator is confronted with the workings of his or her own subjectivity: the work she undertakes to recognise as 'human' another set of names, limbs, signs of racial or class identity and the work of self-constitution that has occurred in order that she might similarly recognise herself.

Conclusion

In this study I have concentrated almost entirely on productions of Shakespeare I have seen live. This is a highly assailable position from which to write about theatre. To acknowledge it is to confess that one's choices have been contingent upon the limitations of time, place and economics. 'And so I begin by being unforgivably arbitrary',[1] says Gary Taylor of his choice to begin a chapter on recent Shakespeare production, in his 'cultural history from the Restoration to the present', with the Berliner Ensemble's *Troilus und Cressida*. 'The chapter might just as easily have begun with the Beijing-Shanghai Shakespeare festival of April 1986 ... but in April 1986 I was in Germany, not China.'[2] What Taylor's whole project, *Reinventing Shakespeare*, suggests, however, is that many of the choices that have led to Shakespeare's dramatic canonisation have been arbitrary, or at least culturally contingent as opposed to entirely predicated upon the genius of one man. If, as performance critics, we acknowledge contingency in this way, then, is it appropriate to privilege the live theatre performance over its more permanent, and thus more permanently readable, traces? By writing on performances at which I was present, do I fail to acknowledge the contingency and constructed nature of presence itself, sentimentally suggesting that 'you had to be there', in the live presence of the actor, soaking up the Magic of Theatre, experiencing a sacred encounter between performer and audience? To the extent that I am examining moments where theatrical illusion, the illusion of presence, appears to be at its strongest then yes, I am privileging the live moment. Central to these case studies and these live illusions are a series of moments where the theatre succeeds by failing, even in productions well received by traditional arbiters of theatrical taste: moments where it fails to transform the actor/Hamlet into the perfect revenge hero, where Sue Wilmington's white box set fails to make the space outside the Other Place anything but a car park or where an audience member refuses

Bolingbroke's signal to stand, where voice, plus voice box, plus body don't quite add up to what we recognise as human. Moments of live performance are what have enabled these speculations as to how far the foregrounding of actorly effort, the performance objective and the failed results of that effort might be integral to the meanings produced by the plays examined here. Moments of live performance are what have provoked me to think about how far the actor and his work are encoded in the literary results of early performance, and so moments of live performance are what I have offered the reader.

It must be acknowledged that my focus on productions at which I have been able to be present places limitations upon this study, however, and only partly because, like Gary Taylor, I am not able to be in China and Berlin at the same time. I am currently, for example, in the frustrating position of not having seen Richard Maxwell's *Henry IV* because, after damning reviews and mass walkouts by its New York audiences, the Barbican's BITE festival saw it and cancelled its run. The production's deadpan delivery, typical of Maxwell's work, and *mise en scène* reminiscent of competent amateur pageantry strike me as interesting interventions in a play in which future kings pretend to be commoners and commoners pageant royalty in the pub. Not all the moments of performance that this project might read as productive failure will be accepted as such by the mainstream theatre and I will have to leave an analysis of Maxwell's (deliberate-sounding) failures to those who have experienced it in its awkward liveness. What I would like this study to enable is a reading of Shakespeare both on stage and from the page that does not attempt to erase the awkwardness and difficulties of the live encounter between performer and audience. I am suggesting here that the awkwardness and difficulties are not only central to the honouring of difference between the present and the four-hundred-year-old play – what is awkward and difficult to us may not have been so to early audiences and I think production can productively acknowledge that – but that they are also central to the plays in their historical moment. 'This is and is not Cressid'; 'This is I, Hamlet the Dane'; 'Then am I kinged again, and by and by/Think that I am unking'd by Bolingbroke/And straight am nothing'. These moments of crisis in subjectivity are most productively felt by the spectator not via the identificatory projections of naturalism but in recalcitrantly theatrical moments of discomfort and disorientation, moments that cannot quite be called 'alienation effects' because of the illusion of real and mutual struggle that they conjure: the struggle to perform socially allotted roles; the simultaneous struggle to perform outside them.

In *Amleto*, Paolo Tonti appears to be doing his best to 'perform human' as he carries out a range of tasks that should mark him as being alive and human: moving, excreting, speaking, writing, having complicated or dysfunctional relationships with family members, contemplating suicide. We are not sure in the moment of performance whether he really urinates or not, whether he really feels too distressed to take a bow and has asked the director to let him off this final moment of exposure, whether he has been told not to. Fundamental questions about agency and subjectivity arise from this performer's work, questions that are fundamental, I have suggested here, to the play *Hamlet* and to the other plays examined here: how far are these figures just 'performing humans'? How far can the human choose the ways in which his humanity is performed, how far is he just a collection of externally conferred repetitions? The first question is asked quite openly in the early modern drama. Jacques and Macbeth famously conclude that, in answer to the first question, we are mere players, poor players, our seven ages allotted to us like seven acts of a play which we had no hand in writing, and in which we strut and fret for an illusory significance.[3] In the plays examined here, the second question of choice and agency is brought into play where the performer/figure, struggling to perform in both the theatre and the fiction, comes into direct contact with an audience, a group of people whose concerns are not immediately those of the dramatic fiction before them and who may refuse either to be trained or tamed.

What do the Societas Raffaello Sanzio's evocations of early modern texts have in common with the theatrically conscious moments I have pointed to in other productions and with the conscious performances embedded in the texts examined here? All produce meaning around a struggle between socially conferred identity and the effect of subjectivity. All depend for their impact upon figures who appear to exist both in the theatre and in the dramatic fiction. They 'talk to the audience' in the theatre from the perspective of a fiction in which their human subjectivities are unstable and worked for, just as their relationships with the audience are. The term 'performing human', a term I use to describe both a figure on stage and an action, has a double resonance for the theatrically conscious performances examined here. It recalls the 'jugglers, dancers, singers, tumblers and related showmen … relatively unconcerned with the symbolic, let alone iconographic, dimensions of their actions' whose mode of performance Robert Weimann regards as in competition with the mode of the actor.[4] These performing humans are performers whose work is always overtly situated in a *platea* performance space shared by the audience; their performances are always

vulnerable to the audience who might lose interest and walk away; their skills may fail them and spoil the show. These are performers whose audiences are also, to an extent, rendered vulnerable in return to this potential for failure. The gasps at the feats of the circus performer or sword-swallower must surely contain some self-interest as well as concern for the performer's safety: will he fall on me, let that bear escape, expect me to help if he injures himself? 'Performing human' also suggests an action, one that takes place in the simultaneously theatrical and fictional world of the early modern theatre: the action of performing the human, performing as if human.

The act of performing human in the plays examined here is an exposing business which in turn exposes the audience. The performer whose job it is to entertain a lit audience with plays about how the human is performed can be laughed with or at, listened to or not, elicit a desired response or fail to do so. This potential for failure is embedded in the fiction that his or her performance unfolds. The early modern spectator can lift her face to eagerly accept the performer's address or turn away in embarrassment, to the glee of the rest of the crowd. A sense of mutual vulnerability is evoked by the texts of the plays examined here, performed and inflected by these vulnerable conditions. What are we when stripped of our conferred identities of gender, family member, social position – whore, son, monarch? What is there to perform other than the parts society, or God, or family allot us? These are disturbing questions for beings interpellated into social being through a process of labelling, of naming. As Terence Hawkes puts it:

> ... if names are tiny 'texts' with which we seek to pin down and permanently fix human beings, they are also words, and thus part of language, and they partake inevitably of language's 'playing' dimension, its ultimate, and untameable, indeterminacy. What threatens to erupt in them is something which fundamentally challenges the notion of the human they, and the economic and social system which gives them currency, seek to enclose.[5]

The untameable and indeterminate is disturbing, as Paolo Tonti is when he refuses to come out and bow. My concluding question concerns how this vulnerability to the fears and tensions regarding the nature of human subjectivity might be restored to the audience watching Shakespeare now.

As I have emphasised previously, it is not the purpose of this study to suggest that a historically authentic reconstruction of earlier performance conditions should be the aim of practitioners involved in Shakespeare production, or indeed the production of any historical text. My choice of the work of the Socìetas Raffaello Sanzio as a paradigm for the previous chapter makes this clear. I have begun with the assertion that the Elizabethan playhouse encourages the mode of direct address and conclude that the plays are written accordingly and achieve their effect of subjectivity in moments of encounter between performer and audience. It is not possible to determine how far today's spectator would recognise in early performances of Shakespeare what Andrew Gurr has called the King's Men's 'naturalism'. This study has suggested that the mode of direct address is central to both the dramatic structure and meaning of the plays examined here, to such an extent that the play cannot be said to demand either the performance conventions or the rehearsal processes that have been associated with this term since the late nineteenth century. In the name of making the plays accessible to modern audiences, the conventions of stage naturalism can close down possible meanings for these audiences, while implying that a particular version of what it is to be human – the consistent, self-contained character – should be recognised as universal, through the work of Shakespeare, most 'universal' of playwrights.

Theatre practices that are not primarily concerned with naturalistic character study not only produce different kinds of dramatic subjects; they produce different kinds of audiences, framing the subjectivity of the spectator differently. The performing humans that I suggest are capable of rendering the post-modern spectator vulnerable to the questions of subjectivity and agency embedded in these plays, behave in ways that will not necessarily earn them plaudits as a good actor in today's theatre. On the other hand there will be moments when they display their virtuosity, triumphing in their abilities to provoke laughter or turn on the tears. A good actor stays in character. His circle of attention will prevent distraction by extra-fictional occurrences in the theatre. He will be able to make mistakes look as though they are part of the play. He certainly never shows off. The performing human may not be a 'good actor' in any of these respects. He or she may appear vulnerable to the material presence of stage and the accidents that might occur there. He or she may have physical or mental qualities that draw attention to themselves: that make meaning when juxtaposed with text and theatre building, rather than being erased in the portrayal of character. In the case of the performances described above, the spectator's work of 'making sense' of the elements presented to her is thus foregrounded, as she consciously constructs meaning rather than having meaning offered to her ready constructed. In the Socìetas Raffaello

Sanzio's work, previously constructed meanings – Marlon Brando's version of Mark Antony, for example, or an imagined performance in which the master's horse mourns his death and women weep uncontrollably over their loved ones' dead bodies – are also acknowledged. These are not parodied, but consciously quoted, recalling past engagements with and reactions to performance, so that the spectator watches herself engaging, reacting, producing effects of subjectivity, behaving like a subject.

The performing human can give a virtuoso performance, like Hamlet with his antic disposition, or the ominous cat with its spinning head in *Giulio Cesare*, playing his or her conferred social and theatrical identities with the confidence that the juggler throws his balls. Closely linked to conscious virtuosity, however, is the possibility of failure, so that the performing human may appear at times awkward in his or her vulnerability to the gaze of the audience. Conferred identity slips away, the king lets slip his crown or Hamlet casts doubts upon the performance tradition that has spawned him. The performing human then stands on stage awkward and vulnerable, like modern clowns or the figures who look shiftily out into the audience as Forced Entertainment's *Emanuelle Enchanted* begins.[6]

A theatrical paradigm shift from 'playing' to 'acting' in the early modern period is taking its academic place alongside the shift from social being to psychological subject that appears in a range of seemingly opposing accounts of the period. If we regard Shakespeare's drama as the first steps along the theatre history trajectory towards naturalistic acting, then of course it is only logical that psychological approaches to character study will be the most suitable for production of the early modern drama and that the technologies of stage naturalism will enhance the audience's focus and attention, essential to appreciate these subtle, sophisticated but ultimately recognisable revelations of inner motivation and character objective. I am suggesting that the dramatic figures in the texts examined here find themselves stranger than that and should be permitted to appear stranger, therefore, to their audiences. We look at Paolo Tonti and cannot find him 'utterly realistic' as Sher does Leontes, a recognisable coherent, self-contained character. As we watch him work, we catch fleeting moments of intention and agency, but we have to work too, to make them 'signify … [some]thing'. It is this work that produces a subject that might stand, teetering awkwardly, just outside ideological transmission.

Notes

1 Actors, academics, selves

1 Anthony Sher, 'How I got into the Mad Bard's Head', *Guardian*, 2 January 1999.
2 Sher, *Guardian*, 2 January 1999.
3 Sher, *Guardian*, 2 January 1999.
4 John Peter, *Sunday Times*, 10 January 1999.
5 Susannah Clapp, *Observer*, 10 January 1999.
6 Adrian Noble, quoted in 'RSC reveals plans for 100m theatre development', *Guardian*, 18 October 2001.
7 Michael Taylor, *Shakespeare Criticism in the Twentieth Century*, Oxford: OUP, 2001, p. 39.
8 For Barker, Pepys' diary exemplifies a social shift towards the 'depoliticised privacy' of bourgeois subjectivity which takes place after the upheaval of the English Revolution. He acknowledges his debt to Foucault in this respect, 'who traces the lineaments of the bourgeois order in studies of two of its essential components – the history of its madness and of its penality', Francis Barker, *The Tremulous Private Body: Essays in Subjection*, London: Methuen, 1984, pp. 11, 13.
9 Stephen Greenblatt, *Renaissance Self-Fashioning*, Chicago: University of Chicago Press, 1980, p. 256.
10 Katharine Eisaman Maus, *Inwardness and Theater in the English Renaissance*, Chicago: University of Chicago Press, 1995, p. 28.
11 Lee dedicates the first third of his *Shakespeare's Hamlet and the Controversies of Self* to a critique of new historicist and cultural materialist work on the early modern period and the 'bleak picture of subjectivity' (p. 84) that he regards it as offering. Lee's particular concern with reclaiming the concept of character relates to the perceived lack of agency afforded to dramatic figures described as 'subjects', John Lee, *Shakespeare's Hamlet and the Controversies of Self*, Oxford: Clarendon Press, 2000, pp. 5–91 and 149.
12 Bert O. States, *Hamlet and the Concept of Character*, Baltimore: Johns Hopkins University Press, 1992, p. xviii.
13 Andrew Gurr, *The Shakespearean Stage 1574–1642*, Cambridge: CUP, 1992, p. 103.
14 See also Gurr, *The Shakespearean Stage*, p. 114, where he asserts:

In playing as in so many other ways, Shakespeare's company, more restrained than their fellows on the public stages, and more life-size, as well as more life-like, than the boy companies, appear to have been the outstanding company of the age in their naturalism.

15 See Robert Weimann, *Author's Pen and Actor's Voice*, Cambridge: CUP, 2000, pp. 31–6.

16 Terence Hawkes, *Shakespeare in the Present*, London: Routledge, 2002, p. 110.

17 John Stephens, *Satyrical Essayes Characters and Others*, London: Printed by E. Alde for Philip Knight, 1615, cit. Hawkes, *Shakespeare in the Present*, and Weimann, *Author's Pen*, p. 135.

18 In his chapter 'Hank Cinq', Hawkes develops the political implications of Weimann's proposed move from playing to acting at the turn of the sixteenth/seventeenth century, suggesting that developing literary modes obscure a populist performance practice from current readings of Shakespeare; see *Shakespeare in the Present*, 2002, pp. 105–26.

19 Hawkes, *Shakespeare in the Present*, p. 110.

20 Robert Weimann, *Shakespeare and the Popular Tradition in the Theatre*, Baltimore: Johns Hopkins University Press, 1978, pp. 73–85 (p. 79).

21 Weimann, *Author's Pen*, p. 180.

22 Weimann, *Author's Pen*, p. 184.

23 See also my discussion of Leah Marcus' work on this issue, Chapter Three, p. 55.

24 I refer here to Raymond Williams' much cited account of society and culture in terms of 'dominant', 'residual' and 'emergent' forms of consciousness, Raymond Williams, *Marxism and Literature*, Oxford: OUP, 1977, p. 132.

25 Alan Sinfield, *Faultlines: Cultural Materialism and the Politics of Dissident Reading*, Oxford: Clarendon Press, 1992.

26 Alan Dessen, *Elizabethan Drama and the Viewer's Eye*, Chapel Hill: University of North Carolina Press, 1977, p. 109, cited in Cary M. Mazer, 'Historicizing Alan Dessen: Scholarship, Stagecraft and the "Shakespeare Revolution", in James C. Bulman (ed.), *Shakespeare, Theory and Performance*, London: Routledge, 1996, p. 154.

27 Mazer, 'Historicizing Alan Dessen', p. 152.

28 Mazer, 'Historicizing Alan Dessen', p. 155.

29 Mazer, 'Historicizing Alan Dessen', p. 155.

30 Peter Holland, 'Brecht, Bond, Gaskill and the Practice of Political Theatre', *Theatre Quarterly*, vol. 30, Summer 1978, pp. 24–35.

31 Bertolt Brecht, 'From the Mother Courage Model', in John Willett (ed. and trans.), *Brecht on Theatre: The Development of an Aesthetic*, London: Eyre Methuen, 1974, p. 219.

32 Mazer, 'Historicizing Alan Dessen', p. 161.

33 Terry Hands, cited in Mazer, 'Historicizing Alan Dessen', p. 159.

34 Brecht, 'From the Mother Courage Model', p. 219.

35 See Margot Heinemann, 'How Brecht Read Shakespeare', in Jonathan Dollimore and Alan Sinfield (eds), *Political Shakespeare*, Manchester: MUP, 1994, pp. 226–54.

36 Graham Holderness, *Shakespeare's History*, Dublin: Gill and Macmillan, 1985, p. 212.

37 Barker, *The Tremulous Private Body*, p. 18.

38 Barker, *The Tremulous Private Body*, p. 20.
39 Catherine Belsey, *The Subject of Tragedy: Identity and Difference in Renaissance Drama*, London: Routledge, 1985, p. 26.
40 Belsey, *The Subject of Tragedy*, pp. 13–18.
41 Brecht 'From the Mother Courage Model', p. 219.
42 Sher, *Guardian*, 2 January 1999.
43 Emile Zola, 'Le Naturalisme au Théâtre' from *Le Roman Experimental*, Paris: E. Fasquelle, 1902, trans. Samuel Draper, in Toby Cole (ed.), *Playwrights on Playwriting: The Meaning and Making of Modern Drama from Ibsen to Ionesco*, New York: Hill and Wang, 1961, p. 6.
44 Strictly historical definitions are insisted upon, for example, in *The Oxford Companion to the Theatre*, Oxford: OUP, 1983, p. 584, *The Oxford Encyclopedia of Theatre and Performance*, Oxford: OUP, 2003, p. 925, *The Cambridge Guide to the Theatre*, Cambridge: CUP, 1988, p. 780. Patrice Pavis, *Dictionary of the Theatre: Terms, Concepts and Analysis*, Toronto: University of Toronto Press, 1998, on the other hand, is happy to admit that the term naturalism 'has developed into a style characteristic of contemporary *mise-en-scène*', p. 235 without dismissing this usage as loose or anachronistic.
45 See Raymond Williams, 'Social Environment and Theatrical Environment: The Case of English Naturalism', in *Problems in Materialism and Culture*, London: Verso, 1980, pp. 125–47 (pp. 125–6).
46 Zola, 'Le Naturalisme au Théâtre', p. 10.
47 Zola, 'Le Naturalisme au Théâtre', p. 6.
48 Patrice Pavis, *Dictionary of the Theatre*, p. 235.
49 Designed by Alison Chitty.
50 Designed by Michael Pavelka.
51 Designed by Rae Smith.
52 Michael Billington, review of *Cymberline* dir. Dominic Cooke, RSC 2003, *Guardian*, 8 August 2003.
53 W. B. Worthen, *Shakespeare and the Authority of Performance*, Cambridge: CUP, 1997, p. 212.
54 Zola, 'Le Naturalisme au Théâtre', p. 6.
55 See Constantin Stanislavski, *An Actor Prepares*, trans. Elizabeth Reynolds Hapgood, New York: Theatre Arts Books, 1970, Chapter 15, 'The Super-Objective', pp. 271–80. See also his *Building a Character*, trans. Hapgood, London: Eyre Methuen, 1979, pp. 276–9.
56 Stanislavski, *An Actor Prepares*, Chapter 13, 'The Unbroken Line', pp. 252–60. This unbroken line is achieved by a combination of close study of the text and a process of 'fill[ing] out' what '[the author] leaves unsaid' (p. 257).
57 Stanislavski, *An Actor Prepares*, Chapter 8, 'Faith and a Sense of Truth', pp. 127–62.
58 Stanislavski, *An Actor Prepares*, p. 312.
59 Stanislavski, *An Actor Prepares*, p. 272.
60 See for example Brecht, 'The Popular and the Realistic', where he questions whether a dramatic story 'is best developed by aiming at an eventual psychological stripping-down of the characters', a characteristic of 'the forms of Balzac and Tolstoy'. His alternative is a 'realist' theatre that 'lay[s] bare society's causal networks' (*Brecht on Theatre*, pp. 109–10).
61 Stanislavski, *An Actor Prepares*, p. 271, original emphasis.
62 Kathleen McLuskie, conference paper for 'Kissing Spiders: Representing

the Female Body On and Off the Early Modern Stage', Warwick University, 29–30 April 2000.

63 Worthen, *Shakespeare and the Authority of Performance*, p. 212

64 Worthen, *Shakespeare and the Authority of Performance*, p. 110.

65 Worthen, *Shakespeare and the Authority of Performance*, p. 212.

66 W. B. Worthen, *Shakespeare and the Force of Modern Performance*, Cambridge: CUP, 2003, p. 100.

67 Joseph Roach's chapter 'Changeling Proteus' in *The Player's Passion: Studies in the Science of Acting*, Newark: University of Delaware Press, 1985, (pp. 23–57) makes particularly suggestive links between early modern biological theory and what might have been considered life-like portrayal of theatrical figures in the period.

68 See Bruce Smith's study of *Shakespeare and Masculinity*, Oxford: OUP, 2000, pp. 7–37 for a useful account of the functions of the word 'person' in early modern English to refer to the physical body, a personage or embodiment of a hierarchical position, a legal agent and the actor of a role.

69 See Adler's interview with P. Gray, 'The Reality of Doing', in *Drama Review*, vol. 9 no. 1, Fall, pp. 137–55; cited in Alison Hodge, *Twentieth Century Actor Training*, London: Routledge, 2000, p. 139.

70 Greenblatt's 'desire to speak with the dead' has become a new historicist trope. See *Shakespearean Negotiations: The Circulation of Social Energy in Renaissance England*, Berkeley: University of California Press, 1988, p. 1.

71 During the research period, the RSC and the National have both produced *Hamlet*. Peter Brook and Peter Zadek have both toured the play internationally. Chapter Three gives accounts of two more London productions, at the Globe reconstruction by Red Shift theatre company and by the Theatre de Jeune Lune, Minneapolis.

72 David Scott Kastan, *Shakespeare after Theory*, London: Routledge, 1999, p. 16.

73 See Jonathan Bate, 'Shakespeare's Foolosophy', in Grace Ioppolo (ed.), *Shakespeare Performed: Essays in Honor of R. A. Foakes*, Newark: University of Delaware Press, 2000, p. 17.

74 The exception is the Societas Raffaello Sanzio's *Amleto. La veemente esteriorità della morte di un mollusco* which, though still in the company's repertory at the time of writing, was first performed in 1992.

2 'Bits and bitterness': politics, performance, *Troilus and Cressida*

1 Trevor Nunn, National Theatre website and publicity, 'Approaching the Millennium: NT Ensemble '99', http://website-archive.nt-online.org/information/ensemble.html

2 Presumably after the range of chicken sauces whose commercials featured a family singing 'I feel like chicken tonight'.

3 National Theatre Programme for 15 February to 10 April 1999, p. 3.

4 Carol Chillington Rutter, *Enter the Body: Women and Representation on Shakespeare's Stage*, London: Routledge, 2001, p. 114.

5 Rutter, *Enter the Body*, p. 115.

6 Rutter, *Enter the Body*, p. 115.

7 Programme notes to *Troilus and Cressida*, directed by John Barton, 1968.

8 *Daily Telegraph*, 22 August 1976, Review of *Troilus and Cresside*, directed by John Barton, 1976.

9 *Guardian*, 21 July 1991, Review of RSC production, directed by Sam Mendes, 1991.

10 *Independent*, 7 November 1998, Review of *Troilus and Cressida*, directed by Michael Boyd, 1998. The exception seems to be the 1980s, during which no such comments are made in reviews held by the RSC archive (Shakespeare's Birthplace Trust library, Stratford-upon-Avon). This is interesting if one considers the political climate of the decade. That the play does not excite commentary on its relevance during this period supports the notion of *Troilus and Cressida* as a play that reflects cultural and political disturbance. At a time of ideological optimism and stability – or complacency and political repression, depending on one's view of the Thatcher years – the press ceases to mark its resonance.

11 Jan Kott, *Shakespeare Our Contemporary*, London: Methuen, 1967, p. 65.

12 E. M. W. Tillyard, *Shakespeare's Problem Plays*, London: Chatto and Windus, 1950, pp. 85–6.

13 I borrow from Rutter again, see above n. 4.

14 Harold Brooks, '*Troilus and Cressida*: Its Dramatic Unity and Genre', in John W. Mahon and Thomas A. Pendleton (eds.), *Fanned and Winnowed Opinions: Shakespearean Essays Presented to Harold Jenkins*, London: Methuen, 1987, pp. 6–25 (pp. 23–4).

15 Elizabeth Freund, 'Ariachne's Broken Woof', in Patricia Parker and Geoffrey Hartman (eds), *Shakespeare and the Question of Theory*, New York: Methuen, 1985, pp. 19–36 (p. 22).

16 Freund, 'Ariachne's Broken Woof', p. 22.

17 Linda Charnes, *Notorious Identity: Materialising the Subject in Shakespeare*, Cambridge: Harvard University Press, 1993, p. 72.

18 Barbara Everett, 'The Inaction of *Troilus and Cressida*', *Essays in Criticism*, vol. 32, no. 2, 1982, pp. 119–39 (p. 274).

19 Charnes, *Notorious Identity*, p. 75.

20 See Brecht, 'Indirect Impact of the Epic Theatre', in *Brecht on Theatre*, pp. 57–8.

21 See Brecht, 'From the Mother Courage Model', in *Brecht on Theatre*, p. 217.

22 Brecht, *Brecht on Theatre*, pp. 219–20.

23 Gary Taylor, *Reinventing Shakespeare: A Cultural History from the Restoration to the Present*, London: Hogarth Press, 1990, p. 299.

24 In his appendix to the *Oxford Shakespeare* edition of the play, Kenneth Muir points out that Pandarus' 'Why but hear you' and Troilus' reply 'Hence broker-lackey! Ignominy and shame/Pursue thy life and live aye with thy name' appear twice in the Folio text, once in the last scene of the play (5.10 in Muir's edition) introducing Pandarus' epilogue and in the same position as in Q, and once in 5.3 where in Q they are omitted. He deduces that where they appear in 5.3, 'they belong to a version of the play in which Pandarus did not reappear' (Kenneth Muir, *Troilus and Cressida*, The Oxford Shakespeare, Oxford: OUP, 1982, p. 189). J. M. Nosworthy argues that 'the Epilogue, which so incongruously brings Pandarus onto the battlefield, is certainly something addressed to the Inns of Court performance ... and that only' (J. M. Nosworthy, *Shakespeare's Occasional Plays*, London: E. Arnold, 1965, p. 84). It seems that Boyd, too, found Pandarus' presence on the battlefield incongruous and his production concurs interestingly with Nosworthy's notion of a tragic version of the play, which Nosworthy

suggests Shakespeare was beginning before being invited to submit a comedy to the Inns of Court for their annual revels.

25 J. M. Nosworthy, *Shakespeare's Occasional Plays*, London: E. Arnold, 1965, p. 84.

26 *Evening Standard*, 9 November 1998.

27 *Independent*, 7 November 1998.

28 *What's On*, 10 November 1998.

29 *Financial Times*, 10 November 1998.

30 *Daily Telegraph*, 9 November 1998.

31 This was an addition for the Pit at the Barbican Centre, London, and for touring. At the Swan, Stratford-upon-Avon, a microphone was not used; the Swan tends to foreground the presence of the audience making a microphone, perhaps, superfluous.

32 Stanislavski asserts that the actor's point of attention must not be in the auditorium, and offers a range of exercises for the development of the actor's 'circle of attention'. See *An Actor Prepares*, pp. 68–9.

33 See below pp. 36–7 for an analysis of transpositions at the end of the production and, for an account of the effect of transpositions in the first half, see Alan Dessen, *Rescripting Shakespeare: The Text, the Director and Modern Productions*, Cambridge: CUP, 2002, pp. 110–1. Dessen argues that Nunn's changes clarify the action but loses some of the 'ironic or deflationary effects built into the script' and 'the impact of various verbal-poetic links' (p. 111). Nunn's reorganised sequence for the first half of Troilus runs as follows: Prologue; part of 1.2 (in which Pandarus and Cressida watch the return of the Trojan warriors); 1.3. up to Aeneas' entrance; 1.1; the rest of 1.2; 2.2; the end of 1.3; 2.1; 3.1; 2.3; 3.2.

34 Designed by Rob Howell.

35 Architect Denys Lasdun describes his 'search ... for a single room embodying stage and auditorium whose spatial configuration, above all else, would promote a dynamic relationship between audience and actor'. This particular design fits well with Lasdun's vision of 'an open relationship that looked back to the Greeks and Elizabethans and at the same time, looked forward to a contemporary view of society ...', Denys Lasdun in Ronnie Mulryne and Margaret Shewring (eds), *Making Space for Theatre: British Architecture and Theatre since 1958*, Stratford-upon-Avon: Mulryne and Shewring Ltd, 1995, p. 120.

36 W. B. Worthen makes this point about period settings where he argues that '[p]eriod production appears to transform 'history' into a metaphor for meanings latent in the text ... [P]eriod staging implies that the dynamics of Shakespeare's plays represent the fundamental forms of human relations, individual and collective action. The apparent changes of history are, in this sense, merely metaphorical – Shakespeare in different clothes', Worthen, *Shakespeare and the Authority of Performance*, p. 67.

37 See Prologue line 2 n. on 'orgulous': '... a fairly common word in the Middle Ages [that] Shakespeare only uses here as part of the consciously elevated style of the Prologue', *Troilus and Cressida*, The Arden Shakespeare Third Series, (ed.) David Bevington, Walton-on-Thames: Nelson, 1998.

38 *Troilus and Cressida*, prompt book note, NT archive.

39 NT programme for 15 February to 10 April 1999, p. 3.

40 *Daily Telegraph*, 25 April 1936.

41 *The Times*, 5 July 1948.

42 See note 24 for explanation of textual variants regarding these lines.

43 Dessen, *Rescripting Shakespeare*, p. 111.

44 Taylor, *Reinventing Shakespeare*, p. 300.

45 Taylor, *Reinventing Shakespeare*, p. 86.

46 Tillyard, *Shakespeare's Problem Plays*, pp. 85–6.

47 The phrase is Lear's Fool's: *King Lear*, 1.4.144.

48 Styan, J. L., *Drama, Stage and Audience*, Cambridge: CUP, 1975, p.153.

49 W. R. Elton, *Shakespeare's 'Troilus and Cressida' and the Inns of Court Revels*, Brookfield: Ashgate, 1999, p. 7 and *passim*.

50 For accounts of how Inns of Court students were educated through the practice of argument, see Philip Finkelpearl, *John Marston of the Middle Temple*, Cambridge: Harvard University Press, 1969, pp. 8–10, Kenneth Charlton, *Education in Renaissance England*, London: Routledge and Kegan Paul, 1965, pp. 174–5 and Wilfred Prest, *The Inns of Court under Elizabeth I and the Early Stuarts*, 'Methods of Aural Instruction', Harlow: Longman, 1972, pp. 116–24.

51 Stanislavski, *An Actor Prepares*, pp. 68–9.

52 For example, G. Blakemore Evans' notes to *The Riverside Shakespeare* (Boston: Houghton-Mifflin, 1974) insists on the sexual meaning in its note to these lines. Muir gives no note in his Oxford edition, but his note to line 54 suggests that Cressida is simply 'wittily evading' talk of Troilus, with no hint of sexual innuendo, whilst Kenneth Palmer's Arden Second Series edition (London: Methuen, 1982) gives the note that Cressida 'deliberately misunderstands' Pandarus but does not suggest a sexual meaning for that deliberate misunderstanding. David Bevington, for the Arden Third Series, notes that she 'perhaps hints at a sexual meaning' and that 'the degree of her sexual knowingness in this scene can be adjusted in performance ...'.

53 A minced man is one 'affected, effeminate, cut up, lacking in virility', l. 243 n., *Troilus and Cressida*, The Oxford Shakespeare, Muir (ed.), 'The lack of dates, an ingredient much used for flavouring and sweetening, would leave the pie sour and shrivelled. Out can also mean "not in", perhaps reinforcing the bawdy implications of a shrivelled bodily part', l. 248 n. Arden Third Series, Bevington (ed.).

54 I should add that I consider the links these students made were rather less spurious than this seeming connection in the RSC production between a metaphor for making Hector drunk and the literal use of blood by Achilles.

55 In an interview with Terry Coleman, *Guardian*, 5 September 1983

56 Sher, *Guardian*, 2 January 1999.

3   The point or the question? text, performance, *Hamlet*

1 General references to *Hamlet* use the Folio line numbering in Paul Bertram and Bernice W. Kliman (eds), *The Three Text Hamlet: Parallel Texts of the First and Second Quartos and First Folio*, New York: AMS Press, 1991.

2 Barker, *The Tremulous Private Body*, p. 36–7.

3 Barker, *The Tremulous Private Body*, pp. 41–2.

4 Terry Eagleton, *William Shakespeare*, Oxford: Basil Blackwell, 1986, p. 72.

5 Terry Eagleton, *Shakespeare and Society*, London: Chatto and Windus, 1970, p. 63.
6 Eagleton, *Shakespeare and Society*, p. 40.
7 Eagleton, *Shakespeare and Society*, p. 40.
8 Eagleton, *Shakespeare and Society*, p. 41.
9 Eagleton, *Shakespeare and Society*, p. 41.
10 States, *Hamlet and the Concept of Character*, p. xviii.
11 Maus, *Inwardness and Theater*, pp. 27–8.
12 My subheading borrows from Worthen's *Shakespeare and the Authority of Performance*.
13 Maus, *Inwardness and Theater*, p. 125.
14 Maus, *Inwardness and Theater*, p. 124. His evidence here is the frontispiece of the Second Quarto, which claims that the text is 'Newly imprinted and enlarged to almost as much/again as it was, according to the true and perfect/Coppie', as opposed to Q1 which advertises the text 'As it hath beene diuerse times acted by his Highnesse ser-/uants in the Cittie of London: as also in the two V/niversities of Cambridge and Oxford, else-where', Paul Bertram and Bernice W. Kliman (eds), *The Three Text Hamlet*, p. 7.
15 Christopher McCullough interviewed by Bryan Loughrey in 'Quarto One in Recent Performance: An Interview', in Thomas Clayton (ed.) *The 'Hamlet' First Published: Origins, Forms, Intertextualities*, Newark: University of Delaware Press, 1992, pp. 123–36 (p. 131).
16 *Hamlet* Q1: 7.114. All references to the First Quarto of *Hamlet* are from the New Cambridge Shakespeare, *The First Quarto of Hamlet*, Kathleen Irace (ed.), Cambridge: CUP, 1998, an edition that divides the text into scenes.
17 Loughrey, 'Quarto One in Recent Performance', pp. 126 and 153–4.
18 *Hamlet* F1: 3.1.55. References to the First Folio of *Hamlet* are from *The Three Text Hamlet*, Paul Bertram and Bernice Kliman (eds). As the first two sections of this chapter deal with productions based on the Q1 and F texts, F is referred to when making a comparison between Q1 and later published texts. Q2 is referenced where Q2 and F are substantially different, again using *The Three Text Hamlet*.
19 These are Christopher McCullough, cited above, Peter Guinness who played Hamlet at the Orange Tree Theatre, Richmond, in 1985 and the director of the Orange Tree production, Sam Walters. They are cited by Leah Marcus in *Unediting the Renaissance: Shakespeare, Milton, Marlowe*, London: Routledge, 1996, pp. 152–3 and Weimann in *Author's Pen and Actor's Voice*, p. 21.
20 Marcus, *Unediting the Renaissance*, p. 155.
21 Marcus, *Unediting the Renaissance*, p. 167.
22 Marcus, *Unediting the Renaissance*, p. 138.
23 Weimann, *Author's Pen and Actor's Voice*, p. 25.
24 Weimann, *Author's Pen and Actor's Voice*, p. 27. Weimann cites Kathleen Irace, 'Origins and Agents of Q1 *Hamlet*', in *The 'Hamlet' First Published*, T. Clayton (ed.), pp. 90–122 (p. 100).
25 Weimann, *Author's Pen and Actor's Voice*, p. 21.
26 Christopher McCullough, interviewed by Loughrey in 'Quarto One in Recent Performance', p. 128.
27 Weimann, *Author's Pen and Actor's Voice*, p. 20.

28 Marcus, *Unediting the Renaissance*, p. 141 and Irace, 'Introduction', *The First Quarto of Hamlet*, pp. 12–13.

29 See Eric Sams' 'Taboo or not Taboo? The Text, Dating and Authorship of *Hamlet*, 1589–1623', *Hamlet Studies*, 1988, vol. 10, pp. 12–46, for a strong argument that Q1 *Hamlet* is the lost ur-*Hamlet*. Leah Marcus suggests a broader range of possibilities for Q1 as an early version or draft of *Hamlet* (Marcus, *Unediting the Renaissance*, pp. 147–50).

30 See Irace, 'Introduction', *The First Quarto of Hamlet*, pp. 6–7. For recent arguments supporting the theory of memorial reconstruction by an actor, see Sidney Thomas, 'Hamlet Quarto One: First Version or Bad Quarto?', in *The 'Hamlet' First Published*, T. Clayton (ed.), pp. 249–56.

31 See Janis Lull, 'Forgetting *Hamlet*: The First Quarto and the Folio', in *The 'Hamlet' First Published*, T. Clayton (ed.), pp. 137–50 for the suggestion that Q1 *Hamlet* is not a 'divided mind or Protestant soul' because the reporters making the memorial reconstruction are not interested in 'the concerns of a relatively bookish elite' (p. 139).

32 I am indebted to designer Neill Irish for technical information here.

33 Loughrey, 'Quarto One in Recent Performance', p. 125.

34 Introduction to *The Tragedie of Hamlet Prince of Denmark* (Q1), Brian Loughrey and Graham Holderness (eds), London: Longman, 1990, p. 24. See also p. 25. Again, this conclusion is taken from Loughrey's interview with the Orange Tree practitioners, 'Quarto One in Recent Performance'.

35 Programme notes, *Hamlet: First Cut*, citing Loughrey, 'Quarto One in Recent Performance', p. 124.

36 Programme notes, *Hamlet: First Cut*.

37 Irace, 'Introduction', *The First Quarto of Hamlet*, p. 12.

38 Though Irace's Q1 text changes Q1 (and Q2)'s 'sallied' to 'sullied', I have retained Q1's spelling here, with its possible meaning of much-tried, exhausted.

39 Robert Miola, *Shakespeare's Reading*, Oxford: OUP, 2000, p. 121.

40 'Master of Play' prepares the play text; 'Master of Voice' works with the actors in rehearsal. It is clear from the accounts of rehearsal provided in the Globe reconstruction's 'Research Bulletin' on the production that the two roles combined in this way amount to something approaching very near the job of the modern director. See Jaq Bessell, 'Shakespeare's Globe Research Bulletin: *Hamlet* 2000', http://www.rdg.ac.uk/globe/research/1999Hamlet2000htm.

41 Giles Block, interviewed by Heather Neill in the Globe *Hamlet*'s programme notes.

42 The F1 text has 'But I have that within, which passeth show; / These, but the trappings and the suits of woe' (F1: 1.2.85–6), where Q1 has 'Him have I lost I must of force forgo,/These but the ornaments and suits of woe' (Q1: 2.38–9).

43 Compare Pauline Kiernan in *Staging Shakespeare at the New Globe*, Basingstoke: Macmillan, 1999, who 'imagines [that this is] because they are not 'boxed in' inside a picture-frame stage [and] also because the distance between playgoer and actor is not as variable' (p. 19).

44 Rylance played Hamlet in the RSC's production of 1989.

45 Marcus, *Unediting the Renaissance*, p. 155.

46 See Chapter 1, pp. 13–15.

47 Rylance is described as 'sensitive-faced and delicate-voiced' (*Time Out*, 5 July 2000), the 'cello-like quality of his verse-speaking' is marked by *Plays International* (Summer 2000), while *The Times* describes him as 'as audible as he is emotionally truthful' (12 June 2000).

48 Kiernan, *Staging Shakespeare*, p. 89.

49 Compare almost any F1 verse passage with its Q2 equivalent; here, for example is F1's grammatical ghost compared with Q2's:

> Do not forget: this Visitation
> Is but to whet thy almost blunted purpose.
> But look, Amazement on thy Mother sits;
> O step between her, and her fighting Soul,
> Conceit in weakest bodies, strongest works.
> Speak to her Hamlet.
>
> (F1: 3.4.110–15)

> Do not forget, this visitation
> Is but to whet thy almost blunted purpose,
> But look, amazement on thy mother sits,
> O step between her, and her fighting soul,
> Conceit in weakest bodies strongest works,
> Speak to her Hamlet.
>
> (Q2: 2490–5)

50 Bessell, notes on 'Verse Work', 'Shakespeare's Globe Research Bulletin: *Hamlet* 2000'.

51 *Morning Star*, 10 July 2000.

52 It should be noted that Block does not, however, advise actors to run sentences on over line-endings: 'Nowadays if a line is not punctuated, we tend to run on the ends, which betrays our ignorance of how the lines are written. The lines are written to help the actor take the time to create the images spontaneously every time they speak the words. [Giles Block] said that this required daring', Bessell, 'Shakespeare's Globe Research Bulletin: *Hamlet* 2000'.

53 *Times Literary Supplement*, 7 July 2000.

54 *Independent on Sunday*, 4 July 2000.

55 Before its completion, Mark Rylance looked forward to the opportunities the Globe reconstruction would provide for direct contact with the audience and explained that '[i]nvolving the audience as one's soul, one's conscience, is a skill I was taught at the RSC', 'Playing the Globe: Artistic Policy and Practice' in Ronnie Mulryne and Margaret Shewring, *Shakespeare's Globe Rebuilt*, Cambridge: CUP, 1997, pp. 169–76 (p. 172). To talk to such a nebulous concept as a conscience strikes me as difficult, and perhaps accounts for the generalised and indirect mode of direct address in the production of *Troilus and Cressida* described in Chapter One. The problem or advantage, according to one's view on the matter, of the lit or day-lit audience is that it is always and visibly a group of people that have paid to come and see a play. See Chapter Four for further analysis of possible roles for the lit audience in *Richard II*.

56 *Times Literary Supplement*, 7 July 2000.
57 Clive Johnson, 'Shakespeare's Big Mac', summer 2000, review of *Hamlet* held at Globe Research Centre, source unknown.
58 Clearly one cannot assume that audience laughter will be elicited at the same point in every performance over the run of a play. Nevertheless, having attended the production twice and examined two other video-recorded performances it is remarkable how uniform the laughter at performances of this *Hamlet* have been, varying in intensity but predictable as to their point in the text. This is not the case with verbal responses to provocations by actors; Rylance cannot guarantee that his direct question to the pit 'Who calls me villain?' will get an individual response; the less threatening uniformity of the laugh seems easy for the Globe performer to manipulate.
59 T. J. B. Spencer, *Hamlet*, The New Penguin Shakespeare, Harmondsworth: Penguin, 1980, 3.2.43–555 n.
60 Or it may be that if a joke about a clown improvising badly was current, it might have disappeared from performance, as clowns across London responded by ensuring they never repeated a joke. It is also possible that, if Q1 is a memorial reconstruction taken on tour out of London by another company, a set of jokes at the expense of a particular set of jokes might have been written down by the reconstruction and lasted that tour, while others might have taken its place in subsequent London productions: others that might have varied from week to week according to what clowns in other companies were making much of.
61 David Wiles argues that around the time of the first performances of Shakespeare's *Hamlet*, the Chamberlain's men had just lost their clown, William Kemp, and that it is for this pragmatic reason that so much clown-like material is written for the tragic hero, *Shakespeare's Clown: Actor and Text in the Elizabethan Playhouse*, Cambridge: CUP, 1987, pp. 57–60.
62 Bert O. States, 'The Actor's Presence: Three Phenomenal Modes', in Philip Zarrilli (ed.), *Acting (Re)considered: Theories and Practices*, London: Routledge, 1995, pp. 22–42 (p. 30).
63 The Globe text here changes F1's 'Who? What an ass am I?' for Q2's 'Why what an ass am I ....'
64 Two other recent productions – Steven Pimlott's for the RSC and Peter Brook's – have used the notion of this speech as Hamlet's attempt at a theatrical performance, which he then undermines at his own expense. Samuel West at the RSC turns to the audience and mimes a clichéd stabbing scene at the point of the 'Bawdy villain' outburst; Adrian Lester precedes the lines with a parody of a meditative yoga and voice warm-up, then speaks them with exaggerated solemnity. Rylance's Hamlet's attempt at a heightened, emotional but non-melodramatic version goes a step further than either of these, by drawing attention to the idea of 'authentic' emotion as performance.
65 Belsey, *The Subject of Tragedy*, p. 42.
66 In both Q2 and F the phrase runs on:

> ... if it be, 'tis not to come, if it be not to come,/it will be now, if it be not now, yet it will come, the readiness is all,/since no man of ought he leaves, knows what is't to leave betimes,/let be.

(Q2: 3669–71)

> If it be now, 'tis not/to come: if it be not to come, it will be now: if
> it/ be not now: yet it will come; the readiness is all, since no/man ha's
> ought of what he leaves. What is't to leave betimes?
>
> (F1: 5.2.221–4)

67 Set and masks designed by Fredericka Hayter, costumes by Sonya Berlovitz.
68 Jeune Lune website, http://www.jeunelune.org/about/, and programme to
    Hamlet.
69 See Peter Brook, *The Empty Space*, London: Penguin, 1990, Chapter 2, 'The
    Holy Theatre', p. 47.
70 I am indebted here to information provided by Barbra Berlovitz, director
    and performer with Jeune Lune.
71 Although Bruce Weber, the *New York Times* critic, evidently couldn't:
    'Accompanying the speaking cast are several robed, masked and silent
    players – I could never figure out exactly how many there were – who func-
    tion as a kind of chorus', *New York Times*, 28 Ocobter 2003.
72 Brook's text uses a Q2-based edition, hence 'sullied', the usual modern
    correction of Q1 and Q2's 'sallied'.
73 Design by Philipe Vialatte.
74 Irace, 'Introduction', *The First Quarto of Hamlet*, p. 12.
75 Peter Brook, interviewed by Margaret Croyden, 'A Certain Path', *American
    Theater*, Vol. 18, May/June 2001, p. 19.
76 Richard Schechner, 'Talking with Peter Brook', *The Drama Review*, vol. 30
    no. 1, Spring 1986, cited in Rustom Bharucha, *Theatre and the World:
    Performance and the Culture of Politics*, London: Routledge, 1993, p. 81.
77 Bharucha, *Theatre and the World*, p. 83.
78 Bharucha, *Theatre and the World*, p. 82.
79 Bharucha, *Theatre and the World*, p. 76.
80 Bharucha, *Theatre and the World*, p. 78.
81 'The essential Hamlet'; review of Brook's *Hamlet*, http://www.
    shakespeare.com/reviews/brook/hamlet.php3.
82 Peter Brook, introduction to *The Mahabharata* by Jean-Claude Carrière, New
    York: Harper and Row, 1987, p. xiii, cited in Bharucha, *Theatre and the
    World*, pp. 74–5.
83 Peter Brook, interviewed by Faynia Williams, *Direct Magazine*, http://www.
    dgg6.co.uk/publications/article9_86.html.
84 Peter Brook, interviewed by Faynia Williams.
85 Charles Spenser, *Daily Telegraph*, 23 August 2001.
86 Bharucha, *Theatre and the World*, p. 70.
87 Kastan, *Shakepeare after Theory*, London: Routledge, 1999, p. 16.

4 The theatre and the Presence Chamber: history, performance, *Richard II*s

1 *Observer*, 2 April 2000.
2 *Guardian*, 1 April 2000.
3 *Time Out*, 5 April 2000.
4 *Independent on Sunday*, 2 April 2000.
5 Set and costumes by Sue Wilmington.

6 Though the text referred to, New Cambridge Shakespeare, 1984, Gurr (ed.) (Cambridge: CUP, 1984) uses Holinshed and Shakespeare's 'Bullingbrook', I use the later 'Bolingbroke', after the spelling in the RSC programme and prompt book.

7 After the Almeida's performances of *Richard II* and *Coriolanus*, these disused studios were converted into shops and flats.

8 Costumes by Paul Brown.

9 *Sunday Times*, 16 April 2000.

10 *Financial Times*, 31 March 2000.

11 *Time Out*, 5 April 2000.

12 *Independent on Sunday*, 2 April 00.

13 *Daily Telegraph*, 31 March 2000.

14 *Evening Standard*, 30 March 2000.

15 *Observer*, 2 April 2000.

16 The phrase is Lear's on meeting Edgar as Poor Tom, *King Lear*, 3.4.106.

17 For interpretations of Richard as 'Player King', an actorly 'character' within the fiction see Ann Barton (née Righter), *Shakespeare and the Idea of the Play*, London: Chatto and Windus, 1962, pp. 123–6; G. A. Bonnard, 'The Actor in Richard II', *Shakespeare Jahrbuch*, no. 87, 1952, pp. 88–99; Leonard F. Dean, '*Richard II*: The State and the Image of the Theatre', *PMLA*, no. 67, 1952, pp. 211–18.

18 Samuel West, 'Richard II', in Robert Smallwood (ed.), *Players of Shakespeare 5*, Cambridge: CUP, 2004, p. 90.

19 The only dramatic location to which the turf does not appear to be naturalistically adequate is Richard's prison in the tower; during 5.5 at the Gainsborough studios, lighting reduces the playing space to a sharply defined oblong where the grass is not so clearly in evidence.

20 Interview with Samuel West, 4 June 2001.

21 This notion of 'presence' is borrowed from Harry Berger Jr, a disagreement with whose article '*Richard II*, 3.2: An Exercise in Imaginary Audition', *English Literary History*, vol. 55, 1988, pp. 755–96, has proved an important inspiration for this chapter. Berger assumes that common sense dictates that Richard cannot be displaying his own narcissism to the audience. Underpinning this study is the belief that a dramatic figure's presence to the audience is not only possible but central to the effects of subjectivity examined here.

22 See below, p. 112.

23 *Daily Telegraph*, 31 March 2000, emphasis added.

24 *Sunday Times*, 9 April 2000, emphasis added.

25 Robert Shaughnessy, *Representing Shakespeare: England, History and the RSC*, New York: Harvester Wheatsheaf, 1994, p. 95. Shaughnessy cites Stanley Wells' comment that the Barton production was 'the most strongly interpretive production of the play I have ever seen' as 'representative of the overall critical response' (p. 95). It is also interesting to note that both productions have been described as 'Brechtian', as though this were a watchword for modern imposition. See *Financial Times*, 31 March 2000 and *Guardian*, 1 April 2000 for descriptions of the 2000 production as 'Brechtian'. See Peter Ansorge, *Plays and Players*, June 1973, pp. 39–41 for a description of Barton's production in similar terms. Robert Shaughnessy's analysis of the Barton production, however, is that to call it 'Brechtian' is a mistake. He points to what he sees as a '... paradox whereby an ultra-conservative

theatrical vocabulary ('Graeco-Elizabethan' was the term used by the directors and the designer) was described by some reviewers as 'Brechtian' (p. 96). While I find much of Shaughnessy's critique of the 1973 production persuasive, it seems odd to condemn an 'Elizabethan' aesthetic as inevitably 'ultra-conservative' given Brecht's own interest in Shakespeare and the Elizabethan theatre.

26 I adapt Benjamin's sense of 'aura' in the celebrated essay 'The Work of Art in the Age of Mechanical Reproduction': 'That which withers in the age of mechanical reproduction is the aura of the work of art' (Walter Benjamin, *Illuminations*, trans. Harry Zohn, London: Jonathan Cape, 1970, pp. 211–43 (p. 223)). The critics cited here find in *Richard II* a nostalgia for an 'aura' of England and kingship, lost in king Richard's new age of financial expedience. This nostalgia, particular to John of Gaunt's 'This England' speech (2.1.31–78), produces a reading of the whole play, not as a dramatic text – contingent and reproduced – but as a medieval artefact that should be lovingly preserved in ways that the Pimlott/West production has failed to do.

27 Graham Holderness, *Shakespeare Recycled: The Making of Historical Drama*, Hemel Hempstead: Harvester Wheatsheaf, 1992, p. 14.

28 E. M. W. Tillyard, *Shakespeare's History Plays*, London: Chatto and Windus, 1944, p. 252.

29 *Daily Telegraph*, 31 March 2000. Compare Tillyard's suggestion that Shakespeare's access to medieval decorative artworks 'would have had a strong, if unconscious, effect on Shakespeare's mind and induced him to present the age of Richard in a brilliant yet remote and unrealistic manner' (Tillyard, *Shakespeare's History Plays*, p. 255).

30 *Observer*, 2 April 2000.

31 Holderness, *Shakespeare's History*, p. 42.

32 Holderness, *Shakespeare's History*, p. 46. Holderness refers to Tillyard, *Shakespeare's History Plays* and Derek Traversi, *Shakespeare from Richard II to Henry V*, London: Hollis and Carter, 1958.

33 Holderness, *Shakespeare Recycled*, p. 15.

34 Tillyard, *Shakespeare's History Plays*, pp. 244–63 (p. 259).

35 Phyllis Rackin, *Stages of History: Shakespeare's English Chronicles*, London: Routledge, 1990, p. 119.

36 Rackin, *Stages of History*, p. 121.

37 Rackin, *Stages of History*, pp. 47–8.

38 Lee Patterson, *Chaucer and the Subject of History*, London: Routledge, 1991, p. 8.

39 *Sunday Times*, 16.4.00.

40 Significantly, the RSC name their whole history cycle 'This England', suggesting that the whole project might be inflected with Gaunt's nostalgia for a lost idyll; it is a suggestion that the Steven Pimlott/Samuel West company succeed in refuting.

41 West, 'Richard II', p. 86.

42 West, 'Richard II', p. 89.

43 For *Hamlet*, a variety of devices have been employed to reduce this distance: the stage was brought forward and the stalls raised for the RSC's summer 2001 season; a walkway was built out into the auditorium, in the manner of the *hanamidri* of Japanese Kabuki theatre; West steps down into the auditorium during one soliloquy and runs up an aisle to address the audience in the stalls; the house lights are brought up momentarily, during Hamlet's advice to the players. Nevertheless, given the traditional circle arrangement,

whose sight lines restrict the walkway to use as an entrance rather than permitting its use for performance, and the fact that the house lights remain off for the greater part of the performance, the effect of pictorial distance is maintained for most of the performance outside of West's soliloquies.

44 *Sunday Telegraph*, 2 April 2000.

45 See *Sunday Times*, 9 April 2000 and *Financial Times*, 31 March 2000. The *Guardian*'s objection was rather more specific: 'I distrust the modern habit, already seen in *Macbeth* this week at London's BAC, of plucking lines from the fifth act to use as a choric refrain' (*Guardian*, 1 April 2000).

46 See above, pp. 36–7.

47 West, 'Richard II', p. 91.

48 In fact there was an alternative ending, in which Troughton spoke Bolingbroke's first line as Henry IV in *1 Henry IV*: 'So shaken as we are, so wan with care …'. This was replaced by the prison soliloquy lines during the run of the production, though occasionally Troughton would revert to the *1Henry IV* ending (Interview with Samuel West, 4 June 2001).

I should also add that this is not Bolingbroke's only transposition. An interval comes between 3.2 and 3.3 in this production and before 3.3, a parallel extra-fictional moment to the first prologue is added wherein Richard and Bolingbroke enter under the purple lighting state and confront one another centre stage. Bolingbroke speaks lines from Richard's dialogue with Isabel on his journey to prison:

> In winter's tedious nights sit by the fire
> With good old folks, and let them tell thee tales
> Of woeful ages long ago betid,
> And ere thou bid goodnight, to 'quite their griefs
> Tell thou the lamentable tale of me.
>
> (5.1.40–4)

Troughton speaks the lines urgently, almost angrily to Richard, as if demanding that his perspective on the tale of *Richard II* now be given. This sits comfortably with the earlier transpositions, emphasising the nature of the play as a 'story' with which the audience may be familiar, whose ending is already known and which is as much Bolingbroke's tale as Richard's.

49 Shaughnessy, *Representing Shakespeare*, p. 102.

50 Holderness, *Shakespeare Recycled*, p. 20.

51 In the previous RSC season to the 'This England' Histories cycle, the Sher/Doran *Macbeth* makes use of the Swan Theatre's external doors. The production uses a range of spaces apart from the stage itself: the stairways connecting the balcony areas behind the stage, the auditorium, and, momentarily, the outside of the building, as the fire doors at the back of the stalls are opened for Macduff and Lennox to confront the Porter (2.3.22). This opening of the doors onto the outside of the building is at the centre of a particularly theatrically conscious sequence in the production, which begins when the Porter confronts the audience with 'Knock Knock' jokes, impersonations of current politicians and television personalities and improvised demands that members of the audience answer him when he addresses them. The effect of the opening doors is jarring. To be placed in the position of spectator to a stand-up routine may be a familiar enough

experience for some in the audience, even though the Porter's difficulty in eliciting responses to his routine suggests that not many expected such a direct burst of improvised clowning at the RSC. To be shown a space so radically extra-diagetic as the outside of the theatre building is an even less common occurrence in 'traditional' theatre practice and, once the very different qualities of light, sound and air of 'outside' are once again shut out, the moment has the unnerving effect of shutting the spectator in: in with the murder that has just occurred in the fiction, into a complicity with the murderer who can make knowing jokes about the king not yet stirring and the fact that it has been 'a rough night' (2.3.61).

52 This effect could not be recreated so startlingly at the Barbican, where the stage left door opened onto the scene dock rather than the outside of the building.

53 *Richard II*, The New Penguin Shakespeare, Stanley Wells (ed.), London: Penguin, 1997.

54 Holderness, *Shakespeare: The Histories*, Basingstoke: Macmillan, 2000, pp. 176–8.

55 West, 'Richard II', p. 87.

56 For definitions of the term in this context see J. L. Austin, *How to Do Things with Words*, Oxford: Clarendon Press, 1962, pp. 4–10 and *passim*; John R. Searle, *Speech Acts: An Essay in the Philosophy of Language*, Cambridge: CUP, 1969, pp. 136–41 and *Expression and Meaning: Studies in the Theory of Speech Acts*, Cambridge: CUP, 1979, pp. 16–20.

57 As opposed to the word's more general use in performance studies, where it now tends to mean 'performed', 'consciously performed or drawing attention to status as performance' or, in the case of events from everyday life, 'containing elements of performance'.

58 Austin describes as 'infelicities' the circumstances in which 'the smooth or "happy" functioning of a performative' cannot occur. He defines the conditions for felicitous performatives in terms of: conditions that all parties to the performative must accept, the appropriateness of the parties themselves, their appropriate thoughts, feelings and conduct and the correct and complete execution of the performative (Austin, *How to Do Things with Words*, pp. 14–15).

59 Judith Butler, *Excitable Speech: A Politics of the Performative*, London: Routledge, 1997, p. 2.

60 Althusser describes how 'ideology interpellates individuals as subjects' in 'Ideology and Ideological State Apparatuses', *Lenin and Philosophy*, pp. 160–5.

61 Butler, *Excitable Speech*, p. 4. Such an understanding of subjectivity gives rise to political questions of agency, of what is to be done to resist hateful and oppressive interpellations; it is these questions that are asked by critics of Althusserian models of subjectivity, and it is with these questions that Butler struggles in her book.

62 Review of *Richard II*, *Spectator*, 8 April 2000.

63 Review of *Richard II*, *Spectator*, 8 April 2000.

64 I call Richard's centre stage position the 'authority position' here, as Kiernan does the centre of the space under the 'heavens' at the Globe (see Kiernan, *Staging Shakespeare*, pp. 63–4). Such a position in a space with seating 'end on', as at the Other Place, is yet more of an authority position,

in fact: whereas at the Globe, some spectators sit and stand where they can view the king in the authority position without being seen by him unless he turns, West's Richard can survey the whole audience with ease.

65 Until 3.2, Richard's main pronoun of self-reference is the 'royal we', shifting noticeably to 'I' as he addresses the earth at the opening of 3.2 on his return from Ireland. This 'I' separates itself from the figure of 'king' at 83–6, as he faces the desertion of the Welsh: 'I had forgot myself. Am I not king?/Awake thou coward majesty! thou sleepest./Is not the king's name twenty thousand names?/Arm, arm, my name!' He reverts to 'we' at line 97, then shifts once more to 'I' where he unkings himself, comparing himself to his subjects and friends: 'For you have but mistook me all this while./I live with bread like you, feel want,/Taste grief, need friends: subjected thus,/How can you say to me I am a king?' (174–7). He then moves from 'I' to 'we' and back until the end of the scene where the first of the third person references occurs: 'Discharge my followers, let them hence away,/From Richard's night to Bolingbroke's fair day' (3.2.215). This recurs in 3.3 at 121 and 143–6: 'What must the king do now? Must he submit?/ The king shall do it. Must he be depos'd?/The king shall be contented. Must he lose/The name of king? A 'God's name let it go'. There then follows the celebrated passage in which Richard suggests that he will swap the trappings of kingship for more humble artefacts and his 'large kingdom for a little grave' (3.3.147–59). As we will see, the relinquishing of externally conferred identity presages death. This figure cannot maintain the subjectivity suggested by the switch to 'I' without contemplating his complete annihilation.

66 See above p. 166, n. 20.

67 West refers to a series of exercises introduced into the rehearsal process by Cicely Berry, whereby a throne was built out of objects in the rehearsal room and dismantled during the scene.

68 West, 'Richard II', p. 95.

69 See Keith Johnstone, 'Status', in *Impro*, London: Methuen, 1981, pp. 33–74, particularly his series of 'letters' improvisations, pp. 51–2; my own experience of working with these improvisations, in which one participant is accused of opening the letters of another, is that they demonstrate the ease with which a range of physical and verbal strategies can undermine the assumed high status of the accuser.

70 John Webster, *The Duchess of Malfi*, 4.2.170.

71 For example, it pushes it beyond acceptable limits for many reviewers with its portrayal of Hotspur as an excessively conformist SAS recruit; it provokes sudden laughter at Richard's addressing Isabel as 'our queen' in a Yorkshire accent; when Bolingbroke is faced with the conflicting appeals of York and his Duchess for the condemnation and pardon of Aumerle, the sense that '[o]ur scene is altered from a serious thing' (5.3.78) is underlined by Bolingbroke pointing a gun at his aunt in his desperation to make her 'Rise up' (5.3.91).

72 For an account of this sequence as comic see Ralph Berry, *Shakespeare in Performance: Casting and Metamorphoses*, New York: St Martin's Press, 1993, p. 83; for an account of the cutting of this sequence and the York/Aumerle scenes to avoid potential comedy see A. C. Sprague, *Shakespeare's Histories*, London: Society for Theatre Research, 1964, p. 42. See Stanley Wells'

account of the 1973 John Barton production in *Royal Shakespeare*, p. 74, for another example of a 'serious' gage-throwing sequence.
73 *Spectator*, 8 April 2000.
74 Bert O. States, 'The Actor's Presence: Three Phenomenal Modes', p. 30.
75 Interview with Samuel West, 4 June 2001.
76 West, 'Richard II', p. 91.
77 In conversation with the keeper of the records of the Tower, William Lambarde, in 1601, Elizabeth makes her much-quoted comparison between herself and *Richard II* – 'I am Richard II, know ye not that?' – and, perhaps with reference to the commissioning of a performance of a Richard II play by supporters of the Essex rebellion of earlier that year, says of Essex 'He that will forget God will forget his benefactors; this tragedy was played forty times in open streets and houses', cited in *Eyewitnesses of Shakespeare: First Hand Accounts of Performances*, collated by Gamini Salgado, London: Chatto and Windus for Sussex University Press, 1975, p. 22.

5 Performing human: the Socìetas Raffaello Sanzio

1 David Savran, *Breaking the Rules: The Wooster Group*, New York: Theatre Communications Group, 1988, pp. 169–220 (p. 192).
2 Willem Dafoe, interview with Philip Auslander in Auslander, *From Acting to Performance*, p. 42.
3 *Julius Caesar*, 3.2.74, 75, 82–7, 96–102, 167–87, 209–11, 214–19.
4 For an account of this theory of autism, see Andrew Meltzoff and Alison Gopnik, 'The Role of Imitation in Understanding Persons', in Simon Baron-Cohen *et al.* (eds), *Understanding Other Minds: Perspectives from Autism*, Oxford: OUP, 1993, pp. 335–6 and Simon Baron-Cohen, *Mindblindness: An Essay on Autism and Theory of Mind*, Cambridge: MIT Press, 1993, *passim*.
5 This obviously would not have been necessary when performing in Italy. The subtitles became part of the *mise en scène* in the London performances, however, where the effect of separating voice from that which produces it drew attention in turn to that which it produces: Shakespeare's words as translation.
6 I refer to theories of voice training that suggest that 'Shakespeare' springs naturally, audibly and comprehensibly from the relaxed, correctly trained body of the actor. The words of Shakespeare, argues Kirsten Linklater, for example, 're-present the aroused internal human condition' that the right vocal training can release (Kirsten Linklater, *Freeing Shakespeare's Voice: The Actor's Guide to Talking the Text*, New York: Theatre Communications Group, 1992, p. 100). This and other examples are cited in Richard Paul Knowles, 'Shakespeare, Voice and Ideology: Interrogating the Natural Voice', in Bulman, *Shakespeare, Theory and Performance*, pp. 92–112. I have borrowed here from his critique of the essentialist philosophies he sees as underpinning the belief suggested by Linklater's writings, 'that if you look sufficiently deeply into yourself, freeing the natural voice and body and discovering your most profound psycho-physical center, you will find Shakespeare' (p. 100).

7 See Stanislavski, *An Actor Prepares*, pp. 163–92 for an account of the 'Emotion Memory' technique, whereby the actor is asked to 'bring back feelings [he] ha[s] already experienced' (p. 168) in order to create the impression of authentic emotion.

8 From Joseph Mankiewicz's Hollywood film of 1953.

9 *Mene mene tekel upharsin (peres)* is the 'writing on the wall' in the biblical story of Balthazzar's feast (Daniel 5.25).

10 Nicholas Ridout, in Bridget Escolme and Nicholas Ridout, 'Performing Humans Historically: Shakespeare and the Socìetas Raffaello Sanzio', conference paper for Performance Studies International 7, State University of Arizona 28 March to 1 April 2000 and adapted for 'Scaena: Shakespeare and His Contemporaries in Performance', St. John's College, Cambridge 9–11 August 2001. My own sections of this paper, written as a dialogue between a critic of Shakespeare in performance – myself – and one whose main interest lies in contemporary devised performance – Nicholas Ridout – form the basis of the argument for this chapter. Extracts from Nicholas Ridout's sections of the paper are clearly cited, as here.

11 Compare Cassandra, whose fate it is to be misread (*Troilus and Cressida*, 2.2.97–129 and 5.3.59–94). However, compare also Portia who writes her own sign upon herself – the wound that proves her 'constancy' and worthiness to be her father's daughter, her husband's wife (*Julius Caesar* 2.1.290–301).

12 The performance breaks at the end of the cut version of Mark Antony's address to the Plebeians, and begins again with a version of 4.2 and 4.3, Brutus and Cassius' quarrel.

13 Ridout in Escolme and Ridout, 'Performing Humans Historically'.

14 Peter Conrad, 'Shakespeare Made Sick', *Guardian*, 6 June 1999.

15 Conrad appears to suggest here that Artaud's concept of a Theatre of Cruelty involves being cruel to performers. When, in his first manifesto for the Theatre of Cruelty, Artaud states that 'There can be no spectacle without an element of cruelty as the basis of every show. In our present degenerative state, meta-physics must be made to enter the mind through the body', he is writing of the effect of his projected performances upon the audience rather than suggesting that performers should be 'stretched and tormented'. See Antonin Artaud, *The Theatre and Its Double*, London: Calder New Paris Editions, 1993, pp. 68–78 (p. 77).

16 Auslander, *From Acting to Performance*, p. 42.

17 Man Ray's photograph 'Violon D'Ingres', 1924. The Cicero figure has the same markings on his back.

18 Cicero, 'L'Oratore', translated for *Giulio Cesare*, surtitles by Valentina Guidi and the Socìetas Raffaello Sanzio.

19 This title translates roughly as 'Hamlet. The Vehement Exteriority of the Death of a Mollusc'.

20 Gertrude's description of Ophelia's death, *Hamlet*, 4.7.166–83.

21 Ridout in Escolme and Ridout, 'Performing Humans Historically'.

22 As Tony Attwood argues: '... rituals and compulsions must be completed or the autistic person can become quite agitated. It appears that he engages in this behaviour to avoid any new experience and maintain a fixed or inflexible routine. This behaviour is "safe" as he has immense difficulty in making sense of the world and in particular making sense of new or

changing information', Tony Attwood, 'Overview and History of Autism', in *Social Education and Training of the Autistic Adult: A Collection of Papers at a Weekend Study Course, 23rd–25th October 1981*, London: The Inge Wakehurst Memorial Trust Fund, 1981.

23 Artaud, ' On the Balinese Theatre', in *The Theatre and Its Double*, p. 43.

24 The Autism Society of America estimates that the syndrome occurs in four times as many boys as girls ('What is Autism?' www.autism-society.org/whatisautism/autism.html).

25 It is certainly part of the disturbing nature of this performance that one suspects that when Tonti urinates, then later defecates, the act may be 'real'. In fact they are a stage effect.

26 Charlotte Moore, 'It forces you to rethink everything you thought you knew about being human', *Guardian*, 16 May 2001.

27 A common manifestation of autism is this repeated speech, whereby the autistic person appears not to understand that a reply or conversational exchange is required of him but repeats what is said to him by another, either immediately or later. See Adriane L. Schuler and Barry M. Prizant, 'Echolalia', in Eric Schopler and Gary B. Mesibov (eds), *Communication Problems in Autism*, New York: Plenum Press, 1985, pp. 163–84.

Conclusion

1 Gary Taylor, *Reinventing Shakespeare*, p. 303.

2 Gary Taylor, *Reinventing Shakespeare*, p. 304.

3 See *Macbeth*, 5.5.24–8; *As You Like It*, 2.7.139–66.

4 Weimann, *Author's Pen and Actor's Voice*, p. 22.

5 Hawkes, *Shakespeare in the Present*, p 126.

6 *Emanuelle Enchanted* begins with a sequence in which the company stand before a gauze curtain, seemingly embarrassed to begin the show. Eventually they pass a piece of paper amongst them and read the credits from one of the Emanuelle porn films. Later in the piece there is a sequence in which identity is instantly and repeatedly conferred on the performers by the holding up of cardboard signs with names, titles or descriptions of possible 'characters'.

Productions cited

Cymbeline dir. Dominic Cooke, RSC, first performed Swan Theatre, Stratford-upon-Avon 2002.

Hamlet dir. Peter Zadek, first performed Berlin Schaubühne, Berlin 1999.

Hamlet dir. Giles Block, first performed Shakespeare's Globe (the Globe reconstruction), London 2000.

Hamlet dir. Peter Brook, first performed Théâtre des Bouffes du Nord, Paris 2000.

Hamlet dir. Steven Pimlott, Royal Shakespeare Company, first performed Royal Shakespeare Theatre, Stratford-upon-Avon, 2000.

Hamlet dir. Ian Brown, first performed West Yorkshire Playhouse, Leeds 2001.

Hamlet dir. Paddy Hayter, Theatre de la Jeune Lune and Footsbarn, first performed Theatre de la Jeune Lune, Minneapolis 2001.

Hamlet dir. John Hazlett, first performed Hull College, Kingston-upon-Hull 2003.

Hamlet Quarto One dir. Sam Walters, first performed Orange Tree, Richmond, Surrey, 1985.

Hamlet Quarto One dir. John Worthen, first performed University College Swansea, 1982.

Hamlet Quarto One: *Hamlet: First Cut* dir. Jonathan Holloway, Red Shift, first performed Watermans Arts Centre, London 1999.

Amleto. La veemente esteriorità della morte di un mollusco dir. Romeo Castellucci, Societas Raffaello Sanzio, first performed Teatro Bonci, Cesena, Italy, 1992.

Henry V dir. Edward Hall, RSC, first performed Royal Shakespeare Theatre, Stratford-upon-Avon, 2000.

Julius Caesar: Giulio Cesare dir. Romeo Castellucci, Societas Raffaello Sanzio, first performed Teatro Bonci, Cesena, Italy, 1997.

Macbeth dir. Greg Doran, Royal Shakespeare Company, first performed Swan
Theatre, Stratford-upon-Avon 1999.

Richard II dir. John Barton, Royal Shakespeare Company, first performed Royal
Shakespeare Theatre 1973.

Richard II dir. Jonathan Kent, Almeida, first performed Gainsbourough studios,
London 2000.

Richard II dir. Steven Pimlott, Royal Shakespeare Company, first performed the
Other Place, Stratford-upon-Avon 2000.

Troilus and Cressida dir. Ben Iden Payne, first performed Shakespeare Memorial
Theatre, Stratford-upon-Avon, 1936.

Troilus and Cressida dir. Anthony Quayle, first performed Shakespeare Memorial
Theatre, Stratford-upon-Avon, 1948.

Troilus and Cressida dir. Glen Byam Shaw, first performed Shakespeare Memorial
Theatre, Stratford-upon-Avon, 1954.

Troilus and Cressida dir. John Barton, Royal Shakespeare Company, first
performed Royal Shakespeare Theatre, Stratford-upon-Avon, 1968.

Troilus and Cressida dir. John Barton, Royal Shakespeare Company, first
performed Royal Shakespeare Theatre, Stratford-upon-Avon, 1976.

Troilus and Cressida dir. Max Wekwerth and Joachim Tenschert, Berliner
Ensemble, first performed Berliner Ensemble 1985.

Troilus and Cressida dir. Sam Mendes, Royal Shakespeare Company, first
performed Swan Theatre, Stratford-upon-Avon 1990.

Troilus and Cressida dir. Michael Boyd, Royal Shakespeare Company, first
performed The Pit, Barbican Centre, London 1998.

Troilus and Cressida dir. Trevor Nunn, National Theatre, first performed Olivier
Theatre, National Theatre, London 1999.

The Winter's Tale dir. Greg Doran, Royal Shakespeare Company, first performed
Royal Shakespeare Theatre, Stratford-upon-Avon 1999.

Bibliography

Primary sources

Unless otherwise stated below, all references to Shakespeare texts are from: *The Riverside Shakespeare*, Boston, Houghton Mifflin 1974.

Where editorial notes and commentary are cited, editions are listed under name of editor.

Kyd, Thomas, *The Spanish Tragedy*, New Mermaid Series, B. L. Joseph (ed.), London: E. Benn, 1964.

Shakespeare, William, *The First Quarto of Hamlet*, New Cambridge Shakespeare, Kathleen O. Irace (ed.), Cambridge: CUP, 1998.

—— *Hamlet, The New Penguin Shakespeare*, T. J. B. Spencer (ed.), Harmondsworth: Penguin, 1980.

—— *Julius Caesar*, The Arden Shakespeare Third Series, David Daniell (ed.), Walton-on-Thames: Nelson, 1998.

—— *Richard II*, New Cambridge Shakespeare, Andrew Gurr (ed.), Cambridge: CUP, 1984.

—— *The Three Text Hamlet*, Paul Bertram and Bernice W. Kliman (ed.), New York: AMS, 1991.

—— *Troilus and Cressida*, The Arden Shakespeare Third Series, David Bevington (ed.), Walton-on-Thames: Nelson, 1998.

Webster, John, *The Duchess of Malfi*, Kathleen McLuskie and Jennifer Uglow (eds), Bristol: Bristol Classical, 1989.

Secondary sources

Alexander, Peter, '*Troilus and Cressida 1609*', *The Library*, 4th series, no. 9, 1928–9, pp. 267–86.

Allsop, Ric, 'On Immobility', *Frankcija Performing Arts Magazine*, no. 15, October 1999, pp. 84–93.

Althusser, Louis, *Lenin and Philosophy and Other Essays*, trans. Ben Brewster, London: New Left Books, 1971.

Ansorge, Peter, review of *Richard II*, *Plays and Players*, June 1973, pp. 39–41.

Artaud, Antonin, *The Theatre and Its Double*, London: Calder New Paris Editions, 1993.

Attwood, Tony, 'Overview and History of Autism', in *Social Education and Training of the Autistic Adult: A Collection of Papers given at a Weekend Study Course, 23rd–25th October 1981*, London: The Inge Wakehurst Memorial Trust Fund, 1981.

Auslander, Philip, *Presence and Resistance*, Ann Arbor: University of Michigan Press, 1992.

—— *From Acting to Performance*, London: Routledge, 1997.

Austin, J. L., *How to Do Things with Words*, Oxford: Clarendon Press, 1962.

Autism Society of America, 'What is Autism?', www.autism-society.org/whatisautism/autism.html.

Barker, Francis, *The Tremulous Private Body: Essays in Subjection*, London: Methuen, 1984.

Baron-Cohen, Simon, *Mindblindness: An Essay on Autism and Theory of Mind*, Cambridge: MIT Press, 1993.

—— *et al.*, *Understanding Other Minds: Perspectives from Autism*, Oxford: OUP, 1993.

Barton, Ann (née Righter), *Shakespeare and the Idea of the Play*, London: Chatto and Windus, 1962.

—— editorial notes to Shakespeare, *Troilus and Cressida*, The Riverside Shakespeare, Boston: Houghton Mifflin, 1974.

Barton, John, *Playing Shakespeare*, London: Methuen, 1984.

Bate, Jonathan, *The Genius of Shakespeare*, Oxford: OUP, 1999.

—— 'Shakespeare's Foolosophy', in Grace Ioppolo (ed.), *Shakespeare Performed: Essays in Honor of R. A. Foakes*, Newark: University of Delaware Press, 2000, pp. 17–30.

Belsey, Catherine, *The Subject of Tragedy*, London: Routledge, 1985.

—— 'Richard Levin and In-different Reading', *New Literary History*, vol. 25, no. 3, 1990, pp. 683–705.

Benedetti, Robert, *The Actor at Work*, 2nd edn, Englewood Cliffs: Prentice Hall, 1976.

—— *Stanislavski*, London: Methuen, 1988.

—— *Stanislavski and the Actor*, London: Methuen, 1998.

Benjamin, Walter, 'The Work of Art in the Age of Mechanical Reproduction', in *Illuminations*, trans. Harry Zohn, London: Jonathan Cape, 1970, pp. 211–43.

Bennet, Susan, *Performing Nostalgia*, London: Routledge, 1996.

Bentley, Gerald Eades, *The Profession of Player in Shakespeare's Time*, Princeton: Princeton University Press, 1984.

Berger Jr., Harry, '*Richard II*, 3.2: An Exercise in Imaginary Audition', *English Literary History*, vol. 55, 1988, pp. 755–96.

—— *Imaginary Audition: Shakespeare on Page and Stage*, Berkeley: University of California Press, 1989.

Berry, Cicely, *Voice and the Actor*, London: Harrap, 1973.

—— *The Actor and the Text*, London: Virgin, 1992.

Berry, Ralph, *Shakespeare in Performance: Casting and Metamorphoses*, New York: St Martin's Press, 1993.

—— *Shakespeare and the Awareness of the Audience*, London: Macmillan, 1985.

Bessell, Jaq, 'Shakespeare's Globe Research Bulletin: *Hamlet* 2000', www.rdg.ac.uk/globe/research/1999Hamlet2000htm.

Bevington, David, editorial notes to Shakespeare, *Troilus and Cressida*, Arden Shakespeare Third Series, Walton-on-Thames: Nelson, 1998.

Bharucha, Rustom, *Theatre and the World: Performance and the Culture of Politics*, London: Routledge, 1993.

Bonnard, G. A., 'The Actor in Richard II', *Shakespeare Jahrbuch*, no. 87, 1952, pp. 88–101.

Brecht, Bertolt, *The Messingkauf Dialogues*, trans. John Willett, London: Methuen, 1965.

—— *Brecht on Theatre: The Development of an Aesthetic*, John Willett (ed. and trans.), London: Eyre Methuen, 1974.

Bretzius, Stephen, *Shakespeare in Theory: The Postmodern Academy and Early Modern Theatre*, Michigan: University of Michigan Press, 1997.

Brook, Peter, *The Empty Space*, London: Penguin, 1990.

Brooks, Harold, '*Troilus and Cressida*: Its Dramatic Unity and Genre', in J. W. Mahon and T. A. Pendleton (eds), *Fanned and Winnowed Opinions: Shakespearean Essays Presented to Harold Jenkins*, London: Methuen, 1987, pp. 6–25.

Brown, John Russell, 'Cross-Dressed Actors and Their Audiences: Kate Valk's *Emperor Jones* and William Shakespeare's Juliet', *New Theatre Quarterly*, vol. 15, no. 59, pp. 195–203.

Bulman, James C. (ed.), *Shakespeare, Theory and Performance*, London: Routledge, 1996.

Burnett, Mark Thornton and John Manning, *New Essays on 'Hamlet'*, New York: AMS, 1994.

Butler, Judith, *Gender Trouble: Feminism and the Subversion of Identity*, London: Routledge, 1990.

—— *Excitable Speech: A Politics of the Performative*, London: Routledge, 1997.

Calderwood, James L., *To Be and Not To Be: Negation and Metadrama in 'Hamlet'*, New York: Columbia University Press, 1983.

Callaghan, Dympna, *Shakespeare without Women*, London: Routledge, 2000.

Carnicke, Sharon Marie, *Stanislavski in Focus*, London: Harwood Academic Publishers, 1998.

Carrière, Jean-Claude, introduction to *The Mahabhareta*, trans. from the French by Peter Brook, New York: Harper and Row, 1987.

Castellucci, Romeo, 'The Animal Being on Stage', *Performance Research*, vol. 5, no. 2, 2000, pp. 23–8.

Charlton, Kenneth, *Education in Renaissance England*, London: Routledge and Kegan Paul, 1965.

Charnes, Linda, *Notorious Identity: Materialising the Subject in Shakespeare*, Cambridge: Harvard University Press, 1993.

Clayton, Thomas (ed.), *The 'Hamlet' First Published: Origins, Forms, Intertextualities*, Newark: University of Delaware Press, 1992.

Cohen, Walter, 'Political Criticism of Shakespeare', in *Shakespeare Reproduced: The Text in History and Ideology*, London: Methuen, 1987, pp. 18–46.

Cole, Toby (ed.), *Playwrights on Playwriting: The Meaning and Making of Modern Drama from Ibsen to Ionesco*, New York: Hill and Wang, 1961.

Coleman, Terry, Interview with Nigel Lawson, *Guardian*, 5 September 1983.

Conrad, Peter, 'Shakespeare Made Sick', *Observer*, 6 June 1999.

Counsell, Colin, *Signs of Performance: An Introduction to Twentieth-Century Theatre*, London: Routledge, 1996.

Cox, John D. and Kastan, David S., *A New History of Early English Drama*, New York: Columbia University Press, 1997.

Croyden, Margaret, 'A certain path', interview with Peter Brook, *American Theater*, Vol. 18, May/June 2001, pp. 18–20.

Dean, Leonard F., 'Richard II: The State and the Image of Theatre', *PLMA*, no. 67, 1952, pp. 211–18.

Dessen, Alan C., *Elizabethan Drama and the Viewer's Eye*, Chapel Hill: University of North Carolina Press, 1977.

—— *Elizabethan Stage Conventions and Modern Interpreters*, Cambridge: CUP, 1984.

—— *Recovering Shakespeare's Theatrical Vocabulary*, Cambridge: CUP, 1995.

—— *Rescripting Shakespeare: The Text, the Director and Modern Productions*, Cambridge: CUP, 2002.

Dollimore, Jonathan, *Radical Tragedy: Religion, Ideology and Power in the Drama of Shakespeare and His Contemporaries*, Hemel Hempstead: Harvester Wheatsheaf, 1989.

Dollimore, Jonathan and Sinfield, Alan (eds), *Political Shakespeare: Essays in Cultural Materialism*, Manchester: MUP, 1994.

Drakakis, John (ed.), *Alternative Shakespeares*, London: Methuen, 1985.

—— 'Theatre, Ideology and Institution: Shakespeare and the Roadsweepers', in Graham Holderness (ed.), *The Shakespeare Myth*, Manchester: Manchester University Press, 1988, pp. 24–41.

Duthie, George Ian, *The 'Bad' Quarto of Hamlet: A Critical Study*, Cambridge: CUP, 1941.

Eagleton, Terence, *Shakespeare and Society*, London: Chatto and Windus, 1970.

—— *William Shakespeare*, Oxford: Basil Blackwell, 1986.

Elton, W. R., *Shakespeare's 'Troilus and Cressida' and the Inns of Court Revels*, Brookfield: Ashgate, 1999.

Escolme, Bridget and Ridout, Nicholas, 'Performing Humans Historically: Shakespeare and the Societas Raffaello Sanzio', conference paper for Performance Studies International 7: 'Translations, Transitions, Transformations', State University of Arizona, 28 March to 1 April 2000.

Evans, G. Blakemore, editorial notes to *The Riverside Shakespeare*, Boston: Houghton Mifflin, 1974.

Everett, Barbara, 'The Inaction of *Troilus and Cressida*', *Essays in Criticism*, vol. 32, no. 2, 1982, pp. 119–39.

Felperin, Howard, *The Uses of the Canon: Elizabethan Literature and Contemporary Theory*, Oxford: Clarendon Press, 1990.

Fineman, Joel, *The Subjectivity Effect in Western Literary Tradition: Essays toward the Release of Shakespeare's Will*, Cambridge: MIT Press, 1991.

Finkelpearl, Philip J., *John Marston of the Middle Temple*, Cambridge: Harvard University Press, 1969.

Foster, Maxwell E., *The Play behind the Play: 'Hamlet' and Quarto One*, Portsmouth: Heinemann, 1991.

Freund, Elizabeth, 'Ariachne's Broken Woof', in Patricia Parker and Geoffrey Hartman (eds), *Shakespeare and the Question of Theory*, New York: Methuen, 1985, pp. 19–36.

Garner, Stanton B., *Bodied Spaces: Phenomenology and Performance in Contemporary Drama*, Ithaca: Cornell University Press, 1994.

Greenblatt, Stephen, *Renaissance Self-Fashioning*, Chicago: University of Chicago Press, 1980.

—— *Shakespearean Negotiations*, Oxford: Clarendon Press, 1988.

—— (ed.), *Representing the English Renaissance*, Berkeley: University of California Press, 1988.

—— 'Resonance and Wonder', in Peter Collier and Helga Geyer-Ryan (eds), *Literary Theory Today*, Cambridge: Polity, 1990, pp. 74–90.

Greene, Gayle, 'Language and Value in Shakespeare's *Troilus and Cressida*', *Studies in English Literature 1500–1900*, vol. 21, no. 2, 1981, pp. 271–85.

Guardian (staff and agencies), 'RSC Reveals Plans for £100m Theatre Development', *Guardian*, 18 October 2001.

Gurr, Andrew, *The Shakespearean Stage 1574–1642*, Cambridge: CUP, 1992.

—— *The Shakespearean Playing Companies*, Oxford: OUP, 1995.

—— and Orrell, John, *Rebuilding Shakespeare's Globe*, London: Weidenfeld and Nicolson, 1989.

Hanson, Elizabeth, *Discovering the Subject in Renaissance England*, Cambridge: CUP, 1998.

Harbage, Alfred, *Shakespeare's Audience*, New York: Columbia University Press, 1961.

Hawkes, Terence, *Meaning by Shakespeare*, London: Routledge, 1992.

—— *Shakespeare in the Present*, London: Routledge, 2002.

Heinemann, Margo, 'How Brecht read Shakespeare' in Dollimore and Sinfield (eds), *Political Shakespeare: Essays in Cultural Materialism*, Manchester: Manchester University Press, 1994.

Hibbard, G. R., editorial notes to Shakespeare, *Hamlet*, The Oxford Shakespeare, Oxford: OUP 1994.

Hillman, Richard, *Self-speaking in Medieval and Early Modern English Drama: Subjectivity, Discourse, and the Stage*, Basingstoke: Macmillan, 1997.

Hodge, Alison (ed.), *Twentieth Century Actor Training*, London: Routledge, 2000.

Holderness, Graham, *Shakespeare's History*, Dublin: Gill and Macmillan, 1985.

—— *The Shakespeare Myth*, Manchester: MUP, 1988.

—— (ed.), *Shakespeare Recycled: The Making of Historical Drama*, Hemel Hempstead: Harvester Wheatsheaf, 1992.

—— *Shakespeare: The Histories*, Basingstoke: Palgrave, 1999.

Holland, Peter, 'Brecht, Bond Gaskill and the Practice of Political Theatre', *Theatre Quarterly*, Vol. 30, summer 1978, pp.24–35.

Hornby, Richard, *Drama, Metadrama and Perception*, Lewisberg: Bucknell University Press, 1986.

—— *The End of Acting: A Radical View*, New York: Applause, 1992.

Howard, Jean E., *The Stage and Social Struggle in Early Modern England*, London: Routledge, 1994.

—— and O'Connor, Marion F., *Shakespeare Reproduced: The Text in History and Ideology*, London: Methuen, 1987.

Innes, Christopher (ed.), *A Sourcebook on Naturalistic Theatre*, London: Routledge, 2000.

Ioppolo, Grace (ed.), *Shakespeare Performed: Essays in Honor of R. A. Foakes*, Newark: University of Delaware Press, 2000.

Irace, Kathleen O., 'Origins and Agents of Q1 Hamlet', in Thomas Clayton (ed.), *The Hamlet First Published (Q1, 1603): Origins, Forms, Intertextualities*, Newark: University of Delaware Press, 1992, pp. 90–122.

—— 'Introduction', *The First Quarto of Hamlet*, Cambridge: CUP, 1998, pp. 1–27.

Jagendorf, Zvi, 'All against One in *Troilus and Cressida*', *English*, vol. 31, no. 141, 1982, pp. 199–210.

Johnson, Clive, 'Shakespeare's Big Mac', Review of *Hamlet*, dir. Giles Block, held at Shakespeare's Globe Research Centre, source unknown.

Kamps, Ivo (ed.), *Materialist Shakespeare: A History*, London: Verso, 1995.

Kantorowicz, Ernst Hartwig, *The King's Two Bodies*, Princeton: Princeton University Press, 1957.

Kastan, David Scott, *Shakespeare after Theory*, London: Routledge, 1999.

Kiernan, Pauline, *Shakespeare's Theory of Drama*, Cambridge: CUP, 1996.

—— *Staging Shakespeare at the New Globe*, Basingstoke: Macmillan, 1999.

Knowles, Richard Paul, 'Shakespeare, Voice and Ideology: Interrogating the Natural Voice', in James C. Bulman (ed.), *Shakespeare, Theory and Performance*, London: Routledge, 1996, pp. 92–112.

Kott, Jan, *Shakespeare Our Contemporary*, London: Methuen, 1967.

Lee, John, *Shakespeare's Hamlet and the Controversies of Self*, Oxford: Clarendon Press, 2000.

Levin, Richard, 'Unthinkable Thoughts in the New Historicising of English Renaissance Drama', *New Literary History*, vol. 21, no. 3, 1990, pp. 433–47.

—— 'Polemic on the New Historicising of English Renaissance Drama: Reply to Catherine Belsey and Jonathan Goldberg', *New Literary History*, vol. 21, no. 3, 1990, pp. 463–70.

Linklater, Kristin, *Freeing the Natural Voice*, New York: Drama Book Publishers, 1976.

—— *Freeing Shakespeare's Voice: The Actor's Guide to Talking the Text*, New York: Theatre Communications Group, 1992.

Loughrey, Brian, 'Quarto One in Recent Performance: An Interview', in Thomas Clayton (ed.), *The 'Hamlet' First Published: Origins, Forms, Intertextualities*, Newark: University of Delaware Press, 1992, pp. 123–36.

—— and Holderness, Graham (eds), Introduction to *The Tragedie of Hamlet Prince of Denmark (Q1)*, London: Longman, 1990.

Lull, Janice, 'Forgetting *Hamlet*: The First Quarto and the Folio', in Thomas Clayton (ed.), *The 'Hamlet' First Published: Origins, Forms, Intertextualities*, Newark: University of Delaware Press, 1992, pp. 249–56.

Mahon, John W. and Pendleton, Thomas A. (eds), *Fanned and Winnowed Opinions: Shakespearean Essays Presented to Harold Jenkins*, London: Methuen, 1987.

Marcus, Leah S., *Unediting the Renaissance: Shakespeare, Milton, Marlowe*, London: Routledge, 1996.

Maus, Katharine Eisaman, *Inwardness and Theater in the English Renaissance*, Chicago: University of Chicago Press, 1995.

Mazer, Cary M., 'Historicizing Alan Dessen: Scholarship, Stagecraft and the "Shakespeare Revolution"', in James C. Bulman (ed.), *Shakespeare, Theory and Performance*, London: Routledge, 1996, pp. 149–67.

McLuskie, Kathleen, conference paper for 'Kissing Spiders: Representing the Female Body on and off the Early Modern Stage', Warwick, 29–30 April 2000.

Melchioni, Giorgio, 'The Acting Version and the Wiser Sort', in Thomas Clayton (ed.), *The 'Hamlet' First Published: Origins, Forms, Intertextualities*, Newark: University of Delaware Press, 1992, pp. 195–210.

Meltzoff, Andrew and Gopnik, Alison, 'The Role of Imitation in Understanding Persons', in *Understanding Other Minds: Perspectives from Autism*, Simon Baron-Cohen *et al.* (eds), Oxford: OUP, 1993, pp. 335–66.

Miola, Robert, *Shakespeare's Reading*, Oxford: OUP, 2000.

Montrose, Louis, *The Purpose of Playing: Shakespeare and the Cultural Politics of the Elizabethan Theatre*, Chicago: University of Chicago Press, 1996.

Moore, Charlotte, 'It forces you to rethink everything you thought you knew about being human', *Guardian*, 16 May 2001.

Mousley, Andy, '*Hamlet* and the Politics of Individualism', in Mark Thornton Burnett and John Manning (eds), *New Essays on 'Hamlet'*, New York: AMS, 1994, pp. 67–82.

Muir, Kenneth, editorial notes to Shakespeare, *Troilus and Cressida*, The Oxford Shakespeare, Oxford: OUP, 1982.

Mulryne, Ronnie and Shewring, Margaret (eds), *Making Space for Theatre: British Architecture and Theatre since 1958*, Stratford-upon-Avon: Mulryne and Shewring Ltd, 1995.

—— *Shakespeare's Globe Rebuilt*, Cambridge: CUP, 1997.

Neill, Michael, *Issues of Death: Mortality and Identity in English Renaissance Tragedy*, Oxford: Clarendon Press, 1997.

Nosworthy, J. M., *Shakespeare's Occasional Plays*, London: E. Arnold, 1965.

Orrel, John, *The Quest for Shakespeare's Globe*, Cambridge: CUP, 1983.

Palmer, Kenneth, editorial notes to Shakespeare, *Troilus and Cressida*, The Arden Shakespeare, London: Methuen, 1982.

Parker, Patricia and Hartman, Geoffrey (eds), *Shakespeare and the Question of Theory*, New York: Methuen, 1985.

Patterson, Lee, *Chaucer and the Subject of History*, London: Routledge, 1991.

Pavis, Patrice, *Theatre at the Crossroads of Culture*, London: Routledge, 1992.

Pfister, Manfred, *The Theory and Analysis of Drama*, Cambridge: CUP, 1988.

Prest, Wilfred R., *The Inns of Court under Elizabeth I and the Early Stuarts*, Harlow: Longman, 1972.

Rackin, Phyllis, 'The Role of the Audience in Shakespeare's *Richard II*', *Shakespeare Quarterly*, 1985, vol. 36, no. 3, pp. 262–81.

—— *Stages of History: Shakespeare's English Chronicles*, London: Routledge, 1990.

Roach, Joseph R., *The Player's Passion: Studies in the Science of Acting*, Newark: University of Delaware Press, 1985.

Roden, David, 'Iconoclasm and the Rhetoric of Energy in Soc. Raffaello Sanzio's *Hamlet*', *Frakcija Performing Arts Magazine*, no. 15, October 1999, pp. 14–21.

Rodenburg, Patsy, *The Right to Speak: Working with the Voice*, London: Methuen, 1992.

—— *The Need for Words: Voice and the Text*, London: Methuen, 1993.

Rutter, Carol Chillington, *Enter the Body: Women and Representation on Shakespeare's Stage*, London: Routledge, 2001.

Salgado, Gamini (ed.), *Eyewitnesses of Shakespeare: First Hand Accounts of Performances*, London: Chatto and Windus for Sussex University Press, 1975.

Sams, Eric, 'Taboo or not Taboo? The Text, Dating and Authorship of *Hamlet*, 1589–1623', *Hamlet Studies*, Vol. 10, 1988, pp. 12–46.

Savran, David, *Breaking the Rules: The Wooster Group*, New York: Theatre Communications Group, 1988.

Schechner, Richard, 'Talking with Peter Brook', *The Drama Review*, vol. 30, no. 1, spring 1986, pp. 54–71.

Schoenfeldt, Michael C., *Bodies and Selves in Early Modern England: Physiology and Inwardness in Spenser, Shakespeare, Herbert, and Milton*, Cambridge: CUP, 1999.

Schopler, Eric and Mesibov, Gary B. (eds.), *Communication Problems in Autism*, New York: Plenum Press, 1985.

Schuler, Adriane L. and Prizant, Barry M., 'Echolalia', in Eric Schopler and Gary B. Mesibov (eds), *Communication Problems in Autism*, New York: Plenum Press, 1985, pp. 163–84.

Scott, Michael, *Renaissance Drama and a Modern Audience*, Basingstoke: Macmillan, 1982.

Searle, John R., *Speech Acts: An Essay in the Philosophy of Language*, Cambridge: CUP, 1969.

—— *Expression and Meaning: Studies in the Theory of Speech Acts*, Cambridge: CUP, 1979.

Sedgwick, Eve Kosofsky, *English Literature and Male Homosocial Desire*, New York: Columbia University Press, 1985.

Shaughnessy, Robert, *Representing Shakespeare: England, History and the RSC*, New York: Harvester Wheatsheaf, 1994.

Shepherd, Simon, 'So What IS the Female Body?', conference paper for 'Kissing Spiders: Representing the Female Body on and off the Early Modern Stage', University of Warwick, 29–30 April 2000.

Sher, Anthony, 'How I Got into the Mad Bard's Head', *Guardian*, 2 January 1999.

Shewring, Margaret, *Shakespeare in Performance: King Richard II*, Manchester: MUP, 1996.

Sinfield, Alan, *Faultlines: Cultural Materialism and the Politics of Dissident Reading*, Oxford: Clarendon Press, 1992.

Siraisi, Nancy, *Medieval and Early Renaissance Medicine: An Introduction to Knowledge and Practice*, Chicago: Chicago University Press, 1990.

Smallwood, Robert (ed.), *Players of Shakespeare 6: Essays in the Performance of Shakespeare's History Plays*, Cambridge: CUP, c.2004.

Smith, Bruce, *Shakespeare and Masculinity*, Oxford: OUP, 2000.

Societas Raffaello Sanzio, '*Amleto*: Post Show Talk', *Frakcija Performing Arts Magazine*, no. 15, October 1999, pp. 22–7.

Soule, Lesley Wade, *Actor as Anti-character: Dionysus, the Devil, and the Boy Rosalind*, Westport: Greenwood Press, 2000.

Spencer, T. J. B., editorial notes to Shakespeare, *Hamlet*, The New Penguin Shakespeare, London: Penguin 1996.

Sprague, A. C., *Shakespeare's Histories*, London: Society for Theatre Research, 1964.

Stanislavski, Constantin, *An Actor Prepares*, trans. Elizabeth Reynolds Hapgood, New York: Theatre Arts Books, 1970.

—— *Building a Character*, trans. Elizabeth Reynolds Hapgood, London: Eyre Methuen, 1979.

—— *Creating a Role*, trans. Elizabeth Reynolds Hapgood, London: Eyre Methuen, 1981.

States, Bert O., *Great Reckonings in Little Rooms: The Phenomenology of Theater*, Berkeley: University of California Press, 1985.

—— *Hamlet and the Concept of Character*, Baltimore: Johns Hopkins University Press, 1992.

—— 'The Actor's Presence: Three Phenomenal Modes', in Philip Zarrilli (ed.), *Acting Re-considered: Theories and Practices*, London: Routledge, 1995, pp. 22–41.

Stephens, John, *Satyrical Essayes Characters and Others*, London: printed by E. Alde for Philip Knight, 1615.

Stern, Tiffany, *Rehearsal from Shakespeare to Sheridan*, Oxford: Clarendon Press, 2000.

Styan, J. L., *Shakespeare's Stagecraft*, Cambridge: CUP, 1967.

—— *Drama, Stage and Audience*, Cambridge: CUP, 1975.

—— *The Shakespeare Revolution*, Cambridge: CUP, 1977.

Taylor, Gary, '*Troilus and Cressida*: Bibliography, Performance and Interpretation', *Shakespeare Studies*, no. 15, 1982, pp. 99–136.

—— *Reinventing Shakespeare: A Cultural History from the Restoration to the Present*, London: Hogarth Press, 1990.

Taylor, Michael, *Shakespeare Criticism in the Twentieth Century*, Oxford: OUP, 2001.

Thomas, Sidney, '*Hamlet Quarto One*: First Version or Bad Quarto?', in *The 'Hamlet' First Published: Origins, Forms, Intertextualities*, Newark: University of Delaware Press, 1992, pp. 249–56.

—— 'Shakespeare Straight and Crooked: A Review of the 1973 Season at Stratford', *Shakespeare Survey*, 1974, no. 27, pp. 143–54.

Thomson, Peter, *On Actors and Acting*, Exeter: University of Exeter Press, 2000.

Tillyard, E. M. W., *Shakespeare's History Plays*, London: Chatto and Windus, 1944.

—— *Shakespeare's Problem Plays*, London: Chatto and Windus, 1950.

Traversi, Derek, *Shakespeare from Richard II to Henry V*, London: Hollis and Carter, 1958.

Vickers, Brian, *Appropriating Shakespeare: Contemporary Critical Quarrels*, New Haven: Yale University Press, 1993.

Watson, Robert, *The Rest is Silence: Death as Annihilation in the English Renaissance*, Berkeley: University of California Press, 1994.

Weimann, Robert, *Shakespeare and the Popular Tradition in the Theatre*, Baltimore: Johns Hopkins University Press, 1978.

—— *Author's Pen and Actor's Voice: Playing and Writing in Shakespeare's Theatre*, Cambridge: CUP, 2000.

Wells, Stanley, editorial notes to Shakespeare, *Richard II*, New Penguin Shakespeare, London: Penguin, 1997.

West, Samuel, 'Richard II', in Smallwood, Robert (ed.), *Players of Shakespeare 6*, Cambridge: CUP, c.2004.

Wiles, David, *Shakespeare's Clown: Actor and Text in the Elizabethan Playhouse*, Cambridge: CUP, 1987.

Williams, Faynia, Interview with Peter Brook, *Direct Magazine*, winter 2001–2, publication of the Director's Guild of Great Britain, http://www.dgg6.co.uk/publications/article9_86.html.

Williams, Raymond, *Marxism and Literature*, Oxford: OUP, 1997.

—— *Problems in Materialism and Culture*, London: Verso, 1980.

—— *Drama from Ibsen to Brecht*, London: Hogarth Press, 1993.

Wilson, Richard and Dutton, Richard (eds), *New Historicism and Renaissance Drama*, London: Longman, 1992.

Worthen, W. B., *Shakespeare and the Authority of Performance*, Cambridge: CUP, 1997.

—— *Shakespeare and the Force of Modern Performance*, Cambridge: CUP, 2003.

Zarrilli, Phillip, *Acting (Re)considered: Theories and Practices*, London: Routledge, 1995.

Zola, Emile, 'Le Naturalisme au Théâtre' from *Le Roman Experimental*, Paris: E. Fasquelle, 1902, trans. Samuel Draper in Toby Cole (ed.), *Playwrights on Playwriting*, pp. 5–14.

Newspaper reviews

Cymbeline

Swan Theatre, Stratford-upon-Avon, dir. Michael Boyd, *Guardian*, 8 August 2003.

Hamlet

New Globe, 'Master of Play', and 'Master of Voice': Giles Block, *Plays International*, summer 2000.
The Times, Benedict Nightingale, 12 June 2000.
Independent on Sunday, Stephen Fay, 4 July 2000.
Time Out, Dominic Cavendish, 5 July 2000.
Times Literary Supplement, Eleanor Margolles, 7 July 2000.
Morning Star, 10 July 2000.
Johnson, Clive 'Shakespeare's Big Mac', review of *Hamlet*, summer 2000, kept at Globe Research Centre, source unknown.
Théâtre des Bouffes du Nord, dir. Peter Brook, *Daily Telegraph*, Charles Spenser, 23 August 2001.
Theatre de la Jeune Lune, dir. Paddy Hayter, *New York Times*, Bruce Weber, 28 October 2003.

Hamlet First Quarto

Red Shift, regional tour, dir. Jonathan Holloway, *Brentford, Chiswick and Isleworth Times*, Malcolm Richards, 10 September 1999.
Guernsey Press, Peter Pannett, 1 December 1999.
Eastbourne Herald, Laura Sonler, 17 March 2000.
as above, Bloomsbury Theatre, London, *Independent*, Paul Taylor, 20 January 2000.
The Times, Ian Michael, 20 January 2000.
Time Out, Charles Godfrey-Fausett, 25 January 2000.

Richard II

RSC, The Other Place, Stratford-upon-Avon, dir. Steven Pimlott, *Evening Standard*, Nicholas de Jongh, 30 March 2000.
Financial Times, Alastair Macaulay, 31 March 2000.
Daily Telegraph, Charles Spenser, 31 March 2000.
Guardian, Michael Billington, 1 April 2000.
Independent on Sunday, Robert Butler, 2 April 2000.
Sunday Telegraph, John Gross, 2 April 2000.
Observer, Susannah Clapp, 2 April 2000.
Time Out, Jane Edwardes, 5 April 2000.
Spectator, Patrick Carnegy, 8 April 2000.
Sunday Times, John Peter, 9 April 2000.
Almeida, Gainsborough studios, dir. Jonathan Kent, *Sunday Times*, John Peter, 16 April 2000.

Troilus and Cressida

King's Hall, Covent Garden, London, dir. William Poel, *Birmingham Gazette*, H.M., 13 May 1913.

Shakespeare Memorial Theatre, Stratford-upon-Avon, dir. B. Iden Payne, *The Times*, 25 April 1936.

Daily Telegraph, W.A. Darlington, 25 April 1936.

Shakespeare Memorial Theatre, Stratford-upon-Avon, dir. Anthony Quayle, *Birmingham Mail*, C.L.W., 5 July 1948.

Daily Worker, 7 July 1948.

The Times, 5 July 1948.

Shakespeare Memorial Theatre, Stratford-upon-Avon, dir. Glen Byam Shaw, *Financial Times*, Derek Granger, 14 July 1954.

Daily Express, John Barber, 14 July 1954.

RSC, Royal Shakespeare Theatre, Stratford-upon-Avon, dir. John Barton, *Daily Telegraph*, Frank Marcus, 22 August 1976.

RSC, Swan Theatre, Stratford-upon-Avon, dir. Sam Mendes, *Guardian*, Michael Billington, 21 July 1991.

RSC, Barbican Pit, London, dir. Michael Boyd, *Independent*, Paul Taylor, 7 November 1998.

Evening Standard, Nicholas de Jongh, 9 November 1998.

Daily Telegraph, Charles Spenser, 9 November 1998.

Financial Times, Alastair Macaulay, 10 November 1998.

What's On, Cheryl Freedman, 10 November 1998.

The Winter's Tale

Observer, Susannah Clapp, 10 January 1999.

Sunday Times, John Peter, 10 Janaury 1999.

Index